Early Education Transformed

Edited by

Lesley Abbott and Helen Moylett

RoutledgeFalmer
Taylor & Francis Group

LONDON AND NEW YORK

First published 1999 by Falmer Press

Reprinted 2002, 2003
by RoutledgeFalmer
11 New Fetter Lane, London EC4P 4EE

Simultaneously published in the USA and Canada
by RoutledgeFalmer, Taylor & Francis Inc., 325 Chestnut Street, 8th floor, Philadelphia, PA19106

Transferred to Digital Printing 2004

RoutledgeFalmer is an imprint of the Taylor & Francis Group

© Abbott and Moylett 1999

Typeset in Times by Graphicraft Limited, Hong Kong
Printed and bound in Great Britain by Biddles Short Run Books, King's Lynn

Cover design by Caroline Archer

British Library Cataloguing in Publication Data
A catalogue record for this book is available from the British Library

Library of Congress Cataloguing in Publication Data
A catalogue record for this book has been requested

ISBNs 0 7507 0844 1 (hbk)
      0 7507 0843 3 (pbk)

Early Education Transformed

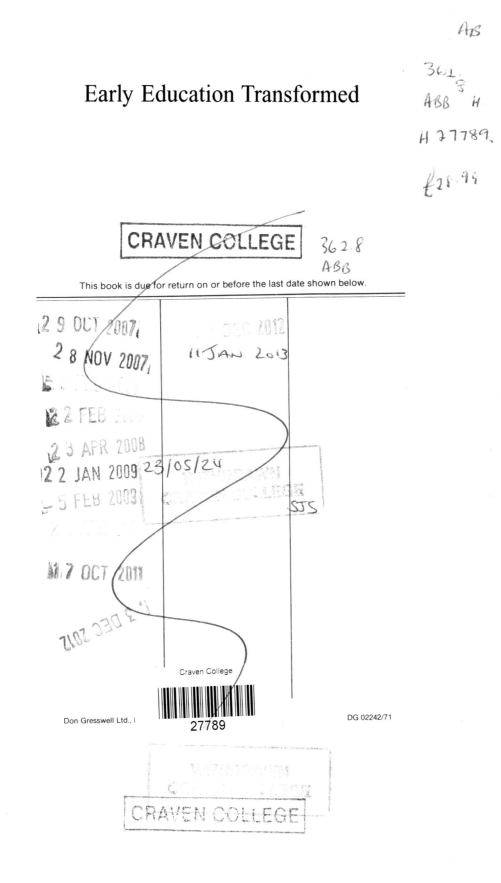

New Millennium Series

How Shall We School Our Children?
Edited by Colin Richards and Philip H. Taylor

Early Education Transformed
Edited by Lesley Abbott and Helen Moylett

The teachers calling me and Thomas into school by Connor Moylett, age 4

This book is dedicated to Ché and Cymion Barratt-Pugh, born at the same time as the book and to all the children of the new millennium.

Contents

Contents

List of Figures

Acknowledgments

This book is one of a series which takes the start of a new millennium as an opportunity to reflect on the influences and experiences which have shaped education thus far. It aims to be visionary in looking forward to the kinds of early experiences we would wish to see in the future.

We are grateful to the many contributors who have provided, what we consider to be a rich tapestry or perhaps 'smorgasbord' would be more appropriate, from which the reader can select at different times according to need and interest.

We are particularly grateful to Trisha Gladdis in the Research Base at the Manchester Metropolitan University for her advice, support and skill in typing, collating and producing the manuscript.

Acknowledgment is made of permission granted by *Co-ordinate*, the *Journal of the National Early Years Network*, March 1998, 64 to publish Figure 1.1. We are also grateful to James Cornford for permission to reproduce *Childhood* by Frances Cornford in Chapter 1. Chapter 15: excerpt from YOU CAN'T SAY YOU CAN'T PLAY by Vivian Gussin Paley, copyright © 1992 by the President and Fellows of Harvard College, reprinted by permission of Harvard University Press.

Lesley Abbott and Helen Moylett
1999

Preface

From the Department of Education and Employment (DfEE)

It is entirely appropriate, as the millennium approaches, to look back at early years education as well as forwards. We all recognize that good preschool education gives lasting educational and social benefits for children. There is valuable experience and practice on which to draw to ensure that these benefits are available for all children. The government made clear in *Excellence in Schools* (1997) that it attaches high priority to making these benefits available to all children, particularly those who are disadvantaged. One of its standards for the new millennium is that all children should have the best possible start in life. This includes childcare of high quality, whether in the hands of parents or carers. The integration of early education, daycare and family services is actively encouraged.

The new Early Years and Childcare Development Plans are tackling our historically low levels of participation. Thanks to the efforts of Partnerships and many nursery schools, preschools, playgroups and other providers, supported by special funding, all 4-year-olds now have access to good quality part-time nursery education for three terms at age 4. The government believes that these and other objectives for early education are best met by cooperation and collaboration between the maintained, private and voluntary sectors, so that we pool and develop our strengths and assist parental choice.

A number of important initiatives will start to bear fruit as we move into the new millennium. Following its comprehensive spending review, the government has undertaken to double the participation rate for 3-year-olds in nursery education from 34 per cent to 66 per cent by 2002. New funding of some £400 million will secure 190,000 new places.

The Sure Start programme for 0–3s is another product of the comprehensive spending review. An inter-departmental Children's Fund of £540 million will support the focusing of healthcare, educational, childcare and other resources on meeting the needs of young children and families in areas of disadvantage. Also this year, Ministers announced the national childcare strategy to support families and children. This too has substantial new funding, and depends on a host of partners working together, principally through enhanced Early Years Development and Childcare Partnerships. The strategy is a major plank in the government's plans for tackling social exclusion, poverty and economic development.

A number of other measures are being taken to improve early years services. OFSTED inspections will continue to support the work of registered providers. The

Qualifications and Curriculum Authority (QCA) is reviewing the Desirable Learning Outcomes for children's learning on entering compulsory education with the aim, among others, of promoting early literacy. We have also asked the QCA to review qualifications and training for the early years, in order to promote a 'climbing frame' of opportunities. Jointly, with the Department of Health, we have consulted extensively on reform of the arrangements for regulating and inspecting early education and daycare. A pilot programme of Early Excellence Centres is being developed to promote models of integrated working for wider dissemination.

We approach the millennium with the promise of historic progress in the development of early years education and other services. This collection of essays reminds us of the importance of that task.

Reference

DfEE (1997) *Excellence in Schools*, London: HMSO.

Foreword: The Importance of Having a Vision

Glenys Kinnock

My interest in, and commitment to, early childhood education is rooted in my experience both as a parent and as a teacher of young children. As a member of the European Parliament I have become increasingly aware of the differences between countries in their policies and provision in relation to the care and education of young children. I am equally aware of the extent to which early childhood education in the UK has been influenced by what happens abroad. Also, as a grandmother of a little girl whose mother is Danish and who is now enjoying the early years support offered in that country, I am most certainly conscious of the need to offer parents and children in the UK a similar level of support.

This book is about vision: we have only to scan the contents page to recognize the range of issues and concerns which are addressed by the contributors. Closer scrutiny shows that there are strands which permeate, themes which recur and influences which are inescapable. Most of the writers, in responding to the request to share with the reader their vision for the future of early childhood education in the new millennium have done so by looking first to the past, recalling some of the formative influences on their thinking, their work, their writing and on their hopes, aspirations and vision for the future. Without exception each chapter makes reference to educationalists, policy makers and practitioners who have had a significant influence upon early childhood provision, philosophy, policy and practice.

From my European perspective I have been struck by the extent to which European influences have, both historically and in terms of future aspirations, influenced early childhood education. There have certainly been significant Europeans whose contribution to our understanding of young children's play, learning and development is inestimable. Pioneers such as Pestalozzi and Froebel with their emphasis on the importance of spontaneous play and child-centred learning have had a profound influence on early childhood education. In contrast, the teaching methods and didactic materials introduced by Montessori in Italy and the notion of 'the prepared environment' continue to influence the design of educational toys. In the UK early childhood care and education owes much to Owen, the McMillans and Isaacs. The work of Piaget, which I studied in the 1960s at the University of Cardiff, continues to be both an abiding influence and a challenge. Many contributors to this book refer to Reggio Emilia in Italy where he is known as 'our Piaget'.

In her exploration of European perspectives on educational provision for young children, David (1993) considers ways in which provision has evolved in Belgium,

Denmark, France, Germany, Italy, Spain, Sweden and the UK. She examines the political and economic influences, the philosophical underpinnings and the effects of research on the lives of the 'Young Europeans' about whom she writes. She says that the status and role of early childhood professionals, as advocates of children's rights, are currently important topics of debate in many of the countries examined and concludes that 'looking beyond national boundaries is a vital ingredient in early years education'.

European funded programmes such as Erasmus and Comenius have done much to increase the opportunities for early years teachers, students and trainers to spend time in other countries to learn from each other and to break down barriers and abolish stereotypes. This opportunity must be both safeguarded and extended in the new millennium.

In his opening address to the Educare in Europe Conference held in Denmark in 1992 John Bennett, the UNESCO coordinator, predicted that early childhood care and education would become an increasingly expanding sector of activity for the majority of countries during the 1990s. The following year in a book entitled *By Faith and Daring* in which I recorded the achievements of some remarkable women, I made the same point, emphasizing the importance of investment in decent, affordable childcare as a central goal and denouncing the then government's aim to get childcare on the cheap and its failure to recognize the fact that it is those who can least afford to pay for care who need to work. It is indeed heartening that, five years on, the present government is fulfilling its commitment to the expansion of childcare and educational provision and is investing in the development of a partnership between the public, voluntary and private sectors which will lead to diversity and choice for parents.

David's final comment in her book is an important one for all who act as advocates for our youngest children, and one which I would certainly endorse:

> The decisions made by governments need to be based not only on the evidence of research, the views of particular pressure groups, or those of experienced pragmatists in the field. They must also be based on arguments concerning the values espoused by a society which claims to care about its children and to require a highly educated workforce of the future. To fulfil questions about the implications of those values, policy makers, parents and practitioners need opportunities to reflect on and discuss the place of the young child in European society, concepts of childhood and the real worlds of childhood inhabited by all our children.

References

BENNETT, J. (1992) Opening remarks — Educare in Europe Conference, Copenhagen, Denmark, October.

BOYDEN, J. (1997) 'Childhood and the policy makers', in JAMES, A. and PROUT, A. (eds) *Contemporary Issues in the Sociological Study of Childhood*, London: Falmer Press.

DAVID, T. (ed.) (1993) *Educational Provision for our Youngest Children, European Perspectives*, London: Paul Chapman Publishing Ltd.

KINNOCK, G. and MILLAR, F. (1993) *By Faith and Daring*, London: Virago Press.

WOODHEAD, M. (1996) *In Search of the Rainbow: Pathways to Quality in Large Scale Programmes for Young Disadvantaged Children*, The Hague: Bernard Van Leer Foundation.

Introduction: A Vision for the Future — Reforming or Transforming?

Helen Moylett and Lesley Abbott

1998, the year in which contributors to this book have been responding to our invitation, as editors, to reflect on the past and to share with us their vision for the new millennium, has been one of rapid change and development for the early years. In 1997 the newly elected government grandly proclaimed in *Excellence in Schools* that:

> Investment in learning in the twenty-first century is the equivalent of the investment in machinery and technical innovation that was essential to the first great industrial revolution. Then it was physical capital; now it is human capital. Our children are our future as a civilized society and a prosperous nation. If they are to have an education that matches the best in the world, we must start now to lay the foundations, by getting integrated early years education and childcare and primary education right. (DfEE, 1997)

In attempting to achieve integration the government has introduced an impressive range of measures. At the time of writing, a guide to current government initiatives in the early years (*Co-ordinate*, March 1998) outlines some 34 cross-sector and departmental developments which must surely warm the hearts of those who sat on committees of inquiry such as Rumbold (1990) and the RSA Early Learning Inquiry (Ball, 1994). The guide states:

> Suddenly early years are on every agenda. The Prime Minister, the Chancellor of the Exchequer and the Secretaries of State in Education and Employment, Health, Social Security and the Home Office, are all generating initiatives that could affect all services for young children and their families.

Figure I.1 indicates the major initiatives which will affect early education into the millennium.

By the time this is published there will doubtless be other initiatives up and running that have important implications for the education and care of young children into the next millennium.

It might therefore seem difficult, in this rapidly changing context, to write with certainty and conviction about the future of early educare. However, the immediate political context is only one aspect, albeit an important one, of the world in which young children live. The contributors to this book can afford, and would indeed

1

Key Initiatives and Developments in the Early Years

Early Education	DfEE	School Standards and Framework Bill	Defines Nursery Education — Creates a duty for LEAs to: • secure the provision of sufficient nursery education • establish Early Years Development Partnerships • produce Early Years Development Plans
	DfEE	Education Action Zones	The School Standards and Framework Bill provides for 25 EAZs to be set up for 3–5 years to create greater educational opportunities by developing innovative solutions to local problems.
	DfEE	Standards Fund	Grants for which LEAs can bid to achieve specific objectives.
	DfEE	Early Excellence Centres	25 local centres demonstrating effective partnerships through the provision of integrated early services with community and parental involvement, training, 'wraparound' care and dissemination of good practice.
	QCA	Desirable Learning Outcomes for young children's learning	Consultation on appropriate curriculum content and experiences for children under 5.
	DfEE	Early Years Development Partnerships and Plans	Collaborative partnerships to demonstrate ways in which local authorities will provide 3 free terms of good quality preschool education for all 4-year-olds.
	DfEE	National Advisory Group on Special Educational Needs	Consultation on Green Paper 1998 — Action plan 1998–2005 to demonstrate ways in which standards will be raised for all children with SEN.
	QCA	Baseline Assessment	Final lists of accredited schemes published March 1998.
Training and Qualifications	DfEE	National Training Organisation (NTO)	Recognition of NTO specifically for Early Years to audit and respond to training needs.
	Teacher Training Agency (TTA)	Recognition of Early Years as a Specialist Subject	Advanced study of Early Years in order to equip Early Years teachers to work across settings for 3–5-year-olds. Particularly important for graduates of integrated degrees e.g. BA Early Childhood Studies to access PGCE Courses.
	DfEE	Standards Fund	Grants for training for early years settings in EY Development Partnerships. Professional development for National Literacy strategy.
Employment	DfEE/DSS	Welfare to Work	The overall strategy for reducing unemployment.
	DfEE	New Deal	Voluntary scheme to help parents to take up work. Compulsory schemes for training 18–24-year-olds. Voluntary scheme for 25+ to take up subsidized employment or training.

Income	Department of Social Security (DSS)	Tax and Benefits Review	Working family Tax Credit for low wage working families to include substantial contribution to childcare costs.
		Child Support Agency	Review of structures and procedures for assessing and collecting parental contributions to child maintenance.
Family Issues	Home Office	Parenting initiative	Ministerial group on the family to: • identify main problems faced by families • review existing policies • identify areas for future action
	DfEE	Education for Parenthood	School based initiative to offer education for parenthood and learning initiatives for parents.
National Childcare Strategy	DfEE	Child care unit	National Childcare strategy 0–14
	DfEE	Out of school childcare initiative	1998–2003 £50 million for creation of out of school care and development of support network.
	Department for Culture Media and Sport	New Opportunities Fund	1999–2003 NOF will provide £400m for out of school provision. £200m for out of school care £200m for out of school learning activity £20m for integrated schemes — childcare and homework support including 8,000 out of school learning initiatives.
	DfEE	Training and Information for childcare	£6.75 million made available.
	Cross Dept Treasury led	Comprehensive Spending Review	Review of spending on 0–7-year-olds — focus preventative action at family and community level.
Health	DoH	Our Healthier Nation — Green Paper	Consultative document on government strategy including healthier schools.
		Health Action Zones	10 Health Action Zones to set measurable targets for improvement in health of local population.
		Healthy Schools Awards	National Scheme to recognize the progress made by schools in achieving and maintaining nationally agreed criteria for healthy schools.
Social Exclusion	Cabinet Office	Social Exclusion unit	Coordinates and improves government action to reduce social exclusion from school.
Disability		Disability Task force	To review ways in which the Disability Discrimination Act applies within education.

Figure I.1:   *Key initiatives and development in the early years*

Source: Table produced with acknowledgment to *Co-ordinate* — March, 1998.

maintain that they had a moral and intellectual duty, to take a longer view than politicians. They are generally unfettered by considerations of political expediency and can therefore concentrate on the things which make true change a process rather than an event. Whilst often welcoming new initiatives, they remind us of the sort of foundations on which they should be built in order to stand as lasting monuments to our developing understanding of the needs of young children. Most of the writers here are mainstream academics, researchers and/or practitioners, many of whom have spent years working closely with national and local government and other agencies for the benefit of young children. They have some important things to say about how we perceive children and childhood at the end of the twentieth century.

Our perception as editors is that those who work with young children generally welcome all the new initiatives, which seem to promise so much and are already delivering badly needed injections of cash and optimism. The government's vision for the future promises much — based as it is on a recognition of the crucial importance of families for an intellectually, morally and physically healthy society. However, once one scratches the surface of the New Left vision, one wonders how visionary it truly is. Indeed some would claim that it is very difficult for politicians to be visionary, driven as they are by political expediency and by global markets. What they can be is reforming. Perhaps politicians find it easier to keep making new things out of the same old plasticene — new and better shapes emerge but they are still fashioned from the same monotonous old stuff, stuff that was once bright and multicoloured but, through over use, has assumed a uniform dull shade. Visionaries go and get something else to play with — they are the people who want to transform rather than reform; who look at the resources and choose what is best for the purpose not just what is out every day. Of course, it takes skill and confidence to challenge the *status quo* — skills of reflection and divergent thinking and the confidence to take risks, among others. All the contributors to this book are visionaries in some way — but they are also realists. For them as for Moss and Penn (1996) '... vision is neither an optional extra nor a self-indulgent distraction. Vision provides answers to essential questions. ... As well as a manifesto for the future ... it is a rejection of the *status quo*' (p. 2). They believe in the reality that if we do not begin to see children and the concept of childhood differently than we have in Britain over the last century, any vision will turn out to have been a mirage — pretty, beguiling, but ultimately deceiving and insubstantial. They argue powerfully for this reality, from different starting points, using different experiences, citing different authorities but all with the same concern for our collective future; our youngest children.

This book is obviously a collection; an assembly of different perspectives and traditions, with writers looking at the early years from different places. They write in differing styles, with different 'voices' and we expect that readers will want to use the book in a variety of different ways. It is difficult in a short introduction to really convey the texture of each individual chapter. Some chapters are very complex; others are more straightforward; some are personal; others give a broad overview. Nonetheless, there are some important common strands that the writers here use in various ways to weave their arguments. The whole book can perhaps be seen as a tapestry which, although obviously worked by different people, gains coherence from the way in which these common colours are used in the various different scenes or chapters. We have chosen what seem to us to be six major 'colours' to introduce readers to the book. These are history, play, children's learning, Information Communication Technology (ICT), postmodernism and research. For the reader's convenience we have chosen groups of chapters to illustrate each of these aspects, although we must stress that these writers range widely and draw upon many different sources; none of them can be neatly categorized and, of course, the strands we have identified overlap. We may, for instance, introduce a contributor in a group of chapters exemplifying current discussions about children's learning, although she may also have important things to say about play, research and history. However, we hope that the way we have organized this introductory chapter helps convey a picture of both the different individual scenes and the whole rich and varied tapestry that will be revealed on reading the rest of the book.

Let us start with the past, with history, which seems essential to an understanding of the present and future. The writers of this book seem to both agree and disagree with Hartley's famous line 'The past is a foreign country: they do things differently there'. Rosemary Peacocke has an abiding interest in history, indeed her chapter starts with her granddaughter's remark about her actually being history! On reflecting on a long career in education, she wonders whether we have really advanced in our thinking since Plowden, and whether we should have done. She highlights the fact that many 'new' initiatives can be seen as cases of history repeating itself — old wine in new bottles; (old plasticene in new shapes!) and suggests that 'At the end of the first millennium it would be a good resolution to learn and act upon many of the sound suggestions made over the previous years, and not constantly rework the mistakes of the past'. What she and other contributors to this book are advocating are new ways of looking at ourselves as well as others. As Peacocke says, we may learn the lessons of history even when we appear to be on a circular path.

In Chapter 2 Caroline Barratt-Pugh draws upon her own personal history in tracing changing perceptions and practices in working with young bilingual learners. Through a series of letters she illustrates how she and others 'did things differently' in the past and how she has come to 'know the place for the first time'. She then projects herself into the millennium as the mother of the twins she was expecting at the time of writing. Her children will be attending a Community Family Learning Centre which is run by the people who use it and where children have a voice in the curriculum. She thus seems to provide a practical example of the childhood institution as public space proposed by Peter Moss in Chapter 13.

Tina Bruce also generalizes from her personal history as she looks back at her own early teachers and appreciates the ways in which they have influenced her present priorities and practice. In Chapter 3 she introduces us to teachers like the Froebel-trained Miss Greaves who were doing the things we know good teachers and educarers do now. 'We really were a caring, learning community . . . She made us feel we could try new, difficult things . . . She gave us, each in our way, the disposition towards learning that lasts for a lifetime, and she valued our childhood play in doing so'. But Bruce reminds us that, despite the lessons we may have learnt from the Miss Greaveses of the world, about respecting children and about the value of play, there 'is still a view that learning can only occur if children are sitting at desks, preferably writing and recording and being graded on what they produce on paper'.

Peacocke, Barratt-Pugh and Bruce all point to the lessons that history should have taught us and, like many other contributors, they refer to an existing powerful example of what can be done in a community that takes these lessons to heart — Reggio Emilia in Italy. Many readers will doubtless have heard about or even visited this extraordinarily successful attempt to put children at the heart of the educational process. What they may not be aware of is that the founders of this child-centred approach to educare have explained that it was the experience of fascism that taught them that people who obediently conform are dangerous. They were therefore determined to translate into reality a vision of questioning children who can think and act autonomously.

Sir Christopher Ball is also determined; determined to change the way in which we look at early education in Britain. In a forthright chapter he looks briefly at his own history as both child and parent and outlines why the Start Right project and its recommendations continue to be so important to him. He wants to know how 'Key Stage 0' can be a time when good quality educare can give children the confidence and self esteem that will equip them to be lifelong learners.

In Chapter 5 Mary-Jane Drummond shares her observations of a context where the confidence and self esteem of children are seen as supremely important. The children in this Steiner kindergarten, like the children of Reggio Emilia, are encouraged to play because play is seen as important — really important; not something to be done after work. Drummond explains how a group of Steiner educarers put into practice their ideas during the hour a day when the children play together without teacher intervention (or interference). She paints a picture of experiences that are rich and fulfilling for the children based on a philosophy that ·values the spiritual and believes that the educarer's role is to find each individual's gifts and develop them. In this setting educarers have to look closely at themselves in order to model the key elements of order, rhythm, good habits and loving consistency. Drummond believes that although she, and presumably, most readers, will never be Steiner educators, we may all learn some important lessons from their loving respect for children and their worlds. She talks about play opening 'the doors through which children pass as their journeys begin'.

Both Rod Parker-Rees in Chapter 6 and John Abbott in Chapter 7 emphasize the importance of continuing to be playful long after our journeys have begun. In fact they maintain that in order to be a successful traveller one must be a playful one. Parker-Rees explores some complex theories about how our minds and our ability to think, develop and grow in intra-individual, interpersonal and socio-historical contexts. He likens learners to trees who need to grow, both up through their branches and leaves, and downwards through their roots. He feels that children should learn to 'enjoy the playful interaction between unpredictable, bottom-up change and the security of top down organising structures' and that 'adults, like children, need to be playful if they are to make authentic choices'. John Abbott is also worried by the British education system which aims for excellence in very narrow areas and therefore fails rather than enables. As a former director of Education 2000 and now as President of the 21st Century Learning Initiative, he warns that 'without deep, rigorous out-of-box thinking about the nature of human learning so many of the present reforms will give us specialists not experts'. He maintains that experts are characterized by their playful curiosity about the world and their ability to make links between different areas of knowledge. Specialists know a lot and stick to the rules — they have forgotten to stretch their minds, to make autonomous choices and links. Both Abbott and Parker-Rees feel that if we want children to become lifelong learners we should be encouraging playfulness in learning.

This concern for the ways in which children learn is of course manifest in all the contributions to this book. Over and over again writers regret the way in which work like Gardner's and Goleman's has been largely ignored in this country, even in the face of evidence from other countries about the deleterious affects of narrowing choice and formalizing the curriculum in the early years. Tricia David, in Chapter 8, reminds us about the power of even very young babies to initiate interaction and about the messages from research about the problematic nature of developmentalism. She refers to Kessen's influential work and claims '. . . the idea that members of a group or society co-construct particular childhoods and that children are active participants in that construction has provided a powerful challenge to decontextualized theories of child development'. She argues that some fundamentally inappropriate and outdated ideas will continue to remain unchallenged by current political initiatives if we do not change our collective ideas about children and begin to value them as people in their own right rather than denigrate them as adults in waiting. Pascal and Bertram in Chapter 9 also pick up this theme. They explain why they are extending the work they have already done on children's learning in the Effective Early Learning (EEL) project and focusing their latest research on how practitioners might measure learning outcomes more effectively by taking a broader view of the qualities that make for lifelong learning. They express concern about the narrowness of most current assessment — 'very few schemes have any reference to attitudes, dispositions or emotional well-being and emotional literacy. . . . Whilst we recognize the importance of skills and knowledge, we believe that such a simplistic focus should not be the sole view of achievement'. They draw upon a wealth of research evidence to support their view that what they call 'the knowledge revolution in early learning' should be shaping policy and practice.

Clearly alongside the knowledge revolution there has been a technological revolution. Children now and into the new millennium are using tools for learning that did not exist even ten years ago. Some readers may have reservations about the rise and rise of information and communication technology, but writers like Mark Vandevelde and Paul Baker would see this as largely misplaced nostalgia for another age. Vandevelde is by far the youngest contributor to this book and presumably the only one who was a proficient computer user at the age of 5! Now at

16 he is considered something of an expert and is still learning. In his visionary view of the classroom of the future he outlines ways in which teaching and learning are already changing. Baker echoes many of Vandevelde's sentiments about the enormous potential of ICT in the early years. He begins and ends with the two girls who 'could hear the lion go roar' and the implications for them and their educarers of those children's awareness of the differences between conventional print and interactive tools. He points to the importance of professional development leading to fewer and fewer 'technophobes' working with young children — who are certainly not technophobes themselves! Both writers stress the importance of the ways in which we apply ICT in the future. Vandevelde's view is that early childhood education has to rise to the challenges of the rapidly changing social and political context, otherwise individuals risk 'the prospect of becoming the downtrodden serfs of the information age'.

Time and place and the way in which we locate ourselves in relation to them also occupy Peter Moss in Chapter 13. He discusses the way in which modernity with its way of understanding the world as a fixed and objective reality, with its emphasis on 'control, order, predictability and certainty' should, and in some places has, given way to an altogether more tentative, contextualized way of seeing things. In the postmodern project, he claims, the world is assumed to be socially constructed. This way of seeing the world obviously has implications for practice. It means we have choices about how we view children and childhood. He maintains that if we choose a way of looking that respects children and families, then we need to develop more democratic and radical ways of looking at public space. In Chapter 14 Philip Gammage shares some of Moss's concerns and reviews the ways in which we are living in a time '. . . when rules, customs, beliefs, values and ideas are subjected to reanalysis, when a greater awareness of their context-dependent, subjective nature is revealed'. In a different approach to Moss's he also regrets the lack of political attention paid to philosophy and research.

Research is the strand we have left till last although it is omnipresent. None of the chapters is research free and most refer to it in pleas for greater understanding of what children's education could be like in the future.

Kathy Sylva in a chapter entitled 'The role of research in explaining the past and shaping the future' identifies the main types of research that have been done in early education as longitudinal studies on the impact of early learning; longitudinal studies on the processes which lead to differential impact on children's lives; discourse analysis and narrative research. She reviews some of the important work done in each of these paradigms and asks 'Which methods or researchers tell us most about the curriculum?' She answers her own question — 'All of them'. All of them are present in this book but we would like to finish this introduction by mentioning two writers who mention other people's research comparatively sparingly but who discuss practical examples of a postmodern way of looking at existing institutions.

Both Margaret Stevens and Gillian Pugh care passionately about what their own research has taught them. They have both spent long careers working with and for young children. In Chapter 10, as well as introducing the reader to the young

Mark Vandevelde (the author of Chapter 11), Stevens outlines some ideas for changing the ways in which inspection might function as part of a locally owned process. These ideas are based on her own experience as an inspector and on a commitment to a more democratic and emancipatory model — similar to that outlined by Peter Moss. Like Stevens, Pugh is keen to listen to the voices of children and parents as well as educarers and politicians. She relates the development of the Thomas Coram Early Childhood Centre to its roots in research and in the needs of the local community. Like Barratt-Pugh's Community Family Learning Centre in Chapter 2 the Thomas Coram Centre seems to be developing new ways of looking at children and families and their needs. In these postmodern projects we seem to see people going some way at least towards more inclusive models of early educare and away from deficit models where change was always demanded from children and parents and not from educarers and policy makers.

This introduction started with a discussion of the pace of change and the way in which the writers of this book remind us of some important ideas about children's learning that transcend the political context. In guiding the reader around the tapestry of this book and introducing its major colours we hope we have already raised questions about how ideas are constructed both socially and politically and about how, why, where and when change takes place. However you construct your reading journey through this book, whether you go straight from first page to last or meander backwards and forwards, we hope you will find much to delight and more to challenge.

References

BALL, C. (1994) *Start Right: The Importance of Early Learning*, London: Royal Society for the Encouragement of the Arts, Manufacturers and Commerce (RSA).

Co-Ordinate, Journal of the National Early Years Network, **64**, March 1998.

DfEE (1997) *Excellence in School*, London: HMSO.

GARDNER, H. (1983) *Frames of Mind: The Theory of Multiple Intelligences*, London: Fontana Press.

GOLEMAN, D. (1996) *Emotional Intelligence*, London: Bloomsbury.

HARTLEY, L.P. (1963) *The Go-between*, London: Heinemann.

KESSEN, W. (1979) 'The American child and other cultural inventions', *American Psychologist*, **34**, 10, pp. 815–20.

MOSS, P. and PENN, H. (1996) *Transforming Nursery Education*, London: Paul Chapman.

RUMBOLD, A. (1990) 'Starting with quality', Report of the Committee of Inquiry into the quality of the educational experiences offered to 3- and 4-year-olds, chaired by Mrs. A. Rumbold CBE, MP, London: HMSO.

1   Inspecting the Future

Rosemary Peacocke

The telephone rang and Rachel, my granddaughter, asked if she might interview me for her project. I agreed to do this and enquired, 'Is this for English or do you want to know about the House of Commons?' 'Oh no,' she replied, 'you're History!' This chastening thought made me think that perhaps, over the long period I have been involved with the early years I have been a part of a lively, exciting and certainly challenging piece of history which is now coming into the new millennium.

As a very new head of an infant school I received a visitor who also wanted to interview me, saying he was a researcher for a committee which was set up under the chairmanship of Lady Plowden. He was interested to learn my views on the most effective ways in which young children learn, and also that he would like to return regularly to observe and ask further questions. I did not know at this juncture that I was about to be a very small part of another important part of history.

Few reports have been so widely quoted and misquoted over the past thirty years in this country. The Plowden Report published in 1967, has been praised and blamed for the development of primary education. Internationally it is still considered one of the most important and influential reports about how young children learn, and the principles and philosophy described are being followed in other countries. Buildings, especially in America, are still being constructed based on those described in the report.

It is worth glancing at the text at the end of the millennium to see a few examples of the thinking at that time. The first two sentences of Chapter 2 are worth quoting, 'At the heart of the educational process lies the child. No advances in policy, no acquisitions of new equipment have their desired effect unless they are in harmony with the nature of the child, unless they are fundamentally acceptable to him' (Chapter 2, p. 7, para. 9). The language may be dated, but this premise still stands.

In the 1960s, a survey showed that 29 per cent of all homes had five books or less. It would be interesting to know if this statistic is similar at the millennium, since reading now has to compete with TV and video. Strong recommendations were made in the Report to foster parental involvement, and many examples of good practice were described.

The 1960 descriptions of the schools in educational priority areas are stark, and unfortunately prophetic. 'We have ourselves seen schools caught in vicious circles and read accounts of many more . . . We noted the grim approaches; incessant traffic noise in narrow streets; the absence of green playing spaces; gaunt looking buildings; often poor decorative conditions inside; narrow passages; un-heated and cramped cloakrooms; . . . it is becoming particularly hard to find good heads of infant or deputy heads of junior schools. We are not surprised to hear of the rapid turnover of staff, of vacancies sometimes unfilled or filled with a succes-sion of temporary and supply teachers of one kind or another' (The Education Committee, 1995). And the above was written not in the 1960s but in 1995!

In 1995 the Select Committee for Education in the House of Commons pro-duced a report on Performance in City Schools. It echoed the words of Plowden, described the depressing effects on the staff and pupils of vandalism, theft and arson in the school. The report goes on to say 'There are significant problems of high teacher mobility in schools in some deprived urban areas, and within individual schools . . . New ways must be found to encourage able, experienced teachers to work in city schools and remain long enough to provide stability and continuity'.

For the purpose of this chapter the most significant recommendation in the Plowden Report is that 'Eventually there should be nursery places for all children whose parents wish to attend from the beginning of the school year after the age of three' (Chapter 9, p. 116, para. 343).

A similar recommendation, except that the age of entry proposed is four, was made by the Select Committee for Education, Science and Arts in a report on *Educational Provision for the Under Fives* in 1988, by the same committee in its report on *Standards of Reading in Primary Schools* in 1991, and also by the Educa-tion Committee in the report *Performance in City Schools* in 1995. It is extraordin-ary that such similar recommendations are being made through the decades and consistently being ignored.

Fascinating and, perhaps, disturbing, though this tour through the highways and byways of the Plowden Report and glances at successive reports can be — and there are many more we could follow — I would like to return to the first quotation 'At the heart of the educational process lies the child . . .' not the curriculum, not subjects, not organization, but the child. It is in this context that I want to consider the social, moral, cultural and spiritual development of the young child and peer through the mist at what might be the inspection priorities in 2000. This is not an area which has only been recognized as an important part of the curriculum in the years in which OFSTED has been inspecting schools. Plowden also had something to say,

> Emotional, social and intellectual aspects are closely intertwined in mental growth: the child is a total personality. Emotional life provides the spur and in many ways gives meaning to experience. Moral development is closely associated with emotional and social development. The child forms his sense of personal worth and his moral sense from early experiences of acceptance, approval, and dis-approval. (Chapter 2, p. 22, para. 65)

The word 'spiritual' is not mentioned in Plowden in this context, and is only used once in the section on Religious Education. The very term 'spiritual' develop-ment causes problems for some teachers, and not only teachers. As long ago as the drafting of the 1944 Education Act, William Temple, then Archbishop of Canterbury tried to find a word that would not offend the members of the Houses of Parliament, and he tried to avoid the word 'religion'. His assistant Canon Hall found the answer, and he wrote, 'The churches were in such a state at that time that we thought if we used the word "spiritual" they might agree to that because they didn't know what it was. They all had very clear ideas about what religion was and they all knew they did not agree with anyone else's definition of it'.

Traditionally, and the use of the word by Canon Hall shows this, spiritual development and spirituality have been associated with religious faith, but the terms are now used in a much wider fashion, though still conveying something belonging to a person's inner life. The National Curriculum Council in 1993 offered the following definition:

> spiritual development needs to be seen as something fundamental in the human condition which is not necessarily experienced through the physical senses and/or expressed through every day language. It has to do with relationships with other people and, for believers, with God. It has to do with the universal search for individual identity with our responses to challenging experiences, such as death, suffering, beauty and encounters with good and evil. It is to do with the search for meaning and purpose in life and for the values by which we live.

We have evidence that spiritual experience is not restricted to those who consider themselves religious believers. As long ago as the end of the 1960s Alister Hardy, an Oxford biologist, carried out a survey inviting responses from the general public on variants of the question, 'Have you ever been aware of or influenced by a presence or power, whether you call it God or not, which is different from your everyday self?' 5,000 responses were received. Since then twelve similar surveys have been carried out showing that 20–48 per cent have claimed to have had some experience of the numinous. Most of the people who responded admitted that they had told no-one of their experiences for fear of being thought either stupid or unbalanced.

From the survey conducted by Hardy all the material which referred to young children, that is the adult's memories of their own experiences, was collated by Eric Robinson in his book *The Original Vision*. It is interesting to note that most of the experiences described were to do with the natural world, and also the very young age these children had these experiences.

This well documented extract from the book illustrates both these points,

> The most profound experience of my life came to me when I was very young — between four and five years old. I am not mistaken in dating this because I remember both the place where it occurred and the shoes I was wearing at the time, of which I was rather fond. Both of these facts relate only to this particular period of my life; I have a dated photograph of myself wearing the shoes in question.
>
> My mother and I were walking on a stretch of land in Berkshire, known locally as 'the moors'. As the sun declined and the slight chill of evening came on, a pearly mist formed over the ground. My feet, with the favourite black shoes with

silver buckles, were gradually hidden from sight until I stood ankle deep in gently swirling vapour. Here and there just the very tallest harebells appeared above the mist. I had a great love of these exquisitely formed flowers, and stood lost in wonder at the sight. Suddenly I seemed to see the mist as a shimmering gossamer tissue and the harebells, appearing here and there, seemed to shine with a brilliant fire. The vision has never left me. It is as clear today as it was fifty years ago, and with it the same intense feeling of the love of the world and the certainty of ultimate good. Of course at the early age of four or five I could not have expressed anything of the experience in the words I have now used. (Robinson, 1983, p. 110)

That last sentence is important. Young children do not have the language to describe their experiences, and we underestimate them because of their inability to talk about it. Some poets and writers however, have described vividly how they viewed the world in the early years, and their perceptions of amazement, awe and wonder. Traherne was one such writer. In *The Centuries* he introduces a section with the words 'Is it not strange that an infant should be heir of the whole world, and see those mysteries which the books of the learned never unfold? . . . The dust and stones of the street were as precious as gold: the gates were at first the end of the world. The green trees when I first saw them through one of the gates transported and ravished me, their sweetness and unusual beauty made my heart to leap, and almost mad with ecstasy, they were such strange and wonderful things' (Traherne, 1963, p. 110).

Although, doubtless, children's inability to express themselves is one difficulty, it can also be relevant that often they do not have anyone to listen if they are prepared to talk. This is becoming even more apparent in the climate of the primary classroom where 4-year-old children are in large groups, and the pressure is towards more formal teaching for the 5-year-olds.

Clive Erricker (1997), in his work in the Children and Worldviews project, suggests that spiritual development is best encouraged by eliciting children's explanations to significant events in their own lives and then relating them to other children who can then reflect on such accounts in relation to their own experience.

The following edited extract, from a much longer contribution, was made in response to another child's comment that she thought her Dad had gone to heaven.

Before my Nan died she told me lots of things because she knew she was going to die. She said she would be happy when she died. On that day she got a picture of her and all the family, stuck it on a postcard and wrote on the back 'I'll see you in my heart'. Now she's always with me. Now I talk to her all the time. I talk to her when I'm lonely. When I've argued with my friends I go and sit on the wall and think about her and talk to her. . . . She says she's going to ring me up. She says things in my head, she rings up my brain and talks to me. When she went up to heaven she took one of her special secrets. She took it with her and she can just ring me up, it's clever. This special secret makes her able to do that. I keep wanting to tell people things but they don't understand. (Erricker, 1997, p. 47)

This remarkable outpouring was only made possible by the fact that another child had stimulated it and there was a sympathetic listener. The child had, with the help of a supportive family, come to terms with her grandmother's death and, in her own way, reflected on her experience using metaphorical language to interpret her feelings.

Death is something which some teachers find it very difficult to deal with, however this is not the only sense of loss with which many children have to cope. The divorce rate now means that the children involved in separation from one parent is increasing. Young children are caught up in an emotional situation that they are unable to understand but of which they are an important part, and often have no-one to talk to because of the relationships of the adults. Personal and social development in schools cannot ignore the pressures some of these children are experiencing, which we know from empirical evidence affect the children's work and relationships with their peers and teachers.

There is evidence to show that in some cases children are struck if they mention to one parent that they wish to visit the other and, often, the children find it difficult to talk about their problems, even to their peers. In another extract from the Children and Worldviews project, where a boy is talking to the researcher about his parents splitting up he says

> Talking's the best way to get it off your mind a lot, cos well you get the chance to talk about things, cos this is the first time we've actually got to discuss it with somebody. But if it was like a group or a class of children, about ten people, I couldn't say anything then cos I'd be scared cos I would think people might take the mickey out of me. (Erricker, 1997, p. 109)

Another boy said 'I talked to N about what happened to me, he was another person I thought I could talk to because he's, his Mum and Dad were on the verge of splitting up and he felt what I felt then, and he, he keeps it a secret'.

The two boys gained such confidence from the discussion that they decided to talk to the headteacher and ask permission to set up a meeting so that they could share problems they had never been able to talk about before. The meetings were arranged and were chaired by the children; the headteacher was present but did not speak unless invited to. The subjects for discussion were placed anonymously in a box during the week.

What do we learn from all this about the needs of the child? Certainly that time must be made to listen to individual children, and then sensitively encourage the children to share their experiences, but perhaps most importantly is that we recognize and respect the children's thinking and in doing so enhance their self esteem. In spiritual, social, moral and cultural development, this is not only the key to enhancing each of these areas, but the fundamental need of every child to have a strong concept of self worth or as they say across the Atlantic 'Feel good about yourself'.

A good self image is just as important for adults to succeed in whatever they are doing, and it can be something said or assumptions made which can affect an individual. An amusing example of this occurred when I was a newly appointed HMI and was visiting a probationary teacher who was having problems with a class of 5- and 6-year-olds. At the end of the morning a valiant, but not very successful, attempt was being made to clear up the classroom after a session which included seven different craft activities. I was sitting silently on a small chair by the door observing all that was going on, when a small girl came over to me and whispered 'Are you learning to be a dinner lady?' It is salutary, but not always comfortable, to see ourselves as others see us, but the self image presented to me that day has lived with me for many years!

If it is accepted that a child will not be able to learn effectively if she has low self esteem, how can this be improved in the early years? There are a variety of ways and perhaps the most important is that other people, and especially the adults who spend a lot of time with the child, take her seriously, listen to what she says and warmly accept her as a person. High esteem also comes from doing things well, knowing that she can trust people and being sure in the knowledge that her friends enjoy her company. Only when the child is secure will she want to learn, be able to learn and be motivated to do so.

With a good self image also comes self-knowledge and an understanding of other people and empathy with them. The poem 'Childhood' by Cornford expresses this well,

I used to think that grown-up people chose
To have stiff backs and wrinkles round their nose,
And veins like small fat snakes on either hand,
On purpose to be grand
'Til through the bannisters I watched one day
My great-aunt Etty's friend who was going away,
And how her onyx beads had come unstrung.
I saw her grope to find them as they rolled;
And then I knew that she was helplessly old,
As I was helplessly young.

Moral development follows closely on from our consideration of spiritual development. Children's moral dilemmas are just as puzzling and just as great as those faced by adults. 'Must I share my sweets just because my friend shared hers?' 'Who will know if I go and eat them all in my secret place?' Children from as young as two or three years begin to understand that other people have their own needs, and from the age of four can put themselves in others' shoes to find a way to help. It is interesting that of the first abstract concepts justice is the first to be understood — 'His pencil is longer, or newer, or sharper than mine. It's not fair!' The child's moral awareness in the early years is shaped mainly by observing others, their peers help them to understand the realities of sharing and cooperating. However, it is the parent and teacher who inform, encourage and help the child, through love and affection, to grow to a moral awareness. The well known phrase 'I can't hear what you say because what you are doing is shouting so loudly' is pertinent here, because it is true particularly in the early years, that while something is being taught, something else is being learnt.

Social development and cultural development both depend on a sense of belonging — to their family and other groups and an understanding and acceptance that other people are different and have their own ways of doing things. One of the joys of working with young children is that they bring a fresh, open and unbiased view to new situations where the adult is tiptoeing over the stepping stones of what she perceives as a dangerous torrent. In a nursery school where there were no children from ethnic minorities the teacher had brought a picture of two little children one black and one white, totally naked, holding hands and walking towards the sea. She introduced the session with an open-ended question about the picture, asking the children to comment on what they saw. The answer came quickly, 'I think they will get a cold and their Mummy will be cross!'

The other important aspects of cultural development are also closely linked with spiritual development. The delight in colour and music, the joy of creativity, the mystery and beauty of the natural world and especially the magic of stories are all experiences which the young child meets at a very early age and is encouraged by the teacher who provides resources and language to extend the child's personal world.

It is the parents, the prime educators who are the first and most important influence in the child's life. The total dependence of the very young child makes the parents concerned for all her physical needs, and they know their child better than anyone else. It is now accepted that children learn more in the first five years of their lives than at any other time. It is interesting to consider how this learning takes place. Some years ago I had the opportunity, while I was in Japan, to observe Dr Suzuki, the violin teacher, teaching a mixed age group of students. Their ages ranged from 7 to 54. After an energetic lesson which involved both Dr Suzuki and the students in dancing, singing, talking and playing he spent time with me discussing his approach to teaching and learning. All teaching, he believed should use 'The mother tongue approach'. When a child learns to talk, the mother, or father, reenforces all learning throughout her waking life with praise, encouragement and consolidation. The parents want the child to learn, she is motivated to do so and she does. The parents, he said, view their child as not only their own in the physical sense, but their own in that they have made her what she is. When I left Dr Suzuki's school in Matsimoto he presented me with an exquisite landscape which he had painted himself, and wrote on the back the translation of the Japanese inscribed on the picture 'Man is a son of his environment'.

The mists will not clear to divulge the priorities which will be given by the government for inspection of early education in 2000, but I would like to close this chapter with a visionary gaze into the millennium. It is not necessary for me to say that literacy and numeracy are of vital importance. I am positive they will be on the agenda, but let us look at the children themselves. In the last forty years, following the example of America, our children have been forced by society to become little adults before they have had time to enjoy and experience childhood. The television in the corner of the room is a major influence in their lives, and they are exposed to explicit sex, violence and vandalism. The so-called nine o'clock watershed means little when many children have a TV set in the bedroom. Neil Postman wrote in

The Disappearance of Childhood about children watching television '. . . having access to the previously hidden fruit of adult information, they are expelled from the garden of childhood'. He refers to them as 'hurried children', and his book ends with these thoughts 'It is not conceivable that our culture will forget that it needs children. But it is halfway toward forgetting that children need childhood. Those who insist on remembering shall perform a noble service'. The culture he refers to is the American culture, but it could just as well be the culture of the United Kingdom.

Young children need time to play, to experiment and discover, to talk and to listen, they need time to linger over the mystery of reflected light and the beauty of a spider's web on a frosty morning. Children need time to make friends, and space to run and shout and jump, they need time to reflect and delight in the warmth of a rabbit, and the trail of a snail. All of this, in the language of the professional, demands a broad and unfragmented curriculum, meeting the needs of the whole child, with opportunity, resources, facilities and space for the young child to learn with the constant and ready support of an appropriately qualified teacher, who ensures that the child has a good self image.

At the end of the first millennium, it would be a good resolution to learn and act upon many of the sound suggestions made over the previous years, and not constantly rework the mistakes of the past.

My crystal ball bursts into a rainbow with the thought that inspection in the millennium could bring new priorities in early education:

- the needs of the child as a person entering this new era — her spiritual, cultural, moral and social development which will enable her to meet new challenges and new situations;
- children given time, and adults giving status, to play;
- childhood being recognized as an important, valuable and essential time of a person's life, which if it is taken away can never be regained.

References

CENTRAL ADVISORY COUNCIL FOR EDUCATION (ENGLAND) (1967) *Children and their Primary Schools*, (The Plowden Report), London: HMSO.

CORNFORD, F. (1973) 'Childhood', *Oxford Book of Twentieth Century Verse*, Oxford: Oxford University Press.

ERRICKER, C. et al. (1997) *The Education of the Whole Child*, London: Cassell.

EDUCATION SCIENCE AND ARTS COMMITTEE (1988) *National Provision for the Under Fives*, first report of The Education, Science and Arts Committee, London: HMSO.

EDUCATION, SCIENCE AND ARTS COMMITTEE (1991) *Standards of Reading in Primary Schools* (third report), London: HMSO.

HAY, D. (1994) '"The Biology of God" What is the current status of Hardy's hypothesis?' *International Journal for the Psychology of Religion*, pp. 6–7.

NATIONAL CURRICULUM COUNCIL (1993) *Spiritual and Moral Development – a discussion paper*, London.

POSTMAN, N. (1983) *The Disappearance of Childhood*, London: W.H. Allen.

PRIESTLEY, J. (1985) 'The spiritual dimension in the curriculum', The Spiritual Dimension in Education, Occasional Papers Series No. 2, University of Southampton: Department of Education.

ROBINSON, E. (1983) *The Original Vision*, New York: Seabury Press.

THE EDUCATION COMMITTEE (1995) *Performance in City Schools* (third report), London: HMSO.

TRAHERNE, T. (1960) *Centuries*, Oxford: Clarendon Press.

2 The Good, the Bad and the Possible? Linguistic and Cultural Diversity: Changing Perceptions and Practices

Caroline Barratt-Pugh

This chapter is an amalgamation of a variety of experiences I have had during the past 20 years of working in the field of language and literacy in early childhood. Thus, the incidents referred to are based on several events at a particular point in time, and do not in any way reflect individual people or institutions. All the children's names have been changed to preserve confidentiality. I could not have made this journey without the children I have worked with, my family, friends and colleagues who enriched every moment and continue to do so.

4 September 1974
Dear Franca,

I'm so excited I can't sleep. I start my first new job tomorrow as a fully qualified Nursery Nurse at Newgate Language Centre for Immigrants, in the reception class.

Mrs Sands (my class teacher) seems really nice. Although she says the immigrant children are really great, they can't hold pencils and scissors, so she does lots of colouring in, tracing, cutting and sticking. In the afternoon she has a play session because they're too tired to do any work and, anyway, apparently they don't play in their culture. Mrs Sands says its a bit chaotic in the first week, but the sooner they settle in the better. They've got to get used to our ways, so they can start learning.

Well I better try and get some sleep, will write more later — on my new typewriter!

What a week! The NESB (non-English speaking background) children are great, I really worked hard trying to say their names. Mrs Sands has nick-names for the really difficult ones and some have English names (Mrs Sands says the parents want their children to be like us). I am beginning to get to know all the children, as every morning they go into the tiny language room in groups of four. It's

Plurals on Monday,
Pronouns on Tuesday,
Adverbs on Wednesday,
Prepositions on Thursday,
And full sentences on Friday.

Guess what, I can do adverbs on Wednesday!

I got into a bit of trouble on Thursday. One of the teachers told me that it's really important that we tell the children not to speak Pakistani (that's not what their language is called, but the children don't know what it is either, so why should we!). So it's important that I keep saying, 'We only speak English here don't we?' It's for their own good. The next generation will speak English and there won't be a problem any more. If only they would speak English at home. As long as parents speak Pakistani the children will take so much longer to replace it with English!

Anyway I made up for not reminding them to speak English by reading, *The Three Little Pigs*. They really enjoyed it. They laughed and giggled all the way through, but they were too shy to move the pigs around on the felt board! I'm really going to enjoy being here. Write soon,
Caroline
PS. Do you know what an ADVERB is?

4 September 1979 (4 years later)
Dear Franca,

I'm so scared I can't sleep, my first very own reception class. What if they won't listen to me, what if they can't understand me, what if they finish all my work cards in a minute, what if they can't do them, what about the ESL (English as a second language) children? I've looked through my old education files and can only find one lecture where they are mentioned, it's called, 'Children with Special Needs'.

Well, I'm so relieved, the children are great. The ESL children are withdrawn for an hour a week, with the remedial children, so they aren't really my problem at all. Apparently they are very clever and will just 'pick-up' English, so I don't have to worry. Mind you, I might be getting Mai Lee, she's eight but can't speak a word of English and is very shy (apparently all Chinese girls are very reserved). She's been to school in Vietnam but really needs a lot of play and simple language so she'll fit in with my lot, though she's rather tall, hope she'll be OK.

It's funny, I still have to keep reminding the ESL children not to speak their home language. Perhaps we should put those children who speak the same language in different classrooms. It's not just my class though, one of the other teachers said, 'they're always speaking gobbledegook, no matter how many times I tell them!' You wouldn't believe it, Amran and Tariq actually wrote something in Urdu, and I found something that looked like Arabic writing. It must be so confusing and really unhelpful. I'm worried they'll never learn to write in English and they'll never 'fit in'. No wonder they don't want to copy words from the blackboard and take them home to learn.

Two of the children in the next class have just come back from a trip to Pakistan, their teacher is really upset. She says all her hard work has been undone, she doesn't know why she bothers. They've forgotten English, won't talk to her about their trip, and will probably start keeping chickens in the bathroom soon!

Anyway, my classroom is beginning to look good. The children did really fantastic pictures of themselves to make into a collage. I tried to mix some paint that matched the hair and eyes, but it didn't seem to matter as most of the girls drew themselves with blond hair and blue eyes! Anyway, the ESL children don't like to feel different, they don't like to 'stand out'. So I'm trying to treat all the children the same, after all, we are all the same underneath. It wouldn't be fair to the other children if I did anything special for the ESL children. Young children don't notice things like colour, do they? I've heard them call each other names in the play-ground, but they don't really mean it. Of course the ESL children don't have to go to assembly or swimming, we're not that insensitive! They just sit in the corridor reading a book until we get back.

We had a great staff meeting and talked about multicultural week. We're going to have a sort of 'sari, samosa and steel band' week. This will include everybody and make the ESL children feel 'a bit special' (just for the week). I'm going to bring in my collection of dolls from around the world in national dress. I'll put some material in the Wendy house for making a Sari (I'm sure the ESL girls will know how to put one on). I'll bring some vegetables in for Mai Lee and she can make a 'stir fry' for us. I'm going to borrow some Indian music from a parent, and some of the girls can show us Indian dancing. I'll try and find lots of books on Pakistan and Bangladesh. We might even do some fund raising for the poor children in those countries, (Oxfam have some great posters). What do you think about a sponsored walk round the mosque? I'm really looking forward to it! Talk to you soon,

Caroline

PS. Big disappointment! After Monday none of the ESL children came to school. I can't understand it, they must have all got flu or something. Oh well, the other children enjoyed multicultural week.

4 September 1984   **(5 years later)**
Dear Franca,

I'm sitting here in a state of trepidation and elation. I think this may be the last time we run a Multilingual/Antiracist weekend. I must admit working as an Advisory Teacher in the Multicultural Centre is a bit like heaven and hell! Working with the rest of the team — I'm constantly confronting my own demons, while my percep-tions about racism, sexism, bilingualism, culture are changing rapidly. There's a constant debate within and across black and white team members. The tensions are always there — who should be saying what to whom, who should be doing which inservice sessions, whether we should take a hard approach (no gain without pain), or a soft approach to bringing about change. Never a dull moment, but one thing's for sure, I'll never be the same again!

I'm a bit nervous about this weekend because things around here are getting really hairy. You may have read about the court case between the Local Education

Authority and a headteacher. It's brought all the racial tensions that were just bubbling under the surface to a head. It might be a good thing, but I guess a lot of kids and parents are at the rough end of it all, and teachers are really divided. Anyway, thank goodness all the team are going to be there, at least we can present a united front. I'll let you know what happens, write soon,
Caroline
PS. I'll just go pack the panadol and the gin, you never know which one will come in handy!

4 January 1986   **(2 years later)**
Dear Franca,

I've been thinking and worrying about you all day and night after we talked. I can't believe Maria won't speak to you in Italian any more, she's so fluent and confident. Could it be somehow linked to her reluctance to go to nursery? I wonder what's happened — have you spoken to her teacher? I can see her grandparents are really upset — suddenly she refuses speak to them in Italian and they only speak a little English. It seems ironic that it's my last day with the Advisory team tomorrow, especially as the bilingual working party has just finished some research looking at ways of supporting ESL and children's home and community languages. Now this — I wonder if I've made the right decision!

Anyway, I've been trying to sort out what to take to my new job at Manchester Poly, and I've come across some work that might help throw some light on what's happening with Maria. I've dug out a report on three language surveys which were carried out by the Local Education Authority. It makes very interesting reading:

- 59 different languages are spoken across all the schools in the local authority;
- 252 out of 284 schools actually have bilingual children; and
- almost all children from Asian communities speak a language other than English when they first come to school — even in nursery and pre-primary centres (just as Maria is/was speaking Italian when she started nursery).

But, but, but . . . something happens in between starting school and leaving school! Even though the council argues that all sections of the community have the right to maintain their own languages and culture, it seems that many older bilingual learners have actually rejected their home language by the time they leave school (even earlier in Maria's case). So what is going on?

Well, a group of bilingual teachers and nursery nurses has been doing a research project on bilingualism in schools. They have developed some resources, done extensive case studies, analysed the children's use of more than one language and interviewed children about their use of home languages. These are some of the things the children said about their languages and their first days at nursery and school. See what you think.

Bilingual Working Party: Talking with Bilingual Children

I started nursery when I was 4 years old. On the first day at nursery was very bad because I wanted to go home, I don't know what to do. Later on I liked it. When I went to First school I was 5 years old. The first day at my school I was scared because when the teacher was telling us what to do, I did not understand what she meant. I didn't want to go and ask what she meant.

Jasvinder

Bilingual Working Party: Talking with Bilingual Children

When I was in the nursery I went to the door and the teacher said, 'Where are you going?' and I said nothing, then I kept saying 'toilet'. I only speak Punjabi to my father, mother, uncle, aunties because they can't speak English very well. When I say something in English, my dad says transfer it to Punjabi. I don't speak Punjabi to my friends because if someone comes they think we are saying something rude or bad. I talk Punjabi if my friend says talk but we go to a safe place to talk so that no one can hear us or see us.

Amran

Bilingual Working Party: Talking with Bilingual Children

When I went to nursery I used to speak Gujarati to my friend. I used to get in trouble a lot by the teacher. I speak Gujarati with my dad and I speak English with my mum. I don't speak Gujarati at home to my mum because I am not very good at speaking Gujarati. I can understand what my dad and mum say in Gujarati. Now I go to Gujarati school I can read a bit of Gujarati and count. I go every Sunday.

Mahendra

Bilingual Working Party: Talking with Bilingual Children

I was born in England. And I learned English when I was in the nursery. And at home I speak Gujarati and at school I speak English. The troubles that I had at my first school were reading. My little sister knew English before she went to nursery because we speak in English and she caught English very quickly.

Nasreen

These are fairly vivid memories of early days at nursery or school! I guess not being able to understand what was going on and not wanting to ask for help could have been very frightening and confusing, no wonder Jasvinder wanted to go home. D'you know if there are any Italian speaking teachers or carers at Maria's nursery? Maybe, like Amran, Maria feels that English is the only appropriate language and using Italian is not acceptable in the nursery. Do they have a nursery policy on children who are becoming bilingual? Of course, I guess someone could be actually discouraging Maria from using Italian, just like happened to the little girl who spoke Gujarati. Have you any idea of how the nursery responds to negative attitudes of staff and children? It looks like Nasreen's experience may have pushed her family into speaking English to her little sister, so she didn't face the same prejudice. It's frightening, really, 'cos I guess all these things affect not only language and learning, but how children actually see themselves and ultimately who they are able to talk to!

Of course there could be all sorts of other things that Maria is worried about! I think talking to her teacher might help work out what's going on. What do you think would be best for Maria? Good luck, let me know what happens.

Caroline

PS. Do you think I'll make it across the Pennines to Manchester in this weather? Headlines: 'Teacher found frozen to death in snow storm, mysteriously wrapped up in hundreds of bilingual writing samples!'

4 September 1996   **(10 years later)**

Dear Franca,

Well here I am, in this beautiful place in this wonderful hotel — panicking. Why am I doing this? What if they ask me a difficult question? What if they don't believe me? What if they fall asleep? Some of my colleagues are here and they've been great. But then, they've never seen me give a conference paper before! Well you're a parent and teacher and you asked me the same question I'm addressing tomorrow at the conference: 'Shall I send Carlo to a bilingual program, especially given the difficulty with Maria?' So I'll tell you what we found in the Khmer-English program for 6–9-year-olds — then you can make your own mind up. All the children, or their parents are from Cambodia and most of them speak Khmer at home.

We've collected lots of writing samples over a period of a year in both Khmer and English from 23 children in the program. Just look at this story written in Khmer and a report written in English by Danny, at the end of year 1. (Sorry I can't send you the pictures to go with the story, the book is in the school library.)

You see how Khmer is based on a highly elaborate script based on Sanskrit and the vowels are written before, above, below or after the initial consonant in a

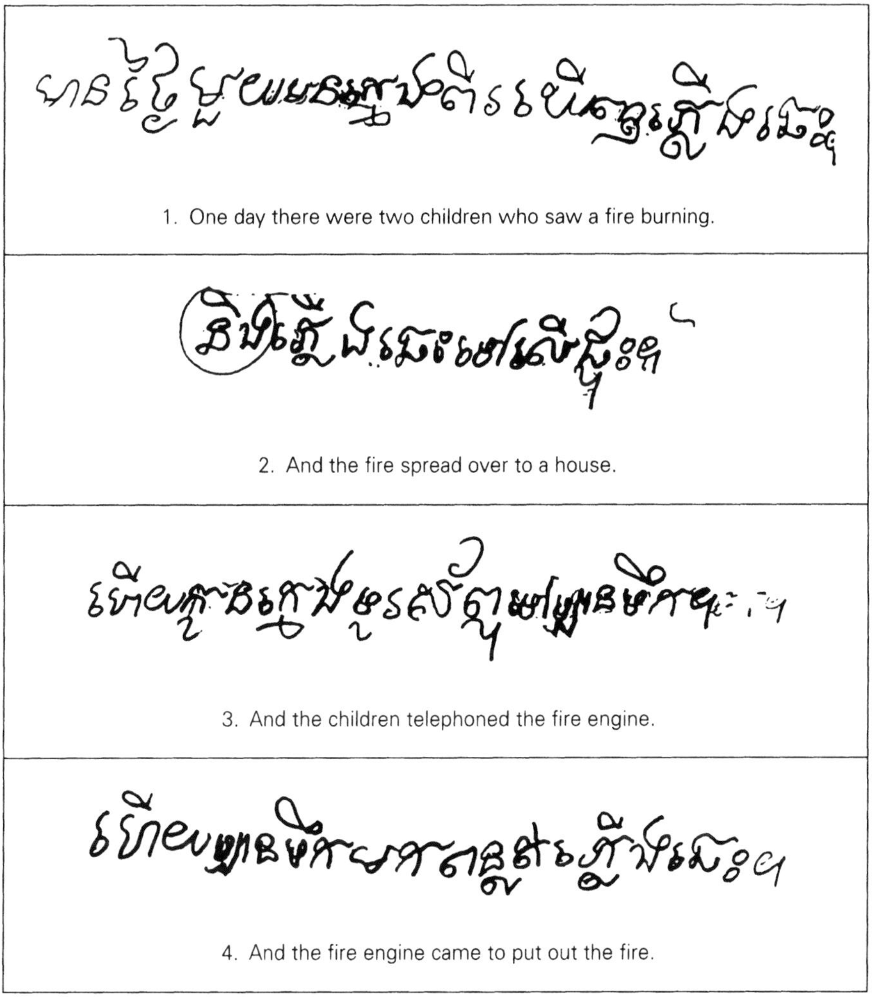

1. One day there were two children who saw a fire burning.

2. And the fire spread over to a house.

3. And the children telephoned the fire engine.

4. And the fire engine came to put out the fire.

Figure 2.1: Danny's story in Khmer (with English translation by the teacher)

syllable. Added to which, there are no spaces between each word, they are joined together in syntactic groups and punctuation marks are quite different to conventional English ones. But, as you can see — even the youngest children have begun to get hold of the complex differences between English and Khmer.

Not only could they write in both languages, but the older children could talk about the differences between the languages. Listen to this:

Vina told me, *'When the English word is at the front, the Cambodian word is at the back, like back to front'*. Chantana gave me an example, *'Like when you say, "We*

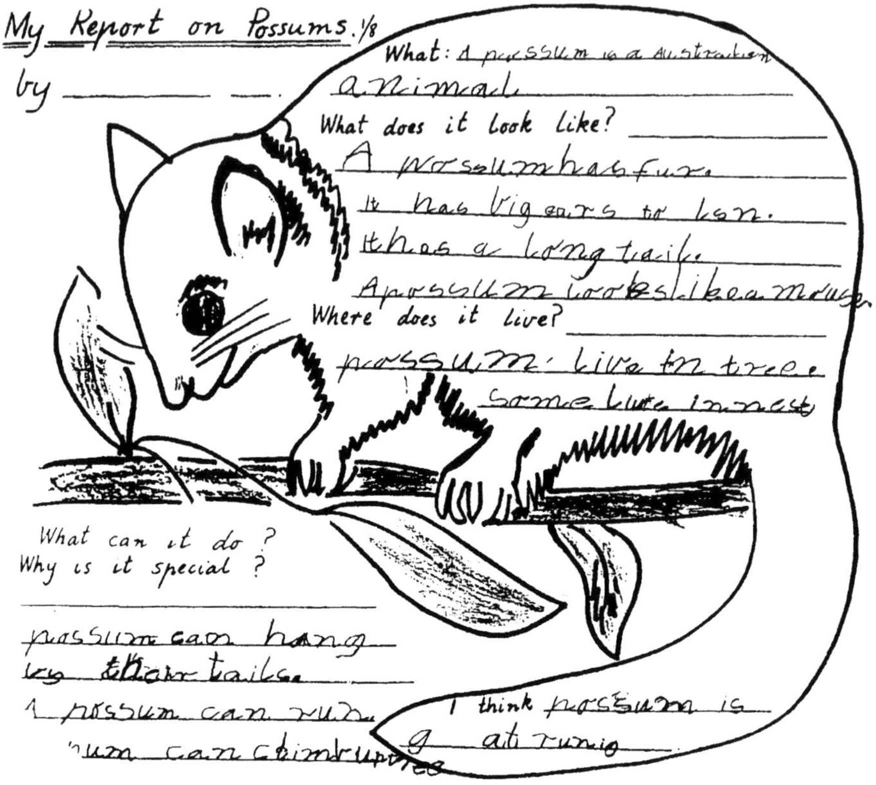

My Report on Possums. ⅛

by _____ _____

What: A possum is a Australian animal.

What does it look Like? _____
A possum has fur.
It has big ears to len.
It has a long tail.
A possum looks like a mouse.

Where does it live? _____
possum' live in tree
some live in nest

What can it do?
Why is it special?

_____
possum can hang
by their tails.
A possum can run.
um can climb up trees

I think possum is
at runig

Figure 2.2: Danny's report on possums in English

are going back home", you can't say it like that, you have to say it the other way
"we are going home back"'. Then she added, 'Like when you're translating, you
don't translate each word or you can't understand what you're saying'. Soriya
pointed out that, 'There's lots more words and lots of alphabets (in Khmer)'. To
which Mira added, 'There's more, more ABC than English'. They're right, 33
consonants and approximately 25 vowels! Even Danny who's only 6, seemed to
recognize this as a difference between English and Khmer. He said Khmer's different, 'Because some words under it'.

Many of the children seem to be able to use both languages very creatively
and to great effect. Several children were able to switch from one language to
another almost spontaneously, depending on who they were talking with. It
was interesting that they also code switched in their writing, but only adding
English to Khmer and not the other way around. I guess that's to do with the power
of English and who they were writing for. Often they switched to English in
their Khmer writing when the word was either 'universal' or didn't exist in Khmer.
Like this:

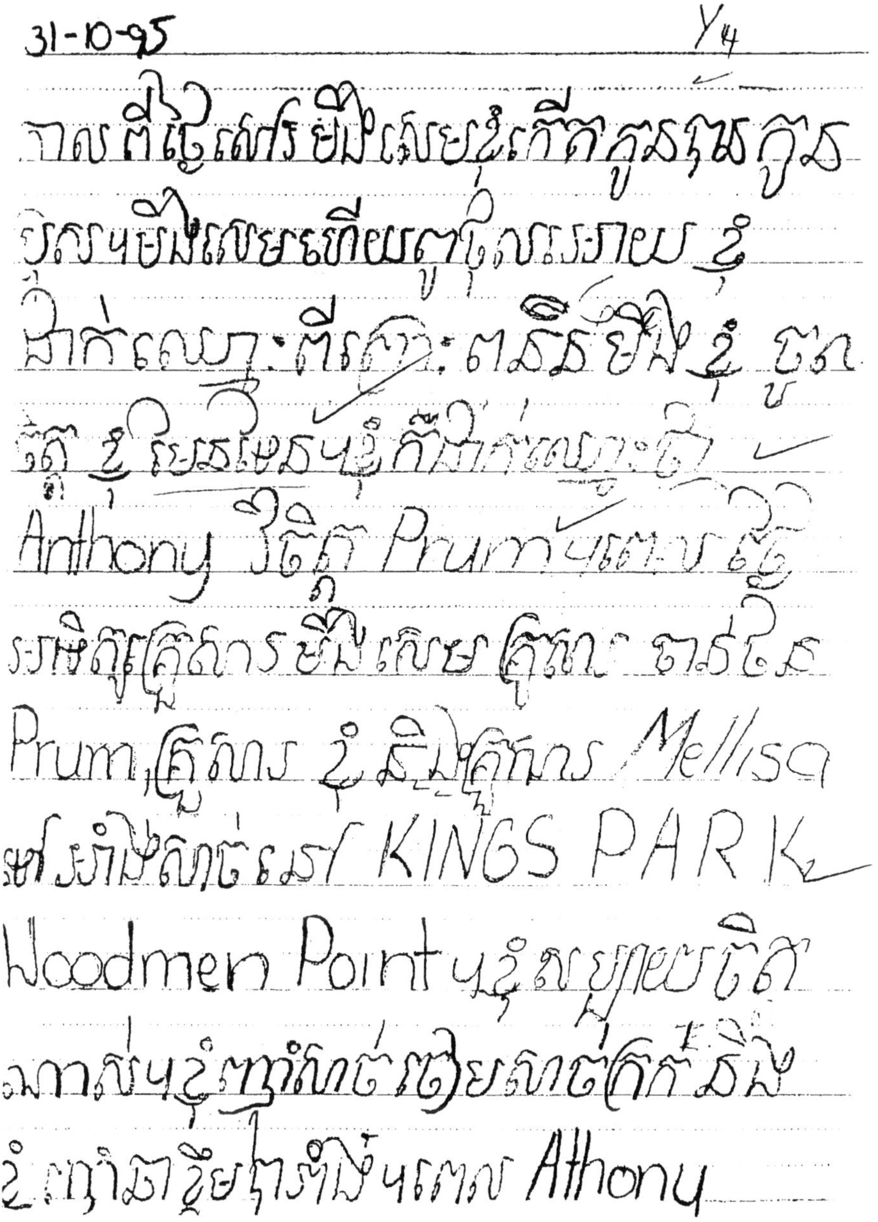
31-10-95
Y4
Anthony
Prum
Prum
Mellisa
KINGS PARK
Woodmen Point
Athony

Figure 2.3: Vina's recount in Khmer (followed by English translation by the teacher)

Vina's recount in Khmer — (English translation, 31 October 1995).

On Saturday my auntie gave birth to a baby boy. Auntie and uncle let me name the baby because my auntie and uncle like me very much. Then I gave the name as Anthony Vichet Prum. On Sunday the same family, Phalla Prum's family, my family and Melissa's family had a barbecue at KING'S PARK Woodman point. I was very happy. I ate lamb sausages and I ate stir fry onions.

In addition, some of the older children did some very clever things with words that didn't exit in Khmer. For example, when writing a narrative in Khmer, *escalator* became *running stair*. Another child sounded out *swap meet* (a sort of car boot sale) in Khmer, and wrote it using the Khmer alphabet. Many of the older children were also able to use appropriate conventions which vary according to the script. For example, in Khmer they were able to signal age and relationships in various parts of speech. In addition, not only were they beginning to write in a range of different genres in both languages, but the majority of children showed parallel development in English and Khmer. In other words, learning in two languages actually enhanced literacy learning!

Finally, the children themselves gave all sorts of reasons for learning two languages. See what you think. Jade who was in Year 1 argued,

'Cos your brain will get more healthier. . . . so you learn. . . . how to speak and you know. . . . and then teach your brothers'. The older children had similar views. Soriya concluded that she learns Khmer at school, 'because we can get smart', and Vichet added, 'You can get better by talking, talking in Khmer'. Mira likes working in two languages because, 'It helps me to learn', and she can use Khmer if she goes to Cambodia. Vina argued that biliteracy is related to future success, 'So you can, um, get a good job and you get lots of moneys'. Chantana touched on the dangers of 'illiteracy', 'You have to know how to read because if they put a sign to go warning, "Don't go in this house because dog might bite you", and you don't know what it says and you go in. And the dog bite you'. Chantana concluded by talking about the social difficulties of being unable to read in two languages! She explained that it's possible for people who can't read to bring back soap instead of corn chips, 'and when your mum eat it, it's very yukky'.

If you want to know any more you'll have to read the book! Wish me luck with the conference presentation,

Caroline

PS. If all else fails with Carlo, bribery and corruption might help: The Khmer teacher kept telling the older children how important it is to learn in two languages. She told them that when they go to university she would take them to a restaurant and treat them something to eat. But Vina knows there's no such thing as a free lunch, he said, 'Free! I think she's um just saying it to let us be good!'

4 September 2004   **(8 years later)**
Dear Franca,

I can't believe I'm still here, 10 years — must be something to do with my work at Edith Cowan University. Or, of course, it could be the beaches, the ocean, the blue sky, the sunshine, the kangaroos, the multicoloured parrots, the muffins! Naturally, I still miss everyone, but I'll probably survive here for a little while longer.

Well, the twins start at the Community Family Learning Centre tomorrow, I'm more nervous than they are! I must admit from our visits I feel very lucky, it seems to have everything I think is important, particularly in relation to language and culture. But we'll have to wait and see — the twins might disagree. I'd like to know what you think, these are a few things that struck me on some of our visits to the Centre.

First of all, there were people from different generations and cultural and linguistic backgrounds who appeared to be working together with each other and with the children on things in which they seemed to be really absorbed. Diversity was the 'norm', and learning was taking place through sort of 'living culture'. Everyone appeared to be regarded as a 'learner' and a 'knower'. I really liked this, not only because it seems to acknowledge everyone's contribution and perspective but, as we don't have grandparents or family over here, I think learning through multiple generations is great. A sort of 'lifelong learning', based on the notion that everyone has something to offer.

I couldn't actually tell who were staff, that is, until someone pointed out that the Centre is run by the people who use it. There are people who have overall responsibility for different aspects of the Centre, but it seems that children and adults are encouraged to develop policies, strategies and structures together. They try and ensure that these meet the community needs in ways which enable everyone to learn what they want, in the way they want. I guess this genuinely enables children to build on what they bring. I don't think I've ever witnessed so many different types of learning going on! There also seemed to be an incredible atmosphere of independence, children making decisions about what they wanted to do, while appearing to respect other children and adults, some achievement! The twins were beside themselves, they couldn't wait to get stuck in. I thought I'd never see them again! Mind you, I'm a bit worried that the twins might just sort of float around from one thing to another, never actually learning anything! They lead a fairly structured life at home — just to keep me sane!

Anyway, as I settled down I realized that the rooms were buzzing with a multitude of languages. The children and adults seemed to be using the languages with which they were most comfortable for a particular purpose. Sharing communication was the goal, which seemed to open up a whole range of possibilities. They appeared to switch between languages quite naturally, being multilingual was the 'norm' rather than the exception. Any hitches in communication seemed to be sorted out with gestures or the help of another child or adult. The children seemed to have built up all sorts of strategies for understanding and making themselves understood. Several of the adults were specifically employed to develop bilingual programs. I know being surrounded by other languages is fantastic for the twins, but I can't help thinking — will being monolingual make them feel inferior? And they already speak their own sort of private language, will anyone talk to them? (I know, I know, I'm full of worries, but I've never been in a situation like this before!)

You'll be pleased to know I'm not worried about the activities I saw! All the activities seemed to be culturally as well as linguistically relevant. One group was making a huge collage of their families. The children were talking about what constitutes a family and who does what. They were also making decisions about how to identify the people in the collage and talking about the meaning of names in different languages. At the same time some of the adults were discussing child rearing practices and concepts of care and education (I really wanted to join in, I keep thinking maybe I've got it all wrong). Another group had visited a Native Plant Nursery which is managed by an Aboriginal co-operative. They were sending thank-you pictures and letters. As one of the older children was explaining what he was writing in Aboriginal English, an adult began to talk about the similarities and differences between Conventional Australian English and Aboriginal English.

But, what I saw, was not quite as easy as it looked. I've found out that this apparent commitment to linguistic and cultural diversity isn't just left to chance.

- The community centre employs caregivers and teachers who speak the community languages fluently. They work hand in hand with members of the family and community to ensure that all children can be understood and can communicate with at least one adult. As the community develops or changes the Centre is able to meet different language needs by the flexibility of those carers and teachers who are prepared to go (within reason) to where their particular languages and skills are needed. And one of the carers is a twin and knows all about twin language, individuality etc. So no worries there!
- The Centre takes into account prior qualifications and experience in order to fulfil the need for qualified caregivers and teachers who speak community languages. Many students take courses which enable them to maximize their bilingualism. Caregivers and teachers who have completed further qualifications such as the course in, Cross Cultural and Mulilingual, Multiliterate Learning (CCAMML), are also employed. Some of the Centre workers are involved in the planning, delivery and evaluation of these courses. I've already been invited to talk about some of our Early Childhood courses.
- Community involvement includes collaboration with near by tertiary institutions. Some students do their teaching practices in the Centre. The experience is seen as a two way process. Students help develop further bilingual programs, share their knowledge of most recent research, try different teaching methodology and discuss new ways of evaluating language. At the same time they are encouraged to plan, implement and reflect upon a range of teaching and learning strategies within this multilingual, cross cultural environment. I'm sure there are lots of ways the university could link with the Centre, I'll have to go and speak to the Community and Client Enterprise Committee.

- The Centre also acts as a lobby group to ensure that the study of linguistic and cultural diversity is a central part of all Early Childhood courses. In addition, the Centre has set up a committee which includes parents, care-givers, teachers, researchers and other advocates of multilingualism, as a means of providing information to other Centres. This group also prepares applications for project funding and sharing of findings though conferences and community meetings. Well, I wonder if they would be interested in our latest publication . . .

- I like the way there is a strong emphasis on equality of outcome through the implementation of what's called a critical curriculum. This involves ways of helping children (and adults) to challenge discrimination, while enabling children to become more responsible for their own education and care. This is done through the use of materials which allow children to explore human diversity and consider ways of being anti-discriminatory. Language is also seen as constructing, as well as conveying meaning and therefore adults are encouraged to model non-discriminatory behaviours as well as challenge biased views. Many activities are based on problem solving in which children are encouraged to think critically about their social world and challenge the things that seem to limit their potential. This would be great for the twins, as much as I try, sometimes I think very little has changed in the last 30 years. Someone asked me if I was going to send them to separate nurseries so that they would be treated as individuals and Ché would be less dependent on Cymion. In fact this is not the case.

- My worries about how I would know what the twins were actually doing were groundless. The Centre sees keeping track of the children's develop-ing understanding at home and at the Centre as central to their continuing progress. Evaluation is a joint process between a carer/teacher who has responsibility for a number of children, family members and the child. The whole team is involved in selecting particular pieces of work, experiences (captured on video or photographs) which reflect development across several learning areas, and language and literacy development throughout the year. Regular 'conferences' with the child, carer and family member are used to focus on achievement and consider what next. Any worries or problems are identified and strategies which might help are discussed. Chil-dren are not evaluated against each other, nor are they measured against a 'norm'. (Thank goodness, it's so tempting to compare the twins to each other all the time.)

- Finally, the Centre also acts as a resource centre. Families are offered support for home languages through the use of resources, workshops and jointly developed research projects. They have access to other professionals who are based at the centre. These include health, parenting information services, counselling, research networks on early childhood, workshop groups which change according to what people want and computer links to access information and other web pages. So I can actually get lots of information and help right here!

I must say I felt very comfortable, didn't feel I was going to be judged or have to explain about why the twins seem to speak in their own language. I didn't feel anyone one was going to prise them apart, but they would still be treated as individuals, (I've been worrying about this for ages!). I feel they will be able to learn through exploring the environment and developing their own interests while learning about others in an atmosphere of mutual respect and trust. And I feel I can go anytime and be part of what's happening. What do you think? Write soon.

Caroline

PS. The twins have sent you their first electronic message and scanned in their drawings of the Centre, just to let you know what it's like from their point of view! They'll probably have a go at reaching you through the virtual Early Childhood Centre, so be warned.

3   In Praise of Inspired and Inspiring Teachers

Tina Bruce

Most adults seem to remember, value and show appreciation of junior, secondary or higher education teachers for whom they felt fondness, value, respect and appreciation. Only a few mention their very earliest teacher. Think of Tony Blair's list of selective celebrities naming their favourite teacher, or the section in *The Times Educational Supplement* called 'My Best Teacher'.

Why is it that most people give the recognition and appreciation to the teachers they had in junior and secondary school, but not their nursery/infant teachers? Perhaps the reasons are purely biological. It may simply be that most adults really can't remember that far back. This is not convincing, because many adults do in fact remember moments and people, even from their toddler times, with quite a degree of accuracy. A more likely reason is that adults living in England do not place much value on the early years of education. Consequently, they don't even try to activate their memories of the first teachers who taught them. Most people are of the view that education does not seriously begin until the junior school years, although they seem to want to try and make younger children perform as if they were 7 or 8 years old, getting them to read, write and do sums as young as 4 years of age.

It seems that it is, in the main, those of us who, in our adult lives, work with very young children and their families who are more likely to remember with appreciation our first teachers. Perhaps our appreciation of some of our earliest teachers inspired us to work with young children and their families. I have always felt a huge rapport with Marie Rambert, who was the 'mother' of English Ballet, and whose life's work has many parallels with that of early years teachers. She was made Dame Marie Rambert sometime after Dame Ninette de Valois, who took the dancers and choreography that Marie Rambert had produced, such as Sir Frederick Ashton, and formed a new company which became the Royal Ballet. Outcomes are rewarded first, and not those who caused them to come about.

It is important, at every point in the educational system, to value good teachers, not just those who are there when we ripen into achievement. Those who contributed to our education in less obvious ways, involving processes which bring long terms results are perhaps the most important of all those who teach us.

I had a good childhood, happy, stimulating, creative anchored in a loving family. My first 7 years were full of doting grandparents, and I attended an AMI Montessori Nursery from 3–5 years of age. My Montessori experience began the

33

term before my younger brother was born in 1951. The Directress, Miss Smith, was a symbol of calm, and provided a predictable, totally secure environment. It may not have stretched my mind, but it calmed me, and I loved her. She played an important role in helping to make my brother's arrival a positive experience. The things I could already do were celebrated, and I felt good being able to walk around the circle marked out on the floor and learnt to tie laces together on a wooden contraption (didactic materials as I now know). Even then I preferred real life to structured, artificial life. It felt good helping young children to tie their shoe laces. I knew I didn't need the wooden contraption. What was wrong with real shoes? I ran messages for Miss Smith, putting the notes for the milkman, and joy of joy, singing, dancing and acting out *Fair Rosie Lived in a Tall Tower* with my friend Stephen being 'a handsome Prince came riding by'.

When I was 7 years old, my mother told me Miss Smith was very ill in hospital. I wrote her a letter in my best writing, thanking her for all she had done. I never had a reply, and later we heard that she had died. Although I was only 7 years old, I somehow knew that by the time she would have received my letter, she would almost certainly have been too ill to register it. Even though I was young, I also knew that this didn't matter. I knew that she knew how I felt about her. The written word can be irrelevant, and even young children know that. If only the adults who have political power to control the curriculum of our youngest children knew that.

The appreciation young children feel for the rest of their lives towards those adults who have contributed in a major way to how they feel about themselves as learners is rarely spoken. It is an abstract, intuitive thing which they take with them through their lives. And yet, it anchors them forever, and it is sometimes called having a sense of well being.

After leaving Miss Smith's Nursery School, I had a miserable time in a large reception class. At least I was fortunate enough to be 5 years old when I went to school. Nowadays children as young as 4 years of age are made to experience such large reception classes. The reception class was certainly a terrible shock, moving as I did from a nurturing, predictable environment with a calm adult and 10 children, to a group of 35 children and one teacher. The post war 'bulge' was working its way through the educational system, and I was part of it.

There was lots of boring lining up, copying, colouring in, having worked ticked, standing in a queue at the teacher's desk before you could go out to play, which was anyway a terrifying experience and greatly to be avoided. Indeed, I quickly worked out that it was better to stay in and queue than to be pinched by girls, or have your skirt lifted by older boys out in the playground. Boredom was preferable to this kind of excitement!

The reception class was followed by a pedestrian year in what was then called the middle infants. Nowadays, I would have had to do SATS at the end of this class, and I would have done very badly. It was expected that children would read fluently by the age of 7 or 8 years, and we did, just as children in the rest of Europe do nowadays. The difference was that then, children were not under pressure to perform before biological development favoured it. They were not forced early as they are now. We were read to; acted out stories in our play scenarios with dolls' houses and farm animals; in dens we had made under tables and in the garden in amongst the mud pies that we patted into shape; or wobbling about on bikes on our way to 'market'; or crouching behind trees; hunting animals in the rain forests (or jungle as we called it); or 'swimming' under the sea playing Jacques Cousteau; or on safari with lions and Elsa stories.

Children throughout the world indulge in play. It comes in different quantities with variations, but it is to be found in Borneo, Nigeria, Finland or Canada or New Zealand etc. Crosscultural research on play (Bruce, 1997) suggests that far from being a privilege of white, western middle class children, this group are increasingly experiencing an erosion of their childhood play. Especially so in the modern UK (*Dispatches*, Channel 4, January 1998) because they are propelled into early performance of adult ways of proving themselves.

At 7 years of age, I moved to the top infants class to be with the Froebel trained Joyce Greaves. We did radio plays, pretending to switch her desk off and on like a wireless. We decorated our handwriting books. She read us poetry and played songs on the piano. We used clay, did collage, made models, grew beans in jam jars, had a shop with lovely work cards for our maths, made patterns with wooden shapes (I now know these were Froebel's Occupations) found places on a globe and looked at artefacts found in different countries and cultures. We did stories in dance, song and drama, and got in rather a mess when making animals out of clay.

But perhaps most important, although she had 40 children in her class, we each felt that we mattered to her. She had long, curly hair, and lovely bright coloured clothes. She never shouted at us and there was no bullying in that class. We really were a caring, learning community. Some children, I now realize, had special educational needs, but we were all expected to, and did, value, respect and celebrate each child's achievement, and not just in the three R's. The expressive arts and experiments in science with ice and plants were much in evidence. She visited each child at home. She made us feel we could try new, difficult things, because we knew that she would see us through and help us to find the courage to have a go. I have always liked fractions because of the care she took to make them manageable for me.

When I was at secondary school, I heard that Miss Greaves had died suddenly. I wished I could have thanked her for all she did for us all — not just for clever, privileged children, but for any child who came her way. She gave us, each in our way, the disposition towards learning that lasts for a lifetime, and she valued our childhood play in doing so.

The junior and secondary years were barren intellectually, with nice teachers and less pleasant ones, but no more inspiration, and no more scholarship — just academic hoops. Once you have experienced a teacher like Joyce Greaves, you know what you are missing when it isn't there, and you yearn for it.

At 18 years of age, I went to the Froebel Educational Institute as it was then called, to train to be a teacher. I was in no doubt. I wanted to be a teacher like Joyce Greaves. There I met Chris Athey, my education tutor, and Sybil Levy, my main subject tutor with whom I studied drama. Between them, and each in entirely different ways, they stretched my mind as it had not been stretched since Miss Greaves' class. I use the word 'stretched' wittingly, because good teachers help you to learn the things you find hardest in ways which are right for you.

These teachers all understood in very deep ways what their pupils needed. They seemed to create a feeling of calm, an anchored feeling, a settled feeling in a group which felt like a real community, and yet they seemed to do this in order to jolt you and make you rethink or think anew in quantum leaps. It was exciting to learn with them. You had a sense you would never be the same again, and you weren't! Their classrooms were full of laughter, but never at the expense of others, and never frivolous or uncontrolled. Their classrooms were also full of expectation. Expectation that people would do their best, that everyone would respect everyone, value each other's efforts, help each other to learn. These were not competitive places but learning communities, full of compassion and care, where each took as much responsibility as was possible. Classroom materials were looked after, people brought food to share and flowers to decorate. These classrooms had heart and soul as well as mind.

These were all teachers who valued childhood play, either by encouraging children to become part of it, or by helping their student teachers to empower children to play, including children who were sick, or who had disabilities. These were not quick fix, get there early, get good outcomes, good SATS results, League Table teachers. These were help-you-to-be-long-term-forever-learner kinds of teacher.

As we approach the millennium things are rather different in the world of education from the middle of the century (the 1950s to the 1970s) the decades wrapping themselves around the 1960s. I can only say how grateful I am to have experienced these decades as both a pupil and as a teacher. I want what I was given by my early teachers for every child, every year of their school life, and I want to be the kind of teacher who sets clear boundaries, has high expectations, has respect for individual children, creates a secure and anchored community which allows creativity and empowers it to flourish, as well as reflective thinking. In such a classroom that is conducive to thinking, these things are relentlessly encouraged and children overcome their fears and manage the things that they find most difficult, becoming autonomous as learners.

Sadly in the 1980s and 1990s, and as we reach the millennium, some aspects of our lifestyle and culture in England (more so than in the rest of the UK) have developed which are rather damaging to the important formative years of childhood. Although we have not returned to the grim conditions of learning experienced by most children at the turn of the century, we have not completely shed its shadow. There is still a view that learning can only occur if children are sitting at desks, preferably writing and recording and being graded on what they produce on paper.

The English have never been renowned for their love of little children, but Italians, Scandinavians, Spaniards have, and their early childhood education systems burst with it. Whilst English 4-year-olds are reading, writing and doing sums in reception classes, in other European countries children are enjoyed and celebrated and are not forced into proving themselves at 4 years of age. This was apparent in the Reggio Emilia Exhibition which was shown at the Bethnal Green Museum of Childhood in association with the British Association for Early Childhood Education in 1997.

In England, children are losing out during the three years from 4–6 or 7 at a point in their development when their play should be moving from symbolic play based on real experience (playing at eating, sleeping, and everyday events) to elaborated, more complex and abstract symbolic play (involving playing at space ships, worlds under the sea etc.). In fact, many children never move from the reality and experience-based play so typical of 2- and 3-year-olds into the more abstract levels of play typical if they are encouraged between 4–7 years of age. Yet we know that it is abstract levels of thinking which count long term in the education process, and which are crucial to any nation in producing outcomes and flourishing.

Children can go beyond the here and now in the thinking, feeling and relating they do in their play in a way that they simply cannot manage in other kinds of abstract or higher order thinking until much later on in middle childhood from 9–12 years and adolescence and adulthood. That is why the human brain is biologically ready with such a propensity for play during early childhood. Play is nature's way of helping emergent forms of thinking in the abstract to develop and take children further from the concrete here and now into higher order thinking. This is an irony, for by eroding childhood play, we are in fact damaging the child's biological means by which to learn effectively.

One central mechanism by which the brain develops and by which children learn is through play. Play gives the child the opportunity to use the learning which has gone before, and to develop it in a number of imaginative and increasingly abstract ways. Between 4–7 years of age, play should be becoming more and more complex. In England it is at this point (4 years of age) that the vast majority of children are put into a school environment where often there is little or no opportunity for the elaboration and increasing complexity of play to develop. When the previous Government and the current Government wring their hands over 'standards', the fact that our children are put into formal schooling some three years earlier than most children in the world, never seems to be mentioned, or questioned, or to be part of the discussion in any way. The predominant view amongst those who control English education seems to be 'the earlier the start to formal education, the better', although the evidence is against this (*Dispatches*, January 1998).

Early years experts, informed by biological and sociocultural evidence, are in agreement that it is damaging to force biology into early performance. Emergent behaviours are just that. They can be 'forced' and speeded up, but why do it? Emergent behaviours lead to better outcomes if they are allowed enough time to be what they are, which is emergent and embryonic. For this reason I should like to see quality early nursery education extended to 6 or 7 years of age, and for children to be given the time, both in early years settings of all kinds as well as at home, that they need to fully develop their play.

If reception classes bulging with 4-year-olds were joined once again with nursery classes, so that 3- and 4-year-olds could learn alongside each other and together as they always have done in British nursery education until recent years, then learning and play could develop effectively and children would be able to help each other to learn in a very deep way. Play deepens in quality when 4-year-olds initiate 3-year-olds into it with ever increasing elaborate play scenes, roles and characters. Three-year-olds drink up all the help they are given by 4-year-olds, and do not seem to mind being biddable, until, that is, they get the hang of what play is about and how to do it. Then the worm turns, and they begin to negotiate play scenes and roles and to initiate the next group of 3-year-olds into deeper symbolic layers in their play.

Susan Greenfield (1997) writes 'humans have the least stereotyped, most flexible lifestyle of all animal species, and it is believed the cortex must therefore in some way be related to liberating the individual from fixed, predetermined patterns of behaviour' (p. 15).

The ability to play is the mechanism which coordinates different aspects of the child's developing brain. Children who do not play do not use their brain fully in the period when it is developing most rapidly. That is why it is so serious that children in England are not encouraged to play once they are in formal school from 4 years of age.

Damaging Play Damages Learning

The insidious thing about this is that the damage does not show until many years later. For example, people do not associate being good at chemistry 'A' level with mixing mud pies, grass, sand and clay in the nursery garden at 3 and 4 years of age; of learning in the doing about reversible and irreversible transformation of state (adding water to earth and making mud, drying it in the sun and making it earth again); of soluble and insoluble matter, sprinkling salt into a puddle; of liquids, bubbles and gases; of sludgy or firm solids; and chatting with adults about all these fascinating things.

Most people do not link role play with making friends, wearing dressing up clothes, negotiating a play theme, elaborating on it, with writing a novel later on. And yet, there are many examples of children storying with narratives and characters which are played out in their childhood, who later become writers, such as the Bronte children or E. Nesbitt and H.G. Wells playing with their wooden blocks. Others are Seymour Papert, who later developed computers, and played with cogs. Frank Lloyd Wright, played with wooden blocks and later became a famous architect.

We need to remember that with the best will in the world, adults can be dangerously damaging to the play of young children. The balance of adults and children playing together is a delicate one. Adults often try to mould a child's play to their shape. They call this guided play, structured play, purposeful play and even educational play. They give this kind of play much greater status than the spontaneous play of children at the bottom of the garden with their mud pies, which is often referred to as purposeless and off task. Whose purpose? The adults of course.

I do not call adult led tasks 'play', which is not to say that they are unimportant. But adult led tasks are different from play. Children need a balance of adult led experiences and spontaneous play, which respects and encourages their ideas, feelings, relationships, reflections on life and what they have learned, and their autonomous learning.

The Effective Early Learning Project directed by Chris Pascal has found that adults are very sensitive to children's feelings, offer stimulating experiences, but find it difficult to allow children the autonomy they need to play or learn deeply.

Over occupied children who are kept busy in teacher led tasks all day in school, and then organized into after school clubs, games, music and dance lessons etc., often from as early as 4 years of age, have no time for their brains to become coordinated and reflective through play. These children have no time to be anchored enough, or to be able to think and feel, to relate to others clearly, for play helps children to unravel their lives and experiences in ways which hold meaning for them. An over taught, over structured life, means there is no time for children to apply and use what they have learnt, for play is primarily about the application of what has been learnt and helps children to sort out understanding.

How do we stop rushing children through their childhood, trying to take short cuts with them and to make quick fixes, propelling them unequipped into adulthood? Children need time to stand and stare, to experience, to live. We would find more settled children (a phrase I like and learnt in New Zealand) with fewer behavioural challenges, calmer children, more focussed children, if we cooled the pace of our young children's lives and stopped trying to pack so much into them.

We need to really look with children at spiders' webs, whether or not the focus of the day is 'knowledge and understanding of the world'.

When we take children to the market, we need to actually look at the fruit, whether or not we happen to be 'doing' numbers in mathematics.

We need to look at the puddle in the street and the drain that takes the water away, whether or not we happen to be 'doing' sound and letter relationships in language and literacy, ug, bug or glug.

For children will use these real experiences in their play. They will replay, adjust through play, experiment and imagine through play, with their real life experiences. They will sort out life's confusions and make sense for themselves as they play. Children, as Susan Isaacs pointed out in the 1930s, in their play can escape into real experience or out of it, and through doing this they learn about reflecting on life, getting a sense of control over their lives, developing self esteem and feeling anchored.

Fein and Kinney (1994) looked at children who are 'high' and 'low' play children. They show Annie with her meticulous, precise style, only able to begin to learn how to play when a safe, social situation is accessed for her by an observant, informed adult. Ellen, with her recurring play theme of dating, going to a dance and taking trips can protect and mentor the low playing Jill and help her become part of the group's social and fantasy life. Ellen helps Jill to unlock from what Fein and

Kinney call her 'prematurely developed self control and adult-like behaviour' and take up the free flow play which they say is a 'risky activity that exposes sensitive emotional issues to public scrutiny'. It is important that the mood, the atmosphere, the moment is right for play to take off and begin to free flow along.

As we reach the millennium, it is becoming increasingly clear through research on the brain as well as in other areas of study, that childhood needs play. Play acts as a forward feed mechanism into courageous, creative and rigorous thinking in adulthood. A quality early years curriculum will be conducive to play. It will need adults who are trained to work with young children and who are informed about how children learn to play, and how children learn in a community together.

Put it this way, if children in England are not encouraged to play and learn with teachers like Joyce Greaves when they are young, I for one predict increased educational failure in the long term. At a job interview, candidates are not asked were you potty trained at one year? Did you read and write and do sums at 4 years of age? They will be asked questions to see if they are autonomous, reliable, able to take responsibility, thoughtful of others, socially competent, competent in the three Rs and able to take initiative and be proactive. These are the ingredients of play in childhood. Play is for long term educators who value learning processes and dispositions much more than they could ever value quick fix outcomes.

So to Miss Smith, Joyce Greaves, Sybil Levy, Chris Athey, my heartfelt thanks for your long term view you take of those you have educated, and for your inspired and inspiring teaching.

References

BRUCE, T. (1997) 'Adults and children developing play together', *EECERAJ*, **5**, 1, Spring.
DESPATCHES (1998) Channel 4 Television, 4 January.
FEIN, G. and KINNEY, P. (1994) 'He's a nice alligator: Observations on the affective organisation of pretence', in SLADE, A. and PALMER WOLF, D. (eds) *Children at Play: Clinical and Developmental Approaches to Meaning and Representation*, New York and Oxford: Oxford University Press.
GREENFIELD, S. (1997) *The Human Brain: A Guided Tour*, London: Weidenfeld and Nicolson.

4 Quality and Professionalism in Early Childhood

Christopher Ball

I was born in 1935. I was well cared for; my parents loved me; I think I was happy. I know I was fortunate. But I remember little of my early years. Few people do. Perhaps that is why we have to rediscover as adults the obvious truth of the importance of early learning. Cultures vary in the value they place on early childhood. I think our culture underestimates the first phase of human life. I would like to change that.

My earliest memory — now heavily overlaid with retelling and embroidery — is of a table wobbling. I think I was sitting beneath it. The wobble bothered me — I like things to be tidy, functional, effective, well organised. I was 3. There is a family story about me playing with a bent stick a year later. When asked what it was, I am reported to have said: 'It is a gun, for shooting babies round corners with.' (My sister had appeared by then.) A year or two later, I remember insisting on sleeping out in a tent for a night all alone — with a chopper under my pillow for protection.

Stories like these — everyone can tell them — reveal the essence of our early learning: making sense of things, attachment and separateness, finding solutions to problems, self-reliance . . . Today, we rather pompously call these things the core and transferable skills and insist that everyone aged 16–19 should practise and develop them. But they really belong in the curriculum of early learning, as part of what I like to call 'Key Stage 0'.

Later still, I was introduced to what we now call 'the key skills' — literacy and numeracy. (IT was unknown to us, though we had the wireless. Ours caught fire one day, so I picked up my baby sister and carried her to safety — thus in one action saving my own skin, and winning undeserved praise for altruism.) I can remember reading for the first time — and the enormous excitement of being able to do so. My first book started: 'John was an airman . . .' It was not politically correct. Numbers fascinated me. They still do. I found it hard to believe that they were infinite. After all, I thought, we know that they start with 1 — it makes sense to think that they must end somewhere. So I tried to count them all in bed at night before going to sleep. (I gave up when I reached 12,000.)

My mother was my first teacher. Indeed, for several years, she was my only teacher. My father was fighting the war overseas. I wasn't really sent to school until I was 9 years old. Then 'shades of the prison house began to close about the growing boy'. It was the end of childhood, innocence and the bliss of early learning. Nothing later has ever matched that infant paradise.

My brother was born just as I entered the second phase of life. Once he had learned to walk and talk and become interesting, I decided to take a hand in his upbringing myself. So I began to study early learning at second hand. I thought that my brother was a genius. (I still do. But in those days I thought him unusual. Now I believe we are all potentially brilliant.) Like me, he was — and is — fascinated by the convolutions of his own mind.

He was a model maker — an infant student of science and technology. On occasions, and somewhat uneasily, our mother would relate how as a 9-year old on holiday he spent a morning trying to fly his home-made kite. The kindly lady next door commented that it was sad to see an ESN boy frustrated by the lack of decent equipment. There is a thin line between different kinds of special needs. What I recall of his childhood is his originality, creative nature and maturity. We were equals — and still are. What is more, we had together stumbled upon the secret of mastery learning.

When I married in 1958, my wife and I were students — and idealists. Like all such people in every generation we wanted to make the world a better place. I was impressed by the challenge of 'absolute pacifism and absolute communism'. So we marched from Aldermaston and supported Oxfam. We promised each other we would never learn to drive. We resigned from the Labour Party in 1965 because it compromised our ideals. And we started a family.

We read Bowlby. John Bowlby had constructed an ethnological theory which asserted the biological basis of early emotional attachments. I was entranced by it. He argued that both mother and baby are genetically programmed to seek contact with one another. From this, a deep emotional bond was thought to develop, which — if broken by even brief separation — led to serious distress for both child and mother. These ideas seemed right to us.

We read Spock. Benjamin Spock was the guru for our generation of parenthood. We trusted him, and applied his rules and guidance most of the time. 'Children know best about food — parents know best about sleep'. 'If your child falls ill, it is probably not serious — but call a doctor in any case'. 'Children need a secure framework of rules, but enough space to be free'. (These are not accurate quotations, but examples of his wisdom distilled by memory.) I was delighted by his paradoxical style.

Like all parents, we discovered the hard way that the advice of experts could only take you so far: one's own strengths and weaknesses — and experience of childhood — were the critical factors. I underestimated the importance of fatherhood, and regret that I did not find more time for the family. With hindsight, I accuse myself of neglect. It doesn't help to guess that I may be typical of my generation of fathers.

We raised six children. They have their own lives to lead — and their own stories to tell. Amid a myriad of particular, fragmented memories of their early childhood, what I remember in general is — our own ignorance and inadequacy, delight, weariness, fascination, the burden of responsibility, the imperative of love.

Nothing in my life has been more difficult than parenthood: we were neither prepared nor trained to meet its challenge. I don't think much has changed in this respect. 'Lifelong learning for all' may be a cliché of our times — but have we yet taken seriously the need to educate parents? Among other things, we tried to teach our children the value of education. We cared deeply about early learning. Although as socialists we never contemplated sending our children to private schools, we cheerfully paid for their nursery education without noticing a possible contradiction to our principles.

I loved the daily walk to school. Most nursery and primary schools welcome parents. Ours certainly did. But I don't remember that they made it their business to help us understand the processes of child development or the 'desirable outcomes' we should look for. For our part, we were a good deal clearer about reading and number than social or moral education. We practised 'times tables' and hard spellings on the way to school: fairness and right and wrong were part of the fabric of family life.

In 1975 our youngest child reached the age of 5 and fulltime education: my wife took a part-time job. We entered a new phase of family life, leaving early childhood behind us as we began to navigate the shoals and rapids of the teenage years. But that is another story.

I never completely forgot what I had learned about the importance of the early years. As a university teacher I was uneasy about the contradiction between the social assumptions (which I shared) of the pre-eminence of advanced education and my private conviction of the fundamental value of early learning. Of course, both are important and valuable. But I suspected that, while higher education may be the glossy fruit, nursery education is the strong root of the tree of learning — and that we neglect it at our peril.

And so I conceived the Start Right project in 1992. The report, published by the RSA in 1994, tells the story — the team of eminent advisers, the support of generous funders, the questions we tried to answer and the conclusions we reached. I believe it is the best piece of work I have ever done. Others must decide whether it has proved to be sound, persuasive and influential. Some recommendations have certainly borne fruit — for example, those on research and the need for an international conference on good practice; others lie dormant — such as those on the need for a Code of Conduct or the education of parents.

Meanwhile, under two administrations the nation inches its way towards a proper provision for the preschool education of all our children. I remain hopeful, and believe, that the case for the importance of early learning, high-quality provision and a universal entitlement will prevail. Let me briefly set it out again.

'Give me a child for the first seven years, and you may do what you like with it afterwards'. This old Jesuit maxim is still apt today. The influence of early learning is so important that, if you give children a good start, there is much less risk of things going wrong later, but if you don't — and things do — it is very difficult and expensive to put them right. Prison doesn't work. Along with health care and parental education, investment in good early learning for all its children is arguably the best investment a nation can make. Why don't we?

I think the answer has more to do with ignorance than money. Most people are unaware of the importance of early learning in our lives. Good preschool education leads to immediate and lasting social and educational benefits for all children — especially those from disadvantaged backgrounds. Investment in high-quality effective early education provides a worthwhile social and economic return to society. A recent research report stated that 'over the lifetime of the participants, the preschool programme returns to the public an estimated $7.16 for every dollar invested' (Schweinhart, Barnes and Weikart, 1993).

Most people are unaware that throughout the developed world — and in some developing nations like India and Brazil — there has been rapid and substantial growth in preschool education during the last 30 years. Denmark stands out as the leader of Europe in the provision of a comprehensive and coherent programme of 'educare': Ireland, the Netherlands and the UK are the laggards. The UK has been close to the bottom of the European league for publicly-funded preschool educational places for three- and four-year olds. This means that those children who most need the experience of good centre-based early learning, and can benefit most from it, are least likely to have it.

People are even less aware of the importance of quality. Quality matters. Poor preschool education is almost as little use to children as none at all. High-quality provision for early learning requires:

- the integration of education and care
- unified responsibility for provision
- effective initial and ongoing training for early years 'teacher-carers'
- an appropriate ('Key Stage 0') curriculum encouraging active learning and purposeful
- play in an environment of 'high challenge–low threat'
- partnership between parents and the teacher-carers
- systematic planning, assessment and record keeping
- continuity and consistency of 'educare'
- adult–child ratios broadly consistent with the RSA rule of thumb
- satisfactory premises and equipment
- regular monitoring and evaluation of performance with the aim of continuous improvement.

Let me plainly state that there is no room for compromise on these ten principles.

How could a universal entitlement to good early learning be provided? Funding often seems to be the problem, but in reality it is a question of priorities. Preschool education is

- a good investment — over time its value outweighs its cost;
- a social priority — like clean water, inoculation and free elections;
- highly effective education — so the education budget should be rebalanced in favour of early learning.

**The rule states that public funding should be used so as to permit class sizes (or learner–teacher ratios) equivalent to one trained adult to the number of children (or students) equal to double their average age — for example, groups of 6 for 3-year-olds, 12 for 6-year-olds, 24 for 12-year-olds, and so on. The intention and effect of such a rule is to tilt public resources back towards early learning, and encourage the increasing use of private funding for higher and adult education, without making substantial new demands on public funding for education over all.

The Start Right report proposed a new solution to the problem by raising the compulsory fulltime schooling age from 5 to 6 and recycling the resources to provide free half-day learning for all children aged three to five in an integrated context of extended day care. We also suggested that, along with parental training, preschool education is so important that it should be made compulsory. These proposals have (so far) fallen on deaf ears.

Instead, and regrettably, both the last government and the present one have tinkered with a problem that requires radical action. Neither John Major's 'nursery vouchers' nor David Blunkett's 'local action plans' take seriously the importance of ensuring good quality provision and honouring the ten principles set out above. We know the indicators of poor quality. They include: the idea that you can teach without caring, or care without teaching; the division of responsibility between Health and Education at local and national levels; the lack of integrated training for early years 'teacher-carers'; introduction to Key Stage 1 of the National Curriculum before the mastery of the fundamental phase of learning I call 'Key Stage 0'; failure to work with parents — and indeed, to help them develop their parenting skills and improve their general education; lack of planning, assessment of children and record keeping; discontinuity and inconsistency (a new supply teacher every month); current primary class sizes; unsatisfactory buildings and a shortage of equipment — including books; complacency, and failure to test oneself against the best. I could go on.

The truth is that few existing forms of provision are up to standard or meet all the elementary requirements of good practice. We have a long way to go. A sensible government would set high standards, but give all concerned — the public, private and voluntary sectors — two or three years to transform themselves to meet the ten principles of good quality.

Some of the best practice is found today in the private sector — which is why I have chosen to work with Jigsaw, one of the leading providers of good 'educare'. I have every hope that we shall find a way of offering places to LEAs for some children from disadvantaged backgrounds as well as developing the growing market for high-quality nursery provision.

Unless or until the government legislates to create 'a statutory responsibility for the provision of free, high-quality, half-day preschool education for all children from the age of 3, in an integrated context of extended daycare' (Recommendation 12 of Start Right), I believe the private sector is best placed to meet the needs of children and their parents — without compromising the ten principles of good quality.

Putting 4-year-olds (and, in due course, 3-year-olds?) into primary schools which have not been designed, equipped or staffed for this age and stage of learning

	high challenge	low challenge
high threat	'anxious'	'dim'
low threat	'bright'	'spoilt'

Figure 4.1: Matrix to show threat/challenge combination

won't do. Early years 'teacher-carers' need special training. Class size and adult–child ratios are a critical issue. 'Key Stage 0' is a prerequisite for Key Stage I. Good early learning provides a foundation stage upon which successful schooling and adult learning can be built. Without it, children become dependent and helpless in the face of adversity and difficulty. High-quality preschool education encourages independence and 'mastery' behaviour — the enjoyment of challenge, perseverance and trust in one's own capability and competence. The Jesuits were right.

Since writing Start Right, I have not ceased thinking about these issues. I am particularly concerned about three of the ten principles of quality, each of which requires more thought and attention than it is receiving at present. They are: the training of 'teacher-carers', the 'Key Stage 0' curriculum, and partnership with parents.

Learning failure occurs when one (or more) of four impediments prevents the achievement of success. These impediments to learning are: (i) lack of confidence and self-esteem; (ii) weak motivation; (iii) inadequate potential; (iv) absence of opportunities to learn. Most educational debate addresses the last two, concerning itself with questions like the 'ability range', IQ, aptitude — or access, equal opportunities, growth of provision. Important as these issues are, they are not the major impediments to learning in the UK (or elsewhere). The real problems are confidence and motivation.

Motivation (wanting to learn) is a by-product of confidence and self-esteem (feeling good about yourself). Look at any happy infant — or self-assured adult. So the challenge to educare is deceptively simple: to foster (or restore) the confidence and self-esteem which babies are born with. An environment characterized by a combination of 'high challenge' and 'low threat' does this.

Adults learn best when they have choice, time, and control of the learning strategy. Children are no different. School often dictates the curriculum, predetermines the time available and imposes a learning strategy (e.g. 'whole-class' teaching). This can increase **the** perceived threat to such an extent that some children respond with the 'fight-or-flight' syndrome typical of any threatened animal. (Educators call this disruption and truancy: it is widespread.)

If 'high challenge' coupled with 'low threat' is ideal (and the reverse is pernicious), the matrix in Figure 4.1 shows each of the possible combinations and the likely effects on the learning child (or adult).

Good preschool educare takes place in the lower left-hand corner of this Figure. It develops and fosters bright (alert, confident, self-assured, well-motivated, happy) children, who are mastery learners. Our task is to develop an appropriate Key Stage 0 curriculum and a workforce of teacher-carers which guarantees this desirable outcome. For those whose lives are lived in the other three boxes become dependency learners, always relying on others for their standards, motivation and self-respect.

Some parents wrongly assume that you can't start too soon on the agenda of Key Stage 1 (e.g. teaching reading and number). Such things can provide excellent challenges, but may instead be disastrous threats, to the young child. Everything depends on the quality of the teacher-carers, who should themselves be role-model mastery learners.

So the questions — for Jigsaw and the UK — seem to be:

- How can we select, train, sustain and retain such excellent teacher-carers?
- Can a dependency-learner (school leaver or adult) be retrained to become a role-model mastery learner?
- How can we re-educate parents to understand and support our teaching and learning strategy?
- What should the Key Stage 0 curriculum look like in detail?
- Who is responsible for finding workable solutions to these difficult problems?

These are formidable challenges. But they should not defeat us, so long as we care enough about the creation of a better future for all our children. Start Right ended: none of these things will happen without an assertion of political will, accompanied by popular support and directed through decisive leadership. The translation of national aspirations into reality cannot be achieved by government alone. It requires the cooperation, effort and enterprise of many agencies and all parts of society. Political will inevitably reflects the general will of society. But political leadership can shape the general will. Progress is possible. Nations have learned to free slaves, end child labour, extend the franchise to women. We can decide to stop neglecting the early education of our children. We may expect a range of economic, social and personal benefits if we do so. But these are not the most compelling reasons for action. We should act because it is right. Our children's children will not readily forgive us, if we decline to face the challenge, or fail.

References

BALL, C. (1994) *Start Right: The Importance of Early Learning*, London: Royal Society for the Encouragement of the Arts, Manufacturers and Commerce (RSA).

SCHWEINHART, L.J., BARNES, H.V. and WEIKART, D.P. (1993) *Significant Benefits of the High/Scope Perry Preschool Study through Age 2–7*, Ypsilanti, MI: High/Scope Press.

5   Another Way of Seeing: Perceptions of Play in a Steiner Kindergarten

Mary-Jane Drummond

Introduction

During a recent sabbatical term, I undertook a series of observations of children's play in a number of early childhood settings, one of which was the Rosebridge Kindergarten, a Rudolf Steiner kindergarten in Cambridge. The quality of play in this kindergarten made a strong impression on me; for at least an hour every morning the children (aged from 4 to 6) were deeply engaged in complex, collaborative and imaginative play. Over the last six months I have revisited the Rosebridge Kindergarten many times, and recorded many hours of observation: I was determined to try to find out why these children's play was so intense, sustained, and varied. I have had many discussions with Steiner educators in the process of this enquiry, as I tried to answer some of the questions that the children's play had raised for me.

In this chapter, I report the fruits of my enquiry, and try to demonstrate the relationship between the quality of the children's play and salient features of the Steiner educators' thinking. I will try to establish connections between what the children do in the kindergarten, during the period dedicated to play, and the key concepts around which the Steiner approach to young children is constructed. I will examine the educators' understanding of children and childhood, the role of the kindergarten teacher, and the whole kindergarten environment, and suggest ways in which mainstream educators, in other kinds of early childhood settings, might learn from their approach.

The influence of Rudolf Steiner (1861–1925) was, of course, immediately apparent in every discussion of which I was part. But my principal interest was in the way in which the educators themselves had assimilated and applied the original inspiration. In this chapter, then, I do not attempt to trace the educators' thinking back to its source in Steiner's own works. Instead, I have tried to explore the ways in which they have made Steiner's thought their own (rather as the educators in Reggio-Emilia speak familiarly of 'our Piaget' — the Piaget they have constructed for themselves, through study and application). I have drawn on the accounts, both oral and written, of practising and former kindergarten teachers, and on my own copious observation notes. I have not attempted to describe the kindergarten programme in its entirety, but have focused almost exclusively on the period spent by the children in spontaneous play, which lasts for about an hour every morning.

Understanding Children: A Steiner Perspective

To mainstream educators, Steiner kindergarten practitioners appear extraordinarily serene and certain when they talk about their work, using the most theoretical and abstract terms with great assurance. The key concepts they work with, deriving ultimately from the writings of Rudolf Steiner, are of the utmost importance to them in shaping their practices, their pedagogical interactions, and their personal responses to individual children. For this reason, any attempt by an outsider to understand the sights and sounds of a Steiner kindergarten must be rooted in an awareness of the same key concepts, however remote they may at first seem from the preferred categories of mainstream early years educators.

Two of the most important ideas appear together in the following extract from the opening pages of a book by a celebrated kindergarten teacher, Freya Jaffke (1996):

(The) whole body acts as a single sensory organ . . . uniting external impressions with the child's internal world. . . . The child's body acts as a sensory organ for the individual, the soul and spiritual being . . . This interaction of external impressions with the child's internal development is revealed in the wonderful power of imitation with which every child is born. Every perception is first deeply assimilated, then grasped with the will and reflected back to the outside. (p. 10)

Here we are being introduced to some of the most complex ideas in Steiner's writing (spirit, soul and body) together with his three fold model of humanity, which comprises the powers of the will, heart and head: doing, feeling and thinking. For children in the kindergarten, before the second dentition, the most important of these is the *will*: young children are essentially in 'doing' mode, exercising their whole bodies, under the control of their will, in sustained, creative, transformative exploration of the world. To the power of the will is added, in this analysis, the power of *imitation*, the second of the two key concepts by use of which I have tried to read my kindergarten observations.

Between the ages of 3 and 5, say the Steiner educators, two new faculties appear: the imagination and the memory. Since these terms are more familiar, I will not elaborate on them further here; their relevance to many of my observations and conclusions will, I hope, be self-evident. However, in presenting this crude, brief summary, I do not want to suggest that the Steiner view of childhood is a modified version of a 'milestones' checklist, in which each child is coolly monitored for the age-appropriate display of will, imitation, imagination and memory. The Steiner view is essentially holistic, almost reverential. The teacher in the Rosebridge Kindergarten, Janni Nicol described it thus:

We think of the child as a spiritual being, who is visiting the earth. The child isn't a product of its genetic material and its home — but so much more. Children come already with their gifts: it's up to us to find their gifts and help them to develop them. Each child has so much to work with and develop — so nothing is suppressed.

She added with a rueful expression . . . 'and mainstream education does do so *much* suppression.' This reverence for the individual, the precious visitor, runs through the Steiner account of childhood like a refrain. It seems to me to illuminate the meanings of their unfamiliar discourse. So Jaffke (1996) writes, emphasizing the unique freedom of the individual child and bringing all these concepts together into one nutshell of conviction: 'Imitation is the activity of the will. The activity of the will is the activity of the "I". The greatest freedom lies in imitation!' (p. 73).

Children's Powers, Children's Play

One of my observations in the Rosebridge Kindergarten focused on a group of children playing close to each other in the clear carpeted space that takes up one half of the kindergarten classroom: an extract follows.

> Ike is building a van. He stacks up two piles of wooden chairs for the driver and his mate, and creates the front with a clothes-horse folded just so that a plank can be placed across to make a dashboard. Here he places a fat round log for the steering wheel, and assembles other smaller logs for brake, accelerator, clutch and radio. All complete, he announces, looking hopefully at Amy playing nearby 'If anyone wants to be a builder with me, I've got a seat for them.' Amy leaves the puppet show she is making and jumps on board. Owen, who has helped with the construction of the van, is not impressed. 'Can *I* play with you?' Ike: 'No, there's only two seats.' Owen: 'But *you're* playing in the puppet show.' Amy: 'But he's *driving* me to the show.' Ike bursts into action with a roar of truck noises, then slams on the brake: 'Here you are!' Amy gets off, Owen gets on. The builders continue their journey to the builders' yard, with the van radio on full blast, while Amy and Caitlin complete the puppet show. They build a space for the audience surrounded by clothes-horse screens, covered with lengths of cloth. They build the stage at the front of this space and close the curtains. Then they assemble the characters and properties for *The Three Little Pigs*, laying them out in exquisite order *from behind* the curtain, facing in, so that to the audience, not yet assembled, they will appear in the right sequence, facing out.

This was by no means an uncharacteristic episode of sustained imaginative and collaborative play. I present it here to illustrate the ideas introduced in the previous section, and to show how the powers of imitation, will, imagination and memory read out, so expressively, in these children's play.

It is not difficult to discern, I think, in this brief extract, a great number of acts, mental and physical, that we could safely describe as learning. We might choose to characterize that learning within any number of categories, drawing for example on the HMI areas of experience (DES, 1985), on the *Desirable Outcomes* document (SCAA, 1996), or the 'foundations for early learning' set out in the recent frame-work *Quality in Diversity in Early Learning* (ECEF, 1998). My purpose here is to show how Steiner educators construct their understanding of the play that occurs so spontaneously and plentifully in their kindergarten classrooms.

In a conference paper, Sally Jenkinson, former kindergarten teacher and currently early years consultant to the Steiner Fellowship, makes a passionate case for the 'creative play of early childhood' (Jenkinson, 1997). Using examples from her own kindergarten, and from a small-scale observation study in another, she documents the way in which the children's imaginative play is 'both a vehicle for human creativity and a vital social force which leads (them) through empathetic thinking and imitation, to the realm of "the other"' (p. 101). She elaborates on this proposition by using specific examples from children's play to show how play can 'awaken social sensitivity and imitation . . . through the playful activity of imaginative empathy.'

> 'You can be the big school girl.'
> (How do big school girls feel and act?)

> 'I'm a spaceship man.'
> (How might a spaceship man behave? What fears might he have? How might he face up to challenges?)

> 'Are you a mouse?'
> 'No, I'm a prince.'
> (So you need to treat me very differently). (pp. 105–6)

My own observations too reveal many such examples of children 'living imaginatively into the experience of the other' — the experience of the avaricious king guarding his gold; the kindergarten friend who mustn't be late for her puppet show; the puzzled mechanics whose flying machine has developed an engine fault and are temporarily baffled. One of my favourite observations, occurred during a long sequence of construction/role play. A magnificent structure involving blocks, chairs, tables, a large chest, screens and long planks (for the wings), with the chairs organized on top of the tables, had occupied five boys for some 25 minutes. They have been talking to each other with their mobile phones (small blocks).

> *Adam to Daniel, the pilot*: 'Can you hear me?'
> *Daniel*: 'Yes, but don't shout, I'm driving.'
> *Adam*: 'I can see a flying saucer, going higher and higher so make that go higher, right? Over.'
> *Daniel*: 'Right. Higher and higher.'
> *Michael*: '120. 105.'
> *Daniel*: 'Adam, Michael, put your seat belts on.'
> *Ike*: 'Put on your seat belts please, or you'll fall out.'

And so on, until the engine develops a fault. They notice that the large chest has a keyhole and is locked.

> *Daniel*: 'It's the *engine*. We *have* to open it up.'

There is an interval here while the boys fetch the materials they need to make a key. ('We need really *stiff* paper') and then return to the flying machine.

> *Sean*: 'The bonnet's not working.'
> *Adam*: 'Oh my God. Let me have a look. [dramatically] There's a *cat* in the engine! There's a *cat* in the bonnet.'
> *Amy*: (playing nearby) 'I'll get the cat out if you like.' (Which she does, much to her satisfaction.)

Jenkinson contrasts this kind of play, in which 'the ability to "read" the thoughts and feelings of others begins to awaken, and the journey towards emotional literacy begins' with 'the cognitive learn as you play model', 'pre-cooked play fare', with predetermined and specific outcomes. She recognizes that children do learn in this way, indeed enjoy this learning, but insists that to use play as a means to an end, to a desirable outcome or an attainment target is, essentially, to miss the point. As children play together, negotiating themes, structures, rules, masterfully manipulating signs and symbols, creating imaginary worlds, peopling and inhabiting them, they are doing more important work than the teacher can set out in advance in her short or medium term plans.

In all this imaginative and imitative activity, the will is strongly involved. Jaffke's (1996) account describes how, in children of 5 and over, the will works to establish a purposeful connection between the idea and the imagination.

> If the will wants to act on an impulse to play, it must now unite with the idea. With the aid of the imagination, it finds or transforms objects into what the idea demands. (p. 66)

For this reason, the Steiner educators provide an environment which can be transformed by the children. They do not provide pre-structured play environments (post offices, launderettes or castles) or ready-made toys. The children arrive each morning into an open space, where they may use the screens, the blocks, the tables, the lengths of cloth, to create their own environments. Similarly, there are few objects that crudely represent the world outside the kindergarten: no toy telephones, or stylized play people. One educator told me: 'Our dolls have no faces,' and another, Joan Almon, described how she had no cars in her kindergarten, preferring the children to rediscover the wheel every day (through the plentiful provision of the right sort of planks and logs). The principle is that it is the child who transforms, rather than the adult who pre-forms. And, indeed, my own observations show how enormously skilled the 4- and 5-year-olds become in using the screens and lengths of cloth, which they secure with ribbons and knots and elastic bands, with great assurance, to shape their own play-spaces, their houses, palaces, flying machines, Euro-Star, racing cars, and boats of all kinds. In the same way the baskets full of conkers, cones, shells and small blocks of wood do duty for food, treasure, credit cards, tickets to the show; I have seen a short length of tree trunk (about as thick as my arm) used by the same child to fill the petrol tank of her car, and then to hoover its interior.

The case the Steiner educators make for play may or may not be convincing to those who hear it for the first time, or who cling devotedly to the categories into which they were inducted in their initial training. But it is certainly a case rooted in the familiar principle of active learning, in that they maintain that children's play essentially involves them in imaginative, transformative and exploratory acts: 'physical thinking' is Sally Jenkinson's (1997) fine phrase. Furthermore, they maintain the crucial power of imitation allows children to become active members of their various communities, to learn the languages of play and social intercourse, to assimilate and reproduce the ways of being, of doing, of representing and expressing, that they see all around them. Without plentiful opportunities for play, Jenkinson writes, children risk cultural, personal and social deprivation.

The Kindergarten Environment and the Role of the Adults

I have already described some aspects of the kindergarten environment and indicated how it is shaped to match what the Steiner educators see as important characteristics of their children's lives. Children, says Jaffke (1996), 'as creatures of the will and the senses, nestle into their environment, whatever it may be.' It follows that the preparation of the environment, and the selection of materials, must be both meticulous and principled. Jaffke claims: 'We carefully select the impressions which confront and surround the children' (p. 11). This claim is no exaggeration, as my own observations amply demonstrate. There are materials which can be transformed, as we have seen, and there are natural objects of great beauty and simplicity; the flowers are fresh, the muslin cloths are neatly hemmed, the dolls have clean (if featureless) faces. The wooden bowls are polished; the bread and jam is attractively served at a table prepared with candles and flowers; the puppets are most beautifully sewn. But it is not just in the provision of material resources that the Steiner educators attend to children's powers of imitation and will. They also maintain that the work of the adult is a crucial force in the children's lives. Accordingly, when the children arrive in the kindergarten, they find the adults sitting calmly at work — sewing, carving, buttering the bread for the children, or mending a broken toy. They are doing adults' work, and doing it with care, enthusiasm, diligence. This work of the adults, say the educators, creates the freedom, the rhythm and the creative space, in which children can play. As Jaffke (1996) neatly puts it, 'the children are left actively in peace'.

This adult behaviour has another function: it models for the children both purposeful activity and 'stewardship' of the world as it appears in miniature in the kindergarten — behaviour that they learn to imitate as they come to join in the routines of setting the table, polishing the wooden bowls, tidying away at the end of the play session, and working in the garden. Sally Jenkinson (1997) describes a further aspect of the educators' practice: that it explains the mystery of adult work. She imagines a child asking her or himself 'What do adults *do*?' or, more urgently, 'What are adults *for*?' In the kindergarten, the children see adults performing ordinary, everyday acts which may no longer be visible in the hurry and bustle of the child's home — slicing and buttering bread, mending clothes, kneading dough, pegging out washing, building and spreading the compost heap, harvesting the fruit and vegetables from the garden. The seeds of stewardship and citizenship are sown in this process of role-modelling, which is, for mainstream educators, an alarmingly dramatic contrast to the typical activities of the hard-pressed teacher in the over-crowded infant classroom.

The principle at work is, once again, imitation, not instruction. The key elements to be modelled, according to Jaffke, are order, rhythm, good habits and loving consistency. The adult exemplifies these acts of the will, deliberately working at a task, such as carving or embroidery, that takes a long time; or a task for the common good, in which she takes both pleasure and great pains. She exemplifies order by working slowly and thinking ahead, not rushing chaotically to catch up with herself. These adult behaviours, writes Jaffke (1996), in a metaphor of great tenderness, act as a *mantle*, which provides protection from external things, and also allows what is inside to flourish, to be strengthened and tended. She writes of 'the mantle of warmth' — physical warmth, soul-warmth, and warmth on a spiritual level, which has to be continually and consciously created (p. 38). She describes too 'the mantle of activity', through which the educators' behaviour, actions and attitudes create 'a world worth imitating'. And she elaborates on the mantle that arises through the educators' use of spoken language. Or, rather, from their extremely judicious, almost parsimonious, choice of language: 'in the context of play we do not need to use many words', she warns. There is no need, in the kindergarten environment, to bombard the children with verbal accounts of sharply defined concepts. Nor is there any evidence, in my observations, of the relentless questioning of the mainstream teacher (benevolently) intent on eliciting a verbal display of understanding from child after child. The familiar question and answer routine (initiation/nomination, response, evaluation) documented in so many studies of classroom interaction (Tizard and Hughes, 1984; Wells, 1986; Bennet and Kell, 1989) is conspicuously absent from the Steiner kindergarten.

The educators are by no means silent, however; it is just that they never speak to the children or to each other in that particular teacher's tone of voice, so caustically satirized by Joyce Grenfell, so ubiquitously heard in mainstream classrooms. The educators talk, laugh, and sing; but they never call for silence in order to issue streams of instructions. The silence that falls when a child lights the candle on the table before eating, or when the whole group is ready to start painting, or just before the fairy story begins, seems to arise from the children themselves, and not from the adult's injunctions. The aim in all cases, according to Jaffke, is to 'organize as little as possible and to regulate daily life as much as possible through real meaningful activity'. This principle runs through the children's lives as well, and *their* real meaningful activity, during the first part of the morning, is the spontaneous, creative, transformative play that I am trying to characterize in this chapter.

At the Rosebridge Kindergarten, the morning session draws to a close with the telling (not reading) of a fairystory, sometimes traditional, sometimes seasonal. These stories are chosen not just for their rich language and their literary worth, but also for their moral meanings; they are stories which 'seek to nourish rather than merely entertain or instruct', as a parent of Steiner school children has put it (Judith Woodhead in Drummond, Lally and Pugh, 1989). Each story is told more than once, sometimes every day for a week, so that the children have time to absorb the formal and beautiful language in which it is told, and to respond to the qualities, or virtues, the story brings, not merely the characters and the plot. With repeated telling, says Janni Nicol, the children come to see the deeper images in the stories, not the outer physical dimensions. The Steiner educator understands the importance of the role of myth and story in the search for deep underlying human truths and values, recognizing that human experience is not confined by the boundaries of the rational world. Sally Jenkinson (1997) writes of 'the realm of the subjunctive — the kingdom of our wishes, hopes, fears and possibilities — (that) is also our real world'. And it is both these worlds that I have been observing, spontaneously represented, in the play of the Steiner kindergarten.

As the educators describe their role in their programme, it is clear how closely they hold to their construction of children's powers — imitation, will, imagination and memory. Everything they do, and do not do, say, and do not say, is imbued with their understanding of children and childhood. Kindergarten teachers have an awesome responsibility: to be genuinely worthy of imitation — not just in manner, but in gesture and in action, in speech and in thought. The daily programme that they shape, through their acts, their speech, their thought, is highly structured, rhythmical and repetitive, and yet at the same time open and responsive; it creates the time and the space in which the child's powers of imitation and imagination are creatively expressed in acts of the will.

Applications, Implications, Explanations

Implicit in this short and selective account of my growing understanding of the Steiner kindergarten programme are some very stark contrasts with taken-for-granted practices in mainstream early years settings. In some ways, it is what the Steiner educators do *not* do that seems most challenging. The absence of printed material, including books, the educators' apparent indifference to the letters and sounds of the alphabet, the lack of adult/child interaction during sustained incidents of complex play: these features are, at first, difficult to assimilate. Seeing and hearing the educators refrain from explicit instruction is another challenging experience. Even when basic literacy and mathematical concepts are, clearly, relevant (in setting the table for example, when each child needs a bowl, a mug and a napkin, or when the last delicious slices of bread and jam are being distributed) the Steiner educators do not initiate didactic exchanges. If the supply of bread and jam runs out while the children are still hungry, the Steiner educators tend to replenish it, whereas my own pedagogical instinct is to embark on early subtraction and division exercises. Joan Almon made a similar point in a conference presentation: 'when we churn butter in the kindergarten', she said, 'it's because we want to eat butter'. She hardly needed to remind the mainstream members of her audience that in other settings the butter-churning enterprise is inevitably tied to a didactic purpose — a project on farms, cows, or People Who Help Us. In mainstream schools and classrooms where I have taught, the children have all experienced baking with yeast, kneading dough and seeing it rise. But not *every* week, as the Steiner children do. Their weekly baking day serves a real purpose in their lives. It is not a fleeting contribution to a topic on Harvest; they need the bread for their regular mid-morning snack. In Joan Almon's words, 'the kindergarten is not a place for empty or arbitrary activities, but for what arises out of life.'

The children's play, in the Steiner account of it, is equally free from explicitly pedagogical purposes. Musing on Sally Jenkinson's warning words about the cognitive model of play, with pre-cooked play fare and specific outcomes, I remembered attending a lecture, not many weeks before, by a well known mainstream early years specialist, with both practitioner and academic credentials. Her account of play included a distinction between *occupational play*, stereotyped, routine, repetitive, non-cognitively complex, mainly effortless, and, in contrast, *learning-centred play*, characterized by its cognitive complexity, its purposefulness and its orientation towards achievement. This latter kind of play, she claimed, needs an adult. The contrast between this position (one of many such in current texts on play) and the Steiner account of play could not be greater, for all that these exponents hold much in common. Their grounds for agreement include the importance of early childhood as a distinct phase in human life, the importance of quality educational experiences for young children, the importance of the adult in structuring and monitoring those experiences, the importance of play. But whereas the mainstream argument for play is constructed around learning outcomes, achievements and cognitive gains, the Steiner advocacy rests on very different premises, which I have tried to outline in earlier sections of this chapter.

After one morning's observation in the Rosebridge Kindergarten (the day the two girls built the puppet show back to front) I sat with the two educators to review the significant events of the session. In the course of this discussion I jokingly referred to the deplorable *Desirable Outcomes* document, and suggested that its requirements were not going to pose any problems for the educators (who are expecting an inspection visit in the coming year). To my surprise and delight, a few weeks later Janni Nicol, the kindergarten teacher, sent me a written account of that same morning's activities, analysed under the *Desirable Outcomes* headings, which she had composed as a demonstration piece for an audience of interested parents and supporters, (and, no doubt, the impending inspector). It is the most fascinating document (and, incidentally, a useful triangulation of my own observations).

First Janni Nicol gives a closely observed, vivid, narrative account of the morning, with many details included that I could not see from my vantage point, some yards away from the table where she had been sitting sewing with a group of children. Next she takes each of the six *Desirable Outcomes* headings and re-describes the children's activities using the official language of the SCAA document. This account too is full of detail; it is precise and definite; it is clear and confident; but the children's living experiences have somehow vanished from the scene. For example, under *Mathematics* she writes:

... the children used mathematical language such as in front of, bigger than, more, through etc. to describe shape, position, size and quantity. They recognized and recreated patterns ... They compared, sorted, matched, used order, sequence ... and so on.

In the final section of her paper, Janni Nicol reverts to her own way of seeing, to the educational discourse she shares with the community of Steiner school parents and supporters. She constructs these concluding paragraphs around the crux of the matter, her conviction, her certain knowledge, that whatever the children 'achieved', in terms of what the DfEE or QCA deem desirable, was not the result of formal instruction:

These are things which *happened*, and which happen every day, through the rhythm of our work ... in the (children's) way of learning, imitating, observing and role playing; in the joy of being, in exploring themselves and each other.

This teacher's written summary seems to me to encapsulate a way of seeing play, and the consequences of play, that is, at the very least, worth serious consideration by a wider audience. She concludes:

And where was it all recorded? Well, for us it was written up in brief in our planning review of the day ... but for the children? We hope it was recorded in their hearts and souls, in their memory and imagination, to be recalled later in their lives and transformed into a creative impulse, in scientific exploration, in the ability to think broadly and widely and to carry a moral impulse to help mankind and the future of the earth. These are OUR desirable outcomes for the children who pass through our kindergarten.

The Steiner educators, whose work I have presented here, have, I believe, much to offer early childhood practitioners in other traditions. The key concepts that have emerged for me, during the months in which I have been trying to learn, trying to understand, are trust and value. It seems to me that the Steiner educators express in every line and every utterance their fundamental trust, in both children and adults. They trust in the pedagogical value of what children spontaneously do in their play, in a harmonious and supporting environment (by leaving them 'actively in peace'); and they trust as completely in the value of their own, adult activities — their story telling, their sewing, their music-making, their calm, sensitive watchfulness, their joyful, loving presences — as they consciously shape the environment in which the children learn by living.

Conclusion

In embarking on this enquiry, I had two distinct purposes: the first, to learn more about children's play, and the second, to learn more about the Steiner kindergarten approach. It was only in the course of the work that I became aware of the relationship between the two, and realized that understanding the Steiner approach would help me to understand children's play. I found, too, that much of what I learned from the Steiner educators complemented and illuminated classic texts on play that I had read in the past but forgotten and set aside. For example, Piaget's great work on play (*Play, Dreams and Imitation in Childhood*, 1951) offers many insights that can almost be read as a commentary on the Steiner position. His emphasis on the child's early fascination with symbolic play (it is important to remember that the book's original title is *La Formation du Symbole*), and his pithy one-liner 'Play is a form of thought' (p. 167) echo the analysis I have presented here. In the same text he writes: 'The conflict between obedience and individual liberty is the affliction of childhood' (p. 149). A Steiner educator, commenting on these words, exclaimed 'Yes! and that's why shop play and restaurant and café play are so important' (for in these contexts, the child can *play* at 'individual liberty').

The concepts of *imitation* and *will*, presented in the first section of this paper, are in a similar way prefigured in the work of Groos (1901) whose immensely long book *The Play of Man* (full of endearing asides — for example, why do children climb trees? 'So that their elders cannot get to them' (p. 88) deserves to be rescued from oblivion. In his meticulous classification of human plays (plural), he includes as a major category *Playful moving of foreign bodies*. Subdivisions of this large group of plays (in adulthood and in childhood) include *Hustling things about*, where he writes of children's play with puddles, revealing their 'joy in being a cause,' and *Throwing plays* where he describes:

> the power of will over matter.... The peculiar satisfaction derived from throwing
> ... projecting our individuality into a wider sphere of action ... The extension of
> motion originated by ourselves ... becomes a part of us. The force which we
> behold at work outside of us is our own. (p. 104)

This passage can be read as an illuminating gloss on the Steiner account of children acting, through their will, on their worlds, transforming them, recreating them, indeed, hustling them about. Later, as Groos painstakingly pursues his immense project of mapping every known form of human play, across the world, from the dawn of time, he brings together, with a simple word-bridge, with a connecting rope of thought, two of the key concepts discussed in this chapter. Arguing that dramatic imitation leads to aesthetic sympathy, he attributes this whole area of human enterprise to the power of imitation: 'Imitation proves itself to be the author of the symbol' (p. 327).

In reporting this enquiry, I have been writing as an outsider, a non-participant observer in more than one sense. I am not a Steiner educator, nor will ever be. I have no intention of settling and putting down roots within the Steiner community of discourse. To conclude this chapter then, rather than reviewing the main features of the Steiner approach, I will offer a brief description of how my own thinking about children's play has developed as a result of trying to learn 'another way of seeing'. My intention here is to take stock of what I have learned, with gratitude, from my friends and colleagues in the Steiner movement, and to outline the ways in which my notebooks full of observations have shaped my present understanding. I do so in the hope that other educators, in any of the great variety of settings where children live and learn, may here find some support for their continuing advocacy of children's play.

I have written elsewhere of the possibility of making an effective case for play in early years education by attending not to the verb form of the word (to play) but to the noun. Then it can confidently be used as an umbrella term for all the thousands of times and places in which children exercise their emotional and intellectual muscles. In play, under a table or up a tree, alone or in small groups, expressing themselves in words, or with blocks, or music or miniature world materials, children think and feel and act in ways of the utmost importance for their learning (Drummond, 1996, p. 138).

My observations in the Steiner kindergarten have enabled me to move on from this formulation, and to adopt a different metaphor, constructing an account of children's imaginative play around the idea of a doorway or, rather doorways. In play, I have come to think, children leave the mundane and everyday world in which their parents give them their breakfasts and button them up in their coats, ready for school, and pass through invisible doorways into alternative worlds. The first of these is the social world of shared play, in which children enter into the feelings, the stories, the creativity of their friends and companions. (Two children, inseparable companions, digging in the soil inside a bush in the kindergarten, create such a world. Sean to Katie: 'Katie, this is our special place'. He says it three times. Sean: 'You be the girl and I'll be the boy'. Katie, in agreement, 'Pretend'. They agree on their names, Adam and Alice. They are *pretending* to be friends!)

Another door opens as the child enters the realm of their own creativity, exploring possibilities, re-living private adventures, past and present, predicting a future, building a whole library of personal symbolic readings of the universe. This is the domain where children discover their individual capacities to act on and transform the world, to represent it in any way they choose, to write their own life-stories, fairy-stories, creation myths and epics of destruction. (I saw many minutes of solitary play in the Steiner kindergarten and am struggling here to represent in words what I believe to be the inner activity of these solitary, not lonely, children, intensely engaged in play.)

Through a third door, children pass into a world that they will share with a wider society than that of their intimate friends. Here they become part, as and when they choose, of their whole society's enduring stories. Through this door, children enter into the wishes, hopes, fears and anger expressed in the legacy of traditional stories, poems and songs that communities have shared together over the centuries. This is the door that opens whenever an educator brings children together to tell them a story, implicitly inviting them to recognize the role of myth, fable and story in humankind's search for meaning, implicitly inviting them to join that search. The themes of these important stories appear again and again in the observations in my notebooks.

As long as children play, and as long as we, their educators, watch them and try to understand what we see, we will go on finding fresh ways to think about and explain the importance of play. In this chapter I have outlined the ways in which Steiner educators conceptualize children's play, and described how their insights have affected my own. In the process, I have drawn on some of the classroom observations and thinking work I have been engaged in over the last six months — a task I set myself, a personal enquiry, an individual journey. The task that faces all early years educators in the coming years is to find the tenacity, and the trust in children, to continue to do such work, co-constructing such robust understanding that we can all stand up as advocates, clear and certain, for 'the beautiful task of play' (a phrase from Groos' (1901) concluding paragraph), confident in our capacity to allow children to pass through the doorways of play on their own infinitely varied journeys into the world.

Acknowledgments: My grateful thanks to Sally Jenkinson and Ute Towriss for the many discussions that have inspired this chapter and taught me so much, and equally to the educators in the Rosebridge Kindergarten, Janni Nicol and Stephanie Grögelein, whose expertise, sensitivity and wisdom in working with children I cannot adequately represent in this brief chapter.

References

BENNETT, N. and KELL, J. (1989) *A Good Start? Four Year Olds in Infant Schools*, Oxford: Blackwell Education.

DEPARTMENT OF EDUCATION AND SCIENCE (1985) *Curriculum Matters 2*, London: HMSO.

DRUMMOND, M.-J. (1996) 'Play, learning and the National Curriculum: Some possibilities', in COX, T. (ed.) *The National Curriculum and the Early Years*, London: Falmer Press.

DRUMMOND, M.-J., LALLY, M. and PUGH, G. (1989) (eds) *Working with Children: Developing a Curriculum for the Early Years*, London: NES Arnold in association with the National Children's Bureau.

EARLY CHILDHOOD EDUCATION FORUM (1998) *Quality in Diversity in Early Learning: A Framework for Early Childhood Practitioners*, London: National Children's Bureau.

GROOS, K. (1901) *The Play of Man*, London: Heinemann.

JAFFKE, F. (1996) *Work and Play in Early Childhood*, London: Floris Books.

JENKINSON, S. (1997) 'The genius of play', in *Realising Children's Potential: The Value of Early Learning*, Conference proceedings, Rolle School of Education, University of Plymouth 5 and 6 September.

PIAGET, J. (1951) *Play, Dreams and Imitation in Childhood*, London: Heinemann.

SCAA (1996) *Desirable Outcomes for Children's Learning on Entering Compulsory Education*, London: HMSO.

TIZARD, B. and HUGHES, M. (1984) *Young Children Learning*, London: Fontana.

WELLS, G. (1986) *The Meaning Makers*, London: Heinemann.

WOODHEAD, J. (1989) 'Approaches to the curriculum (Steiner)' in DRUMMOND, M.J., LALLY, M. and PUGH, G. *Working with Children: Developing a Curriculum for the Early Years*, London: NES Arnold in association with the National Children's Bureau.

6   Protecting Playfulness

Rod Parker-Rees

> *Playfulness* is a more important consideration than play. The former is an attitude
> of mind; the latter is a passing outward manifestation of this attitude. (Dewey,
> 1909, p. 162)

It may be useful to sharpen the distinction between play, the behaviour which
we grow out of as we grow up, and playfulness, the attitude of mind which can
continue to influence our thinking and our behaviour throughout our lives. Play is
often seen as a childish 'pre' behaviour which we leave behind when we learn
how to do things properly. When schooling begins, the young child's largely
self-directed exploration of things, people and situations is displaced by a more systematic induction into social patterns of meaning. The pressures of a prescribed
curriculum then make it increasingly difficult to allow children to find their own
way around what they need to know, so play is removed from work activities and
isolated in playtimes and playgrounds. Play becomes a recreational form of activity
earned by the completion of work.

Playfulness, on the other hand, is fundamental to our ability to function within
social groups throughout our lives. Playfulness can be seen as a disposition (Katz,
1995) but it is more than just a habitual way of thinking; it is a way of coping with
the tension between personal freedom and social constraints which characterizes all
forms of interaction.

Recent work on mastery motivation (Messer, 1993; MacTurk and Morgan,
1995; Hauser-Cram, 1998) and on the long-term social effects of the High/Scope
programme (Sylva, 1992; Schweinhart et al., 1993) has highlighted the importance
of giving young children opportunities to practise making choices and decisions. I
will argue that this ability to choose is rooted in the disposition to be playful, to
recognize opportunities for play in the structures which shape our behaviour at
every stage of our lives. Adults who work with young children are particularly well
equipped to appreciate the value of playfulness, not only in children's early exploration of cultural systems but also in their own efforts to cope with the pressures of
externally imposed constraints. We can learn about playfulness from young children and we may find that we can find opportunities to be playful in our work but
we also have a responsibility to share our understanding with a wider audience
beyond the world of early years education. Children's playfulness may provide a
valuable model to help all adults to understand their own interaction with the
cultural forms which both influence and are influenced by their behaviour.

I have chosen to constrain my own play with playfulness within Helen Haste's taxonomy of three levels in the process of generating meaning: 'the sociohistorical, the interpersonal and the intra-individual' (Haste, 1987, p. 173). Beginning at the intra-individual level, I will consider the scope for playfulness in the interaction between subconscious and conscious mental processes: the informing of brain activity which results from thinking and which enables us to think. At the interpersonal level I will explore the playful interaction between personal meanings and the social structures or languages which enable us to represent these meanings, both to ourselves and to others: the transforming of meaning which results from communication and which enables us to communicate. Finally, at the sociohistorical level, I will consider the implications of playfulness in the interaction between the behaviour of individuals and the constraints imposed by cultural expectations: the performing of roles which results from engagement in social activities and which enables us to engage in social activities. Being playful at each of these levels involves seeing the forms which organize our experience not as rigid rules to be obeyed but as tools or 'thinking devices' (Lotman in Wertsch and Penuel, 1996, p. 424) to be used for, and refined by, making and sharing meaning.

Informing: Playful Interaction between Subconscious and Conscious Mental Processes

Guy Claxton's recent study of pre-conscious mental processing (Claxton, 1997) presents a strong case for reappraising the significance of the 'undermind', the mental processes which underpin (and sometimes undermine) our thinking. Claxton contrasts the fuzzy, complicated workings of the undermind with the relatively tidy, ordered patterns of deliberate thought, echoing Hofstadter's image of a tree of knowing:

> We can liken the ... thought processes to a tree whose visible part stands sturdily above ground but depends vitally on its invisible roots which extend way below ground giving it stability and nourishment. In this case the roots symbolize [!] complex processes which take place below the level of the [conscious] mind — processes whose effects permeate the way we think but of which we are unaware. (quoted in Hodgkin, 1985, p. 77)

Our brains are made up of an immensely complicated web of neurons, each with its own 'root system' of dendrites which connect it with as many as 20,000 others (Claxton, 1997, p. 137), so the complexity of the three-dimensional forest of the brain is already vastly simplified in Hofstadter's model. But this sort of simplification seems to be an essential feature of our thinking at all levels. As whole populations of neurons react to stimuli a complicated mass of activity is progressively filtered and encoded (Howlett, 1998) into increasingly coherent structures until the signal triggers a reaction or emerges into consciousness (Claxton,

1997). What we are aware of knowing is always tidier, more organized and simpler than the brain activity which gave rise to our knowing: 'The world of experience must be greatly simplified and generalized before it can be translated into symbols' (Vygotsky, 1962, p. 6).

The word 'simple' originally meant 'without folds'. It is related to the words 'implicit' and 'complicated' (folded together, entangled) and 'explicit' (unfolded), all of which draw on the same metaphor; representing ideas as pieces of cloth which can be smoothed out tidily in two-dimensions or folded up into three-dimensions so that the relationship between parts is more difficult to trace. Holyoak and Thagard use the terms 'implicit' knowledge and 'explicit' knowledge to distinguish between 'the ability to *react* to something and the ability to *think* about it' (Holyoak and Thagard, 1995, p. 21). Implicit knowledge is 'tacit' (Polanyi, 1958), largely acquired through direct experience and not accessible to conscious reflection but even implicit knowledge must be abstracted from experience. We inform our perception by choosing what we will notice and what we will tune out as irrelevant. Holyoak and Thagard refer to Jorge Luis Borges' story, *Funes the Memorious*, to illustrate the importance of this kind of simplification in the relationship between perception and thinking:

> The fictional character Ireneo Funes is described as having a prodigious memory for every detail of his everyday experiences, for he 'remembered not only every leaf of every tree of every wood, but also every one of the times he had perceived or imagined it'. But his memory for specific details carried a heavy cost: He was incapable of abstract thought. 'Not only was it difficult for him to comprehend that the generic symbol "dog" embraces so many unlike individuals of diverse size and form; it bothered him that the dog at three fourteen (seen from the side) should have the same name as the dog at three fifteen (seen from the front).' For Funes, every situation was perceived in such excruciating detail that any cross-situational commonalities were totally obscured. His mind was shackled by the power of specific sensory experience, unable to break free to see abstract patterns of similarity that we normally take for granted. Instead of enhancing his thinking power, Funes's amazing memory abilities seemed to be cognitive chains, binding him to the particular. (Holyoak and Thagard, 1995, pp. 19–20)

Our brains are plastic or adaptive because play in the genetic programming which organizes the growth of networks of neural connections allows us to tune ourselves to the particular environment we inhabit: 'the play of life depends . . . on both rules — order — and play within these rules' (Lambert, 1997, p. 32; my translation). By the age of 12 months we lose our earlier ability to recognize a wide range of differences between speech sounds. By focusing our attention on the phonemic distinctions which are meaningful in the languages we hear, we are able to recognize the abstract patterns of similarity between different pronunciations of the same word (ibid.). Pre-conscious learning is 'the ability to distil out of our everyday experience useful maps and models of the world around us' (Claxton, 1997, p. 21). These maps allow us to escape the shackles of sensory experience, to 'see the wood for the trees' but they can also narrow our perceptions so that we risk mistaking the map for the territory (Claxton, 1984, p. 19) limiting our thinking to the level of artificially tidy stereotypes.

Playing with the 'real world', moving around in it, manipulating bits of it and deliberately changing and recombining our perceptions of objects and events, allows us to abstract richer, more subtle and more complicated interpretations. Play with 'treasure baskets' (Goldschmied, 1992), which contain both natural objects and simpler, made things, enables very young children to explore the abstraction of patterns of similarity; to re-map and re-tell their perceptions in different ways. This exploratory or epistemic play (Johnson, 1990) is a two way process, driven by both the bottom-up induction of affective and sensori-motor schemes and by curiosity, the top-down, deductive process of developing and testing emergent schemes and concepts. Playful sorting and classifying activities can supplement the relative simplicity of structured sorting materials by emphasizing the possibility of different organizing principles (not 'Which is *the* odd one out?' but 'How could *each* item be the odd one out?'). This playful approach not only helps to preserve our sensitivity to the subtleties of our feelings and perceptions (the complexity beneath the simplicity of ideas) but it can also help us to become more aware of the conventions of map-making and story-telling, the cognitive tools which enable us to make sense out of our perceptions. Recognizing that all information, fact as well as fiction, is 'made up' allows us to construe the stories told by our undermind more playfully so that they inform our thinking rather than instruct it.

Playfulness is a luxury which we can only enjoy when we are free from the more urgent demands of survival. Neurons, like people, respond to crises by clustering into functional teams which 'pull together' (Claxton, 1997, p. 148). Individual neurons are then more easily stimulated by activity in their neighbours so our thinking may be simpler, sharper and quicker but it is also less complicated, less flexible and less creative.

Transforming: Playful Interaction between Personal and Social Meanings

The Piagetian model of the child as 'little scientist' smoothing the tangle of everyday experience into increasingly tidy, cool and formal concepts is itself only one of many possible ways of mapping the complexity of cognitive development. Vygotsky insisted that this 'natural line' of development was accompanied by a 'cultural line' (Wertsch, 1991, p. 25) because we construct our ways of interpreting experience within a cultural environment which is deeply rutted by the social process of communication. The flow of our perceptions is channelled into shared forms or disciplines as we tune our interpretations and adopt common ways of organizing what we know: 'The unique feature of the social world is that it increases the likelihood that we will perceive certain features of the environment, of ourselves or of our social partner' (Fogel, 1993, p. 76).

Communication both generates and depends upon common ways of simplifying and making sense of experience; words mean what people mean when they use them. But communication also depends on a certain amount of play in the cultural machine; word meanings are far from fixed or static. Our personal sense making can never correspond exactly with another person's because, although we may share a broad system of simple definitions, the colour, richness and warmth of the meanings and connotations which we attach to these is rooted in our own, unique, subterranean tangle of experiences. This inevitable looseness of meaning is what makes conversation both interesting and emotionally rewarding; it is 'just what is needed to allow change to happen when people with different analyses interact' (Newman et al. in Bliss et al., 1996, p. 62).

By communicating with others we can explore the patterning of the cultural landscape of made sense (Parker-Rees, 1997) but when we encounter ruts which have not been worn by our own experience we have to connect these 'scientific', top-down concepts (Vygotsky, 1962) to the root system of our 'spontaneous', bottom-up understandings:

> In working its slow way upward, an everyday concept clears a path for the scientific concept and its downward development. It creates a series of structures necessary for the evolution of a concept's more primitive, elementary aspects, which give it body and vitality. Scientific concepts in turn supply structures for the upward development of the child's spontaneous concepts toward consciousness and deliberate use. (p. 109)

As we grow *up* we also grow *down*; the growth and organization of our root system informs and is informed by the air and light of conscious, communicated thought and our branching understanding of common meanings informs and is informed by the earth and water of immediate personal experience. Play, like metaphor and analogy, enables us to imbue cool, smooth, explicit concepts with the warm, dirty, immediacy of implicit connotations: 'a good analogy is not only understood; it is also felt' (Holyoak and Thagard, 1995, p. 78).

The disembedding, abstracting processes which inform our experience enable us to decontextualize our thinking, to free it from the shackles of the here-and-now, but we also recontextualize our ideas (Richards and Light, 1986, p. 185) in the branching structures which we share with others and which enable us to communicate. Articulated ideas are 'composed of distinct parts which may move independently of each other' (Claxton 1997, p. 43); ideas which have been dismembered in the process of abstraction can be re-membered in different ways in the stories we tell ourselves and others (ibid.). Organizing or informing experience also enables us to transform it, to take things apart and reassemble them; connecting our roots to the branches of shared structures:

> The capacity for transformation, for the imaginative and often bizarre refashioning of everyday experience, was originally the child's unerring, ineluctable talent for making something of his own from whatever he finds (the given is inert until it becomes the made). (Phillips, 1998, p. 6)

Children play with sand, water, dough and construction kits, forming and transforming materials and exploring their possibilities, but they can also transform the more abstract, cultural properties of objects, playing with what things are meant to mean. When a child uses a leaf to represent a plate in her play she can observe similarities and differences between her direct perception of the leaf and remembered information about plates, becoming more aware of physical properties such as flatness, smoothness, hardness and rigidity. She may also, if only implicitly, inform her understanding of the metaphorical, transformational nature of representation.

Playful transformation of experience depends on, and gives access to, the '100 languages of children' (Edwards et al., 1993), the patterned forms of representation which make communication possible. Adults are responsible for 'making and protecting the child's space' but also for 'introducing into it appropriate structural elements which derive from the surrounding culture' (Hodgkin, 1985, p. 26): 'open materials in suggested order — the adult's order that need not be maintained — leave the most room for children to create their own ideas in play' (Jones and Reynolds, 1992, p. 20). Jones and Reynolds emphasize the importance of a plentiful supply of 'loose parts' which can be combined and recombined in different ways (ibid., p. 23) and this is precisely what the languages of representation provide (Parker-Rees, 1997). Children who have been encouraged to use these languages in playful ways, as construction kits which can be deconstructed, transformed and reassembled, may feel more confident about choosing how to make sense of problem situations by re-membering possible ways of responding:

> Transfer seems to involve grasping the structural features of a task, comparing these with analogous tasks, and taking the risk of 'going beyond the information given' and applying the old skills to the new situation where they may possibly be useful. (Meadows, 1996, p. 93)

This sort of risk taking requires both confidence and flexibility; the mastery orientation which children are more likely to develop if they have opportunities to practise and represent decision making in play situations (Sylva, 1992). Children can also be encouraged to transform artefacts and situations in their imaginations: How *else* might things be done? What else could be used? What else might have caused this? Playing with 'what might be' helps children to escape from the shackles of 'what is' but it also deepens their understanding of why things are the way they are (Parker-Rees, 1997). By holding open a space within which we are protected from the stresses and pressures of 'everyday life', playful activities can allow us to wander between the well trodden paths which we must use when we are hurried. The looser, more complicated and more interconnected knowledge which results from this sort of wandering (or wondering) prepares us to cope more creatively when we find our path blocked: instead of giving up, we are able to strike out in a different direction, using *both* our implicit knowledge of the terrain *and* our explicit mental map of established tracks to re-member another route (Claxton, 1997).

Performing: Playful Interaction between Behaviour and Cultural Rules

On a cold winter's day, a group of porcupines huddled together to stay warm and keep from freezing. But soon they felt each other's quills and moved apart. When the need for warmth brought them closer together again, their quills again forced them apart. They were driven back and forth at the mercy of their discomforts until they found the distance from each other that provided both a maximum of warmth and a minimum of pain. (Arthur Schopenhauer quoted in Eigen and Winkler, 1982, p. 153)

The tension between individual freedoms and social obligations is well represented in the stories which inform our culture. The classical tradition celebrates the precarious triumph of civilization over the heart of darkness which still pumps beneath the frail veneer of our smooth, clean world. The romantic tradition, on the other hand, regrets our expulsion from the garden of innocent, unmediated experience, the price we must pay for tasting the fruits of the tree of knowledge and binding ourselves in the swaddling bands of conformity. But we do not have to think in terms of conflict between decorum and passion, light and dark or up and down; instead of seeing culture as the smooth skin which contains and conceals the awful energy of life, we should perhaps think of it as the skeleton which, by limiting the movements of the flesh, enables us to move.

We begin by tuning our brains to the environment we inhabit: choosing what we will filter out as irrelevant 'noise'. We go on to choose how we will reduce the complexity of life to 'mind-sized bites' (Johnson, 1990, p. 215) in our play. Later we negotiate 'play frames' (Garvey, 1977) with our friends, again choosing our own constraints but also enjoying the meeting of minds which we can experience in the creative, transforming process of communication. As we begin to play games with rules, our freedom to choose changes but it is not lost. While we may have less freedom to choose the rules, we are still free to choose how we will interpret them. Rules are simple, overground structures which organize what players can do but they are nourished and complicated by the roots of each player's personal experience: 'When one observes real individuals playing . . . the subtle variability and emergent creativity leap out almost in mockery of the supposed rules of the game' (Fogel, Nwokah and Karns in Fogel, 1993, p. 35).

The rules of a game define a space, providing a structure which, like the pillars of a cathedral, may be heavy and oppressive or light and airy. Within the space contained and protected by this structure the players can escape the pressures and complexity of everyday life and 'lose themselves' in the game. But it is not only in formal games that we can choose to interpret rules playfully, to play the game. Mihalyi Csikszentmihalyi (1992) has argued that the everyday conflict between differentiation (the desire for space) and integration (the desire for structure) can be reconciled if we choose to treat social constraints as the rules of a game:

What we tend to forget is that these rules and obligations are no different, in principle, than those rules that constrain behaviour in a game. Like all rules, they exclude a wide range of possibilities so that we might concentrate fully on a selected set of options.

Cicero once wrote that to be completely free one must become a slave to a set of laws. In other words, accepting limitations is liberating. For example, by making up one's mind to invest psychic energy exclusively in a monogamous marriage, regardless of any problems, obstacles, or more attractive options that may come along later, one is freed of the constant pressure of trying to maximize emotional returns. . . . As a result, a great deal of energy gets freed up for living, instead of being spent on wondering how to live. (Csikszentmihalyi, 1992, pp. 179–80)

To understand how this play with rules can be seen as performing, we need to consider the important distinction between dressing and dressing up. To dress is to organize, tidy up or simplify; we arrange plates on a dresser and we dress stone blocks by squaring them up and smoothing their faces so that they will fit together. When people talk of dressing for dinner they do not mean that they have spent the day naked, although changing into smooth, starched, formal evening dress can be seen as a way of covering one's complications. Dressing, in this older sense, is conforming and, although it *can* allow the wearer to concentrate on more important matters, freeing up energy for living, there is always the danger that it may lead to uniform thinking; the single vision of cults, gangs, mobs and armies which is the antithesis of playfulness.

Dressing *up*, on the other hand, involves playing with roles and rules. When children dress up they retain their freedom to choose how they will interpret the branch-work of social expectations represented by the clothes and props they choose to use. They per-form in the sense that they dress up in the structure of a role, expressing themselves *through* the forms they choose to interpret. Dressing up in a set of constraints, deliberately limiting our degrees of freedom within a bounded play world, allows us to explore the relationship between the simple structure of the role and the messy, fuzzy complexity of our own experience. Colwen Trevarthen (1995) has shown how 3-year-old children use imitation to share their play ideas and to demonstrate interest in each others thoughts before language takes over this role. But we continue to use imitation to play our way into new roles throughout our lives: 'The first stage of learning can be called, in Freud's language, identification; the student becomes like someone who knows these things' (Phillips, 1998, p. 55). This is the top-down discovery of made sense but the second stage requires 'dream work', the 'continual transfiguring of the facts of life by the fantasies of life' (ibid., p. 107). This is the bottom-up process of making our own sense of those aspects of the role which our undermind identifies as significant to us.

When we learn to be teachers we begin by dressing up as teachers and our understanding of the role develops all too slowly as we strive to shore up the gap between the branches of what we know teachers do and the roots of our own feelings, knowledge and experience. In Vygotsky's terms, it is only by bluffing our way into the interpersonal social processes of teaching that we can begin to benefit from guided participation (Rogoff, 1990), the engagement with competent practitioners that enables us to organize and internalize our understanding of the rules that inform the practice of teaching.

Dressing up as a princess, a pirate or a mum can help children to develop playful approaches which will help them to learn how to 'dress up' as a son, daughter, pupil or friend. For adults, dressing up in the rules of a game, in the fantasy world of a play, film or novel or in the formal structures of music and poetry can also serve as a reminder that the purpose of rules is to make play possible, not to constrain it. The rules of football, play scripts and musical scores all provide structures which are brought to life by being performed. The skeleton of rules can only dance when it is fleshed out by the life of players who lose themselves and find themselves in their interpretation and communication of meaning. Watching this sort of performance can inspire an audience, reminding them of the energy and excitement that can result when the management of constraints is skilful enough to appear playful. As individuals influence each other's performance they contribute to the development of culture, as the conversations between neurons in the undermind influence conscious awareness. If, however, cultural forms and constraints are more imposed than chosen, if conforming is valued more highly than performing, then the joints stiffen and the tension between what we want to do and what we are allowed to do becomes stressful and oppressive. Instead of dancing with rules we can only follow them.

Performing as an Early Years Teacher

Those who work in early years settings may be particularly sensitive to the contrast between children's playfulness and their own attempts to cope with the increasing burden of regulation and constraint imposed from on high. Responding to teachers who have told him that 'teaching's no fun anymore', Peter Woods has argued that creative teaching can help to 'transform constraint into opportunity' (Woods, 1996, p. 8) but, as Angela Anning has observed, this kind of creativity requires exceptional levels of commitment and can exact a heavy price, frequently resulting in burn out (Anning, 1996). Choosing to perform one's duties as a teacher, to play the game rather than simply obey the rules, may make teaching more enjoyable by reintroducing a feeling of personal control:

> To treat an order, or any kind of rule or instruction, as merely suggestive — to turn it into something a little more to one's taste — is radically to revise the nature of authority (obedience would be merely fear of interpretation). (Phillips, 1998, p. 87)

We can play the Desirable Learning Outcomes and the National Curriculum orders as a musician interprets a score but we are not free to ignore them. Margaret

Buchmann (1993a) reminds us that dressing up as a teacher involves putting on a role which is to some degree independent of the person:

> the moral nature of teaching — which also requires being genuinely oneself — does not remove the need for role orientation. Instead, a proper understanding of authenticity in teaching builds in the idea of external standards within which teachers make authentic choices. (p. 157)

Adults, like children, need space to be playful if they are to make authentic choices. The British Psychological Society, in its report entitled 'Fostering Innovation' argues that 'individuals are more likely to innovate where they have sufficient autonomy and control over their work to be able to try out new and improved ways of doing things' (West et al. in Claxton, 1997, p. 212) and there are striking parallels between the conditions required for playfulness at all levels. Schooler's observation that 'verbalization may cause such a ruckus in the "front" of one's mind that one is unable to attend to the new approaches that may be emerging at the "back" of one's mind' (Claxton, 1997, p. 87) might equally refer to the ruckus created by legislation which drowns out what practitioners have to say: the noise made by the branches makes it difficult to hear the roots.

Stig Boström has observed that too much insistence on realism in pretend play (e.g. giving the right change when playing shops) can detract from the 'essential dimensions of make believe and fantasy', reducing play to a 'mechanical and narrow reproduction of reality' (Boström, 1998, p. 34) and at the sociohistorical level, 'living by the rules is another way of hoping that the future will be more like the past' (Phillips, 1998, p. 88). Insistence on conformity limits the play of behaviour, resticting growth both up *and* down: 'adherence to consistency brings a lot more regimentation than is needed to rise above randomness' (Lakoff and Johnson in Buchmann, 1993b, p. 223). Increasing the play in the system need not result in chaos or anarchy but it can allow the tidy logic of consistency to be enriched by the looser 'human sense' of coherence (Buchmann, 1993b).

Floden and Buchmann (1993) argue that we must prepare teachers to cope with uncertainty if they are to walk the tightrope between routines and anarchy in the classroom but it is by no means *only* teachers who could benefit from learning to enjoy the playful interaction between unpredictable, bottom-up change and the security of top-down organizing structures. Preparing children to cope with uncertainty must begin in the early years because dispositions are acquired early and appear to be highly resistant to change later in life (Katz, 1995). If we want the children who will grow up in the next millennium to develop the mastery orientation which will enable them to play their part in keeping their culture alive and growing, then we must hold open space for playfulness so that they, their teachers and education itself can grow down as well as up. Policy can grow down if it responds to the interpretations of the practitioners who perform it; language can grow down if it responds to the speakers who transform it and we can all grow down if we can still the chatter of our minds long enough to let us listen to the undermind roots which inform our thinking.

References

ANNING, A. (1996) 'Being the best in the worst of times', *Oxford Review of Education*, **22**, 1, pp. 113–16.

BLISS, J., ASKEW, M. and MACRAE, S. (1996) 'Effective teaching and learning: Scaffolding revisited', *Oxford Review of Education*, **22**, 1, pp. 37–61.

BOSTRÖM, S. (1998) 'Frame play in early childhood education', *International Journal of Early Childhood*, **30**, 1, pp. 27–35.

BUCHMANN, M. (1993a) 'Role over reason: Morality and authenticity in teaching', in BUCHMANN, M. and FLODEN, R.E. (eds) *Detachment and Concern: Conversations in the Philosophy of Teaching and Teacher Education*, London: Cassell.

BUCHMANN, M. (1993b) 'Coherence, the rebel angel', in BUCHMANN, M. and FLODEN, R.E. *Detachment and Concern: Conversations in the Philosophy of Teaching and Teacher Education*, London: Cassell.

CLAXTON, G. (1984) *Live and Learn*, Milton Keynes: Open University Press.

CLAXTON, G. (ed.) (1997) *Hare Brain, Tortoise Mind: Why Intelligence Increases When You Think Less*, London: Fourth Estate.

CSIKSZENTMIHALYI, M. (1992) *Flow: The Psychology of Happiness*, London: Rider Books.

DEWEY, J. (1909) *How We Think*, London: D.C. Heath and Co.

EDWARDS, C., GANDINI, L. and FORMAN, G. (eds) (1993) *The Hundred Languages of Children: The Reggio Emilia Approach to Early Childhood Education*, Norwood, NJ: Ablex.

EIGEN, M. and WINKLER, R. (1982) *Laws of the Game: How the Principles of Nature Govern Chance*, London: Allen Lane.

FLODEN, R.E. and BUCHMANN, M. (1993) 'Between routines and anarchy: Preparing teachers for uncertainty' in BUCHMANN, M. and FLODEN, R.E. *Detachment and concern: Conversations in the philosophy of teaching and teacher education*, London: Cassell.

FOGEL, A. (ed.) (1993) *Developing through Relationships: Origins Of Communication, Self and Culture*, Hemel Hempstead: Harvester Wheatsheaf.

GARVEY, C. (1977) *Play*, Cambridge MA: Harvard University Press.

GOLDSCHMIED, E. with HUGHES, A. (1992) *Heuristic Play: Children of 12–20 Months Exploring Everyday Objects*, London: National Children's Bureau.

HASTE, H. (1987) 'Growing into rules', in BRUNER, J. and HASTE, H. (eds) *Making Sense: The Child's Construction of the World*, London: Routledge.

HAUSER–CRAM, P. (1998) 'I think I can, I think I can: Understanding and encouraging mastery motivation in young children', *Young Children*, July, pp. 67–71.

HODGKIN, R.A. (1985) *Playing and Exploring: Education through the Discovery of Order*, London: Methuen and Co. Ltd.

HODGKIN, R.A. (1997) 'Making space for meaning', *Oxford Review of Education*, **23**, 3, pp. 385–99.

HOLYOAK, K.J. and THAGARD, P. (1995) *Mental Leaps: Analogy in Creative Thought*, Cambridge, MA: MIT Press.

HOWLETT, R. (1998) 'Simple minds', *New Scientist*, **158**, 2139, pp. 28–32.

JOHNSON, J.E. (1990) 'The role of play in cognitive development', in KLUGMAN, E. and SMILANSKY, S. (eds) *Children's Play and Learning: Perspectives and Policy Implications*, New York: Teachers' College Press.

JONES, E. and REYNOLDS, G. (1992) *The Play's the Thing: Teachers' Roles in Children's Play*, New York: Teachers' College Press.

KATZ, L. (1995) *Talks with Teachers of Young Children*, Norwood, NJ: Ablex.

LAMBERT, J.-F. (1997) 'Des règles et du jeu', *International Journal of Early Childhood*, **29**, 1, pp. 26–33.

MacTURK, G.A. and MORGAN, R.H. (1995) *Mastery Orientation: Origins, Conceptualizations and Applications*, Norwood, NJ: Ablex.

MEADOWS, S. (1996) *Parenting Behaviour and Children's Cognitive Development*, Hove: Psychology Press.

MESSER, D.J. (ed.) (1993) *Mastery Motivation in Early Childhood: Development, Measurement and Social Processes*, London: Routledge.

PARKER-REES, R. (1997) 'Making sense and made sense: Design and technology and the playful construction of meaning in the early years', *Early Years*, **18**, 1, pp. 5–8.

PHILLIPS, A. (1998) *The Beast in the Nursery*, London: Faber and Faber.

POLANYI, M. (1958) *Personal Knowledge: Towards a Post-critical Philosophy*, London: Routledge and Kegan Paul.

RICHARDS, M. and LIGHT, P. (eds) (1986) *Children of Social Worlds*, Cambridge: Polity Press.

ROGOFF, B. (1990) *Apprenticeship in Thinking: Cognitive Development in Social Context*, New York and Oxford: Oxford University Press.

SCHWEINHART, L.J., BARNES, H.V. and WEIKART, D.P. (1993) *Significant Benefits of the High/Scope Perry Preschool Study through Age 27*, Ypsilanti, MI: High/Scope Press.

SYLVA, K. (1992) 'Conversations in the nursery: How they contribute to aspirations and plans', *Language and Education*, **6**, Nos. 2, 3 and 4, pp. 147–8.

TREVARTHEN, C. (1995) 'The child's need to learn a culture', *Children and Society*, **9**, 1, pp. 5–19.

VYGOTSKY, L.S. (1962) *Thought and Language*, (trans. E. Hanfmann and G. Vakar), Cambridge, MA: MIT Press.

WERTSCH, J.V. (1991) *Voices of the Mind: A Sociocultural Approach to Mediated Action*, London: Harvester Wheatsheaf.

WERTSCH, J.V. and PENUEL, W.R. (1996) 'The individual-society antinomy revisited: Productive tensions in theories of human development, communication, and education', in OLSON, D.R. and TORRANCE, N. (eds) *The Handbook of Education and Human Development*, Oxford: Blackwell.

WOODS, P. (1996) 'The good times: Creative teaching in primary schools', *Education 3 to 13*, **24**, 2, pp. 3–12.

7 The Search for Expertise: The Importance of the Early Years

John Abbott

The advantage of being an English academic working outside the United Kingdom is essentially twofold. Firstly, it is normally several days before I see the English daily papers — and by that time news is generally too dated to merit comment — and secondly, because it is easier to relate British events to what is happening in other countries. Distance certainly lends a sense of perspective, if not always enchantment!

'In a global economy knowledge is everything. It is the country which knows how best to educate its young people that will compete most successfully in the global marketplace' (Ryan, 1996, p. 2). This is as much a statement of national aspiration amongst the tarnished 'tiger economies' of the Pacific Rim as it is in the new Emerald Tiger economy of Ireland, or in Puerto Rico's bid to become the financial centre of the Caribbean, or in Estonia anxious to be a bridgehead to the East, as ever it is in the United Kingdom. The pressure is obviously intense. We are all, it seems, after the same thing.

Defining this 'thing' clearly is hard, and its essence elusive like quicksilver. Some time ago President Clinton remarked that, 'What you earn depends on what you learn.' In late April of 1998, in *The Independent* newspaper, Chris Woodhead, the Chief Inspector of OFSTED, battled with Seamus Hegarty, the Director of the National Foundation for Educational Research, to prove that most educational research was a waste of time. We, the English, it appears to Mr. Woodhead, know what we have to do — the only thing is we have to do it harder, more efficiently, and in a more closely prescribed manner. Yet, on *The Independent*'s previous page, a report on the Committee set up the previous year to advise on 'Creativity and Cultural Education' showed that this interesting group of people was obviously not so sure; 'How do you manage to tap students' creativity in an education system which is consumed with the very basics?' they were asking themselves. Good question, especially as — in times gone by — critics have seen earlier attempts to do this in primary schools as being responsible for a perceived fall in standards.

For years the debate has lurched backwards and forwards between the advocates of progressive, experiential-learning (presumed to be on the political left, but good for creativity) and disciplined, content-specific directed studies (presumed to be on the political right, and essential for basic skills). England has lurched along with all the others but, because we are a thoughtful and imaginative people more addicted to innovation than we are to application, our teachers in their search for both basics and creativity, have often been at the forefront of these swings. Yet, because we are not good at taking innovations through to application, others have gained more than we have from such ideas. We tend to lose our nerve long before an innovation has had time to become established.

In the mid 1970s so effective were good state primary schools seen to be at implementing the recommendations of the Plowden Commission that many middle class parents, concerned with 'value for money', started forsaking independent preparatory schools in such numbers as to leave some such schools struggling for pupils. Many another country, from Germany to America, from Scandinavia to New Zealand, still speak with awe of the 'imaginative, creative responsibility' created amongst pupils in 'good' state English primary schools of that era.

But such reforms were, within 15 years, seen as the scapegoat for Britain's failing education system. Why? As I, and others, have argued it wasn't that the theory was wrong, rather it was the over rapid application of a 'whole new way of doing things' that was beyond the capability of most teachers at the time to implement, and for most parents to understand. Experiential learning got a bad name and soon came to be seen as synonymous with 'play'.

Then, in 1977, Her Majesty's Inspectorate (HMI) attempted to come to terms both with learning theory and with epistemology when it published *Curriculum 11 to 16* ('The Red Book') and listed what it saw as eight essential Areas of Experience. It was a good list, and reflected the intuitive understandings of many wise people, and is probably not too different to that list which Professor Robinson's Committee on Creativity and Cultural Education would now produce. However, six years later Howard Gardner (1984) from the Harvard Graduate School of Education produced his list of seven innate, autonomous but interrelated intelligences. His theory was based not on intuition but on many years of laboratory experimentation. The lists sounded similar, but the methodology was very different. One was a 'wish list', the other was the first fruits of that serious study of the biological nature of intelligence and the functioning of the human brain which is currently exciting scientists. For years England took little notice of this work preferring instead to hold tight to our 'wish list' rather than research — especially American research. It was easier for the English to view intelligence as a single factor . . . we liked talking about 'the gifted', 'the average', the 'less able'; to make a distinction between interpersonal and intrapersonal skills unnecessarily complicated our thinking.

Separately England took an early lead in the use of technology to support distance learning with the Open University, something which still, for all its enormous achievements, does not seem quite 'proper' to English expectations. Developing countries, however, know that they have to make every pound count, and they are not so squeamish. It often seems that the further one goes from Milton Keynes the more well-known is the Open University! Again, to all intents and purposes, it was the English who invented the computer and certainly it was the English who pioneered the use of computers in schools. But we have failed to capitalize, yet again, on its amazing potential. Why? Simply because it challenges the *status quo* and the accepted way of doing things, and that, it seems, is not a good thing to do. Let me give you an illustration.

My eldest son has been using a computer at home since he was 8. Three years ago at the age of 15, when we were still living in England, and he was coming up to GCSE, his form teacher took him to one side and recommended that he should stop using the word processor and instead get used to writing out the answers in his homework 'right the first time'. 'That,' said the most concerned teacher, 'is how you will be marked in the exams.' Later that evening a very annoyed, and very articulate, son said, 'Dad, doesn't anyone understand? It's not that I write so much faster with the keyboard than ever I can freehand, but I just don't think in a straight line anymore. I'm always moving my ideas around as the argument develops.' He then looked at me very seriously. 'Don't worry, Dad, I'll still do okay but the exam won't show the best I can do. It's really stupid. Now I know why you do the job you do, but it must be depressing to see just how slowly things change!'

Indeed it is. We are still living with a curriculum designed for a paper and pencil technology; we hold fast to a belief that learning is dependent on instruction, rather than the individual's ability to construct their own meaning. If you change your technology, as any manufacturer will tell you, then your overall working practice — in the case of education, the curriculum — must also change. If it doesn't, then frustration will only increase.

At the heart of England's present search for a better education system is the elusive quest for transferable skills. At a time when the half-life of useful scientific knowledge is thought to be less than 7 years, it's not only what you know when you leave school that matters, it's also your ability to understand how to go about solving problems in areas you've never experienced before that is critical. We have been on this quest for a long time. It is interesting to note that so many of the innovations that English educators have tentatively attempted to introduce over the past 30 years do actually contribute something towards possible solution. In current jargon the issue we have to face is that of meta-cognition — the ability to think about your own thinking, and so develop skills that are genuinely transferable and not tied to a single body of knowledge; skills which can be applied in different and novel settings. It is linked to a specific form of intelligence that is becoming known as 'reflective intelligence'.

In a world of continuous change, the ability of individuals to plan and implement their own learning without external instruction has to be the fundamental factor. Learning is nothing if it is not a deeply reflective activity in which every new idea is internalized and used to refine, or to change, or to upgrade, earlier, more naïve understandings in ways which give the learner a greater sense of mastery and control. Learning is sterile if it is not active; it is about problem solving; it is about making sense of other, often disconnected, ideas. Learning is about changing, and survival. Humans are the planet's pre-eminent learning species simply because we are 'better at it' than any other species.

Learning, real learning, has to be personally challenging; if we are too comfortable, too complacent or too threatened nothing much happens. Kauffman (1993), writing in *The Origins of Order*, states, 'If the dynamics of the system are too chaotic no learning occurs because there is not enough stability to conserve information. If the dynamics are too static, no learning occurs because no change occurs in response to new inputs.' In other words, powerful learning occurs at the junction of order and chaos . . . midway as it were between the intuitive, open, experiential tradition, and the highly rigorous, content-specific disciplines favoured by the political right. Meta-cognition feeds off both, neither 'side' is all right, or all wrong. The trick is to know how to create the appropriate mixture.

If England is to lead with the issues raised both by Woodhead and Hegarty, and those raised by the Committee on Creative and Cultural Education, then England has to stop lurching between two polarized extremes and look very hard indeed at the evidence now emerging from a wide range of research which helps us to understand this 'middle ground' better, and what can be learned from earlier, if only incomplete, initiatives.

Central to the issue of Creativity is the old hoary conundrum of Transferability. Before considering Transferability, however, there are two key concepts which themselves have to be properly understood; these are Specialization and Expertise.

We English, with our infatuation for a reductionist, easily understandable world of sub-components, have lived comfortably with self-contained specializations, and the importance of specialists — people who know just everything there is to know about probably an ever smaller and more self-contained area of study. Our advanced standard of living is the direct result of specialized inquiry into a multiplicity of topics resulting in new products, new medicines, new technologies, and new understandings from everything from Astronomy through to Zoology. 'Advanced' levels are the first, almost remorseless step, in a young person's gravitation to becoming a specialist. Yet as a society we are fast coming to recognize that over-specialization also creates real social problems. We sense that the single mindedness of specialists has become a root cause of our disconnected, fragmented way of life. Such problems come under the rubric of unintended consequences. What is good for the specialist may not be good in all its aspects for the wellbeing of society. In years gone by many of us tried, in the Sixth Form, to stitch our own fragmented studies together with General Studies, but we were largely unsuccessful, because youngsters had already learnt that what society really valued was the skill of analysis, not synthesis.

Recent work by two Canadian cognitive scientists, Bereiter and Scardamalia (1993) on Specialization and Expertise, further extended by the findings of neurologists and systems thinkers, is especially helpful in understanding the subtle and highly significant difference between those two concepts which, in the public mind, are frequently assumed to be the same thing.

We have to understand these differences if we want to understand Woodhead's responsibility to develop basic skills, and the Committee's desire (which I would argue has also to be a national necessity) to understand Creativity. The argument goes like this: A specialist, by working within the well-defined parameters of a specialism 'knows the subject from the top to the bottom'. Specialists know all the rules, all the tests, and all the possible combinations and formulae. Their authority rests on the depth of their knowledge, and the understanding of the rules and is uncluttered by the need to assess extraneous influences. Such a person exudes a confidence in their competence — in some, this comes through as arrogance. No one can better them. Discussion with such people is often difficult. Just where their specialisms fit in a bigger picture does not trouble such a person, for that is essentially unquantifiable, imprecise and highly uncertain; there are no rules for that kind of thing, so these are questions best left unanswered.

A caricature perhaps, but in essential aspects often true. So the world has come to be fearful of specialists for, in some hard-to-define way, we sense they are just not 'real'. Their single mindedness gets us into trouble. They 'think the world apart', and that makes us personally schizophrenic.

Experts, argue Bereiter and Scardamalia (1993), possess certain additional qualities that make them very special people . . . the kind of people Professor Robinson is looking for, and who Messrs Woodhead and Hegarty need to know far more about.

Experts start off as specialists. They know an awful lot about their own subjects; you can't fault them on detail, any more than you can fault a specialist, but they have one vital attribute — they're able to 'get outside themselves and their subjects' and look at their specialisms from a distance. They are essentially quizzical. They ask themselves uncomfortable questions about their specialization's significance, and its possible relevance. They are intentionally 'playful'. In a sense they know so much about their subject that their natural inquisitiveness makes them inquisitive about many other things. They are quick to grasp the overall situation, rather than just dealing with single parts; 'big issues' fascinate them. Howard Gardner (1984) defines them as people who think about a concept by drawing on insights from several forms of intelligence. I think of them as I think of craftsmen of old — proud in their skills, humble in their attitudes, essentially inquisitive, and as concerned for the quality of what is not seen as much as that which is seen. People who I would trust my life to because they're not afraid of responsibility. People able both to have their feet on the ground, and their heads in the skies.

Bereiter and Scardamalia (1993) explain this in their own way,

> Experts, we propose, tackle problems that increase their expertise, whereas (specialists) tend to tackle problems for which they do not have to extend themselves (by going beyond the rules and formulae they accept). Experts indulge in progressive problem solving, that is they continually reformulate a problem at an ever-higher level as they achieve at lower levels, and uncover more of the nature of the issue. They become totally immersed in their work (flow), and increase the complexity of the activity by developing new skills and taking on new challenges. (pp. 182–220)

Experts with such high level 'open thinking' are vastly important people in a culture which is changing so rapidly that it is hard to see where we are headed. Unlike the specialist's supreme confidence within a specialism (not much use when the walls of that specialism are falling apart!), the expert is essentially humble and questioning, more aware of what he doesn't yet know rather than what is already known. Experts of course know the rules but they also know how to reformulate them, even when to break them so as to fit new circumstances. They are persistent, industrious, and always curious, and they are always searching for perfection. 'Let's back up on this problem. Think this one through again. See it from another perspective; imagine it in another way. Give ourselves a breather, and ask somebody else what they think.' These are the words of the true craftsman. These are real experts.

There aren't too many of such people around . . . that's why Professor Robinson has his Committee. And, unless Messrs Woodhead and Hegarty appreciate the difference between a specialist and an expert, we may actually end up having even less of them in the future. Remember the explanation Oscar Wilde gave of the cynic? 'The person who knows the price of everything, and the value of nothing.' Without an imaginative, constructive resolution of these issues we are indeed in great difficulty.

Here, however, are clues to the Committee's dilemma. So long as creativity continues to be thought of as separate from expertise, then there will always be a market for various brands of 'creativity-enhancing snake oil'. Creativity is essentially an aspect of expertise. Creativity can't be taught. You gain creativity through the experience of problem solving within a specific domain, but then stepping outside and looking at this with a fresh eye; only then do you see things to which the specialist with his tightly defined rules and procedures is blind. That's when the young specialist starts to mature and begins to formulate the vision of the expert.

The creation of conditions in which expertise can develop needs both the practices of open experiential learning, and the rigours of subject-specific disciplines. It is in the study of expertise that we find the clue we need to both creativity and transferability of knowledge. And its roots start very young. Expertise is a frame of mind that starts forming in the nursery, and begins to mature in the primary school.

It is not so much new research that Seamus Hegarty needs to worry about; rather it is finding people with minds broad enough to make sense of the valuable, highly interconnected, research which is already available and which can be gleaned from several lands. We don't need Chris Woodhead's dismissive words about 'the sociology of education (that) is a subject without a future'. Making better sense of research already available is vitally important in helping us to shape the future. If that knowledge was blindingly obvious we wouldn't have a problem, for we would have seen it long ago. But this research is 'heavy duty' stuff. We have to come to terms with many new ideas if we are to understand the apparent paradox that, if as a nation we want to increase the level of real learning that individuals are able to do, we should actually do less teaching. I guess Professor Robinson's team understand that paradox, for many of them will know from their own experience that what drives them is their own inner personal desire simply 'to make sense of the world around them'. It is that inquisitive desire that actually makes us human.

While specialization has become a feature of modern society, it is not, however, particularly natural to the human brain which has evolved over the millennia to be a multi-faceted, multi-tasked organism that is predisposed to think about any piece of data, or idea, from very many perspectives. It works in terms of wholes and parts simultaneously. The glory of human learning is that it is essentially a complex, messy, non-linear process. A further story to make my point.

For several summer holidays when my three sons were young, we swapped our home just outside Cambridge with friends in Virginia. To our children, America was a land of long summer days, plenty of ice cream, and visits to national parks and historic sites. Late one evening back in England we were driving home from a day in Derbyshire with the children. My wife was playing a Garrison Keillor tape — the one describing his fictitious one-room school house in Minnesota. 'At one end of the room was a portrait of Abraham Lincoln and at the other one of George Washington beaming down at us like two long-lost friends', Keillor drawled in his best Lake Wobegon style. 'That's wrong', piped up seven-year-old Tom. 'They weren't alive at the same time, so they couldn't have been friends!'

Amazed I asked Tom how he knew that. 'Well', he said, 'when we went to Mount Vernon they said how sad it was that Washington didn't live into the nineteeth century — and when we went to Gettysburg, Lincoln talked to his army and that was 1860 something, wasn't it?' His logic and the connections he had built fascinated me.

Several years later, at a dinner party in Seattle, I recounted that story. 'How I wish American elementary schools taught history as well as that!' mused our host, a Professor of Education. 'No', said Tom. 'It's not school that taught me that. I just like everything to do with America!' Our host then asked, 'What do you like best at school then?' 'Math', replied Tom, 'because our teacher always gets us to think about connections and patterns. That's really interesting. I can see how things come together.'

Patterns and relationships, emotions, the need to make sense, intrinsic motivation, formal and informal learning, history dates and mathematical formulae — these elements in my son's learning defy any logical structure. That's what makes learning such an exciting thing. That is why to put faith in a highly directive, prescriptive curriculum is to so 'go against the grain of the brain' that it will inevitably inhibit creativity and enterprise, the very skills needed in the complex, diverse, knowledge society for which we desperately need to prepare our children. As Professor Sylwester of Oregon writes, 'Get rid of that damn machine model of the brain. It's wrong. The brain is a biological system, not a machine. Currently we're putting children with biologically shaped brains into machine orientated schools. The two just don't mix. We bog the school down in a curriculum that is not biologically feasible' (Sylwester, 1995).

Please, Mr Woodhead and others of a similar disposition, take notice. For without deep, rigorous, out-of-the-box thinking about the nature of human learning so many of the present reforms will give us specialists, not experts. Note my choice of words. I'm talking about experts, not generalists, and as someone who used to think of himself as a generalist I now realize that I was wrong. In a knowledge society, where everyone has to be able to function at ever higher levels of thinking, it is not an early bifurcation between specialists and generalists that is needed, rather it is to take specialists beyond their comfort zones into being real experts that modern society requires.

So you, and others, have got an enormous amount of studying to do if you are to get the nuances of all this sorted out. If you don't do this, I respectfully submit you won't be able to fully appreciate what real experts might report back to you. I know, from my own hard experience, that this is difficult, very difficult. Earlier assumptions and belief systems have to be suspended. But this is essential. In the long run it would pay your employers handsome dividends for you to take time out to do just this. Don't be content just to condemn present research; think through the consequences of a whole new way of arranging learning opportunities.

Watching so many current well-intentioned innovations, I worry that you are trying to put new linen patches onto old wineskins; and your classical education will tell you what a disaster that was. Too much has already changed for us not to recognize that we have to deal systemically with the very institutions of learning themselves. These may, all unwittingly, be frustrating the validity of the new linen simply because they are more concerned with their institutional identity than they are with the interests of learners. The lives of our young people — their essential creativity and search for meaning — is simply too precious for you not to find the time to do the studying you need to do if you and others are to shape English education in ways that 'go with the grain of the brain'. Other countries are preparing to leapfrog the very arrangements that you are trying desperately to sustain. From an 'offshore' perspective I'm aware of those countries which are preparing 'to think smarter, not just harder'. They are starting to grab at these ideas. They want to leapfrog us . . . and they could do so relatively quickly. Their objective? Creativity and Expertise.

Drawing all this together; given what we now know from all our previous experience and from a massive body of current research, I do not believe that we have the moral authority to carry on with what we are now doing. It's simply too limited. We have literally to turn our current practices upside down and inside out. Above all, we have to explore a sweeping pedagogic shift that develops meta cognitive skills in everyone, from the very youngest age. We have to do this urgently, or we will not be able to look the younger generation in the face. They will hold us accountable for our timidity if we do not use every strategy available to us to apply these new understandings.

References

BEREITER, C. and SCARDAMALIA, M. (1993) *Surpassing Ourselves: An Inquiry into the Nature and Implications of Expertise*, Chicago: Open Court.

BRUER, J. (1993) *Schools for Thought: A Science of Learning in the Classroom*, Cambridge, MA: MIT Press.

DIAMOND, M. and HOPSON, J. (1998) *Magic Trees of the Mind*, New York: Dutton.

GARDNER, H. (1984) *Frames of Mind*, London: Hutchinson.

GARDNER, H. (1991) *The Unschooled Mind: How Children Think and How Schools Should Teach*, London: Basic Books.

KANIGEL, R. (1997) *The One Best Way: Frederick Winslow Taylor and the Enigma of Efficiency*, New York: Viking.

KAUFFMAN, S.A. (1993) *The Origins of Order, Self-organisation and Selection in Evolution*, New York: Oxford University Press.

LABAREE, D.F. (1997) *How to Succeed in School Without Really Learning*, New Haven, CT: Yale University Press.

PALMER, P.J. (1998) *The Courage to Teach*, San Francisco: Jossey-Bass.

PERKINS, D. (1995) *Outsmarting I.Q.: The Emerging Science of Learnable Intelligence*, New York: The Free Press.

PLOTKIN, H. (1997) *Evolution in Mind*, London: Penguin Press.

RYAN, T. (1996) 'The case for a mindshift', *Education 2000*, p. 2.

SYLWESTER, J. (1995) Conference Proceedings, Wingspread Conference, Reston, VA, USA.

TATERSALL, I. (1998) *Becoming Human: Evolution and Human Uniqueness*, New York: Harcourt Brace and Co.

Web Site:

http://www.21 learn.org.

8   Valuing Young Children

Tricia David

Much of what we take for granted in our lives as in some way fixed, is in fact a social construction. The millennium itself is occurring because our ancestors decided to call what they conjectured to be the year of the birth of Christ as year zero — hence we end up celebrating the year 2000. Events such as this are seen by some as having mystical significance. However most of us view the millennium, it can be the catalyst for reflection on how our society has been, and is, developing. Among other debates, it can cause us to pause and consider our country's attitude to and treatment of the youngest children in our society. More than ever before politicians of all parties are beginning to take an interest in educational provision for children in their earliest years. Not only is daycare for working mothers high on the agenda, as women overtake men as a proportion of the workforce, evidence that early learning promotes children's later achievements (e.g. Ball, 1994; Shorrocks, 1992; Schweinhart and Weikart, 1993a) is at last recognized by top levels of government.

Early Childhood: Perceptions and Expectations

What happens to, or is thought to be 'right' for, young children in any society or subcultural group is related to the childhoods constructed by that society (Nunes, 1994; Tobin, Wu and Davidson, 1989). For many years babies and young children were not accorded the powers psychologists now acknowledge. For example, Deloache and Brown (1987) and Singer (1992) have documented the ways in which developmental psychology, because of its underlying assumptions and methods, failed to access those powers. Now Gardner (1983) has added a further dimension to this issue by proposing the idea of multiple intelligences, most of which we in the West appear unable to foster because we cannot 'see' and do not value many of the 'intelligences' Gardner identifies. As Gardner explains,

> The time has come to broaden our notion of the spectrum of talents. The single most important contribution education can make to a child's development is to help him toward a field where his talents suit him best, where he will be satisfied and competent. We've completely lost sight of that. Instead, we subject everyone to an education where, if you succeed, you will be best suited to be a college professor. And we evaluate everyone along the way according to whether they meet that narrow standard of success. We should spend less time ranking children and more time helping them to identify their natural competencies and gifts, and

cultivate those. There are hundreds and hundreds of ways to succeed, and many, many different abilities that will help you get there. (from an interview quoted in Goleman, 1996, p. 37)

The dominant view of very young children in the UK tends to be based on limited and out-dated theories and beliefs. Ideas about maternal deprivation and children's emotional needs (Bowlby, 1953) have been used as arguments against the provision of nursery education in the past. Further, the idea that young children are active learners capable of constructing their own view of the world and of participating in the creation of knowledge is not informing a coherent policy for our youngest children. It appears that in UK society, it does not matter if children in this age group experience numerous changes of settings during their first five years, some even spend time in two different educare settings within a single day, in order to cover their parents' work hours. Further, there is a notion that the learning achieved in the first five years is not 'real education' and that the purpose of nursery provision is to prepare children, to lick them into shape in a number of ways, so that 'the reception class can begin the proper process of education' (*The Times*, 1995, p. 17).

Constructions of Childhood and Societal Values

Once we become aware of the ways in which childhood itself is constructed in different societies or at different times, we also begin to ask ourselves why children are treated in certain ways, what is considered an appropriate education for children at different stages in their lives and what does all this tell us about that society.

Unfortunately, our value system is implicit in the view of children as 'adults in waiting'. This represents a particularly western/northern approach to both child-hood and learning (Hazareesingh et al., 1989) and, in its rationalist stance, an education system which separates the intellect from the emotions denies the holistic nature of human being.

> Perspectives on childhood that include the concept of children as 'adults in wait-
> ing' do not value children as learners and therefore create systems of educating, and
> designing curricula, that can be narrow minded rather than open minded and which
> transmit to children, rather than challenge children to use their powers as thinkers
> and nurture their humanity. (Nutbrown, 1996, p. xiv)

Recent research indicates that babies and young children will live 'up or down' to societal and family expectations, that they will try to please the adults around them in order to be valued, loved and accepted (e.g. Bruner and Haste, 1987; Trevarthen, 1992). So the curriculum we decide on for young children, both its content and its teaching approaches, may have crucial long term consequences for our society. We have to decide what kind of people we want our children to be and to become. We have to ask ourselves how they will cope with a world we will not be here to see and experience and, above all, we have to remember they may be small but they are not our possessions. They are people who are actively trying to make sense of their world. And as the poet Kahlil Gibran writes:

> You may give them your love but not your thoughts, For they have their own thoughts . . . For life goes not backwards nor tarries with yesterday. You are the bows from which your children as living arrows are sent forth. (Gibran, 1926, in the 1994 edition, p. 20)

Childhood in Contemporary Britain

Using both international comparisons with other western/northern nations and comparisons with our own national records, we find that:

- the reported infant mortality rate is higher in the UK than in Sweden, Norway, Switzerland, and the Netherlands and higher proportions of the UK population live in relative poverty than in those countries — and the divide between rich and poor has increased during the last fifteen years;
- the UK and Denmark have the highest percentages of lone parents in the European Union (EU) and there are links between lone parenthood and poverty (Utting, 1995);
- studies have shown that there is evidence of a decline in average reading standards unaffected by teaching methods but related to the rapid increase in relative deprivation (Wilkinson, 1994) and achievements (or lack of them) in the later years of school are also related to socio-economic factors;
- more than half the children in London's poorest boroughs are entitled to free school meals (Brindle, 1994) and the growing differentials in access to a healthy environment and diet carry risks such as increased risk of early death (Kumar, 1993);
- the UK has the fastest increase of maternal employment outside the home, yet more than a third of fathers of children aged between birth and nine years work more than 50 hours a week — the highest levels in the EU (Cohen, 1990). The result can be little time to spend together as a family — yet we have known for many years that isolation can lead to parental depression;
- meanwhile, parental anxiety about the potential for child physical abuse as a result of the stress caused by unemployment has been documented by the NSPCC — the UK has the second highest proportion of unemployed fathers of children under nine in the EU (Moss, 1996);
- the risk of homicide for babies under one year old is four times that of any other age group. We have the fifth highest rate of infant homicide in the European Union (Butler, 1996).

This litany serves to show how the childhoods experienced by all our children are not the same. Just as diet casts a long shadow forward, so too does the family and community's ability to provide emotional, social and intellectual stimulation.

If, as a parent or carer, you do not have sufficient information or resources, how can you help your child? If our society fails to provide the necessary support is it a sign that the construction of different and unequal childhoods is useful to those in power?

Biology, Culture and Theories of Child Development

'That children have certain characteristics, that adults have others, and that it is natural to grow from one to the other, are messages that we receive from all forms of mass communication' (Morss, 1996, p. 29). In each of his challenging studies, John Morss (1990 and 1996) questions the taken-for-granted nature of development-alism in western/northern thinking about children. He cites Rom Harré's (1983; 1986) argument that

> stage-based accounts of childhood make the pretence that a sequence of stages unfolds through some natural process. . . . The world or worlds of the child, Harré argued, have to be described not as if biologically determined but more as forms of culture. (Morss, 1996, pp. 33–4)

Just over a decade ago Harré and others (for example, Harré, 1983, 1986; Ingleby, 1986) were challenging the roots of developmental psychology and its biological basis. Before this the social construction movement, which was especially strong in Britain with its foundations in sociology, had been ushered in by the publication of Berger and Luckmann's (1967) *The Social Construction of Reality*. Yet even this book propounded a view of babies as part of their mothers and as largely biological beings, who **become** human through socialization in the culture.

However, it was probably the ground-breaking paper *The American child and other cultural inventions* by William Kessen (1979) which really put the cat among the pigeons. Kessen could see that childhood is defined by a particular society at a particular time in a particular way. In fact, according to studies, such as that by Aries (1962), childhood did not exist at certain times in the history of Western Europe. And according to Postman (1985) childhood was invented with the printing press, since children then required a period of time in which to become literate. What Kessen, who in the mid-1970s led a delegation visiting educational settings for children in communist China (Kessen, 1975), was really highlighting was the question of why different societies construct childhood in particular ways and why certain childhoods are assigned to particular children. By claiming that one version of childhood is a correct or true version and by demanding conformity, developmental psychologists and early years practitioners appear to have operated in a culture- or context-blind fashion. As Morss (1996) remarks, developmentalism may be hegemonic. We must ask if in defining stages in development and in seeking to protect young children, we also limit their achievements. Concluding that we end up with 'the children we deserve', Ros Miles (1994) argues for greater attention to children's rights and personhood.

What has been especially powerful about many western academic studies of child development has been the assumption that findings can be generalized and applied to other societies. The impact of cultural context and the beliefs about young children permeating the shared meanings in any social group or nursery have been largely ignored. There have been some notable exceptions however. Psychologists were attempting, as early as the 1960s to show how parents and small children together create their own meanings and family culture (for example, Newson and Newson, 1963; 1967). Another member of Kessen's delegation to China, Urie Bronfenbrenner (1975 and 1979), attempted to bring together context and biology in his ecological theory of child development. He proposed that each child's 'ecological niche' is unique because each will experience the relationships and processes of interaction between home, nursery, wider world and the ideology in which all these are embedded. He also argued that children themselves, like the others around them, actively influence this 'ecological niche'. Since that time, the idea that members of a group or society co-construct particular childhoods and that children are active participants in that construction has provided a powerful challenge to decontextualized theories of child development.

Yet despite these challenges, most research about young children and their learning has continued to be dominated by assumptions and approaches derived from the natural sciences. The problem is that this has led to underestimates of their potential and capabilities (Deloache and Brown, 1987). Morss (1990) shows how even Piaget ignored his own evidence when it did not fit contemporary preconceptions about young children's thinking. Watching two-and-half-year-old Arthur helping my 18-month-old grandaughter onto a garden bench, where he had never been before nor seen an adult model this behaviour, I was spurred to reflect on the reported egocentricity of Piaget's children. Similarly, we see numerous examples of babies and young children hypothesizing in extremely sophisticated ways. An exhibit from the Reggio Emilia nurseries at the Bethnal Green Museum of childhood in summer 1997 consisted of a series of photographs of eight-month-old Laura. In the first she is looking at a catalogue with an educator. The page displays a range of watches. Laura then looks at the worker's watch, which by chance is the type which ticks. The worker puts her watch to Laura's ear. In the final photo Laura has laid her ear on the page of watches.

It may be that alliances between early years professionals from a range of fields and disciplines will move us on even further in our ability to comprehend and respond reflectively to young children. For example, stimulating new ideas concerning the complementary nature of genetic and epigenetic factors in children's brain development are being researched by psycho-physiologists such as Lambert (1996) in Paris. He suggests that contrary to the notion that babies and young children have to wait for their nervous connections to grow and for interaction with the environment to stimulate that growth, there are in fact many connections already in existence and it is through the complementarity of biology and experience that just one nervous connection (for a particular muscle action let's say) survives — the others die off. We can see how such a theory makes sense in the way human babies display all the sounds necessary to speak any language — but by around twelve months of age a child will begin to lose all the sounds not used in the home language or languages.

Earlier this century professionals who worked with babies and young children were told that newborn babies do not feel pain, that young children cannot understand the world from another's viewpoint, that they cannot communicate or interact with others. However, recent research suggests that children come into this world 'programmed' to make sense of the situation in which they find themselves and to communicate with other human beings (Trevarthen, 1992) and that they learn more in their first five years than in all the other years of their lives. As Howard Gardner (1993) remarks, we need to throw out limiting old assumptions and respect the flexibility, creativity, adventurousness, resourcefulness and generativity of the young mind.

It would appear that young children have dispositions to learn different things, that they are not simply bundles of biological urges slowly being transformed, as they pass through universal pre-set stages of development, until they become fully formed humans as adults. On the contrary, once we have decided what kind of society we want, it is in everyone's interests to pay attention to the impact of policies on young children and those who share their lives, even those policies which appear irrelevant to early childhood. It is, perhaps, one of the responsibilities of early childhood educators to act as advocates for young children by ensuring policy makers and parents have access to new ideas and research information.

It seems likely that we, as a nation, underestimate the learning capacity of children in these first years of life, because of our assumptions and accepted notions about young children. Received wisdom about very young children in UK society, or established 'regimes of truth' (Foucault, 1977), have resulted in our having one of the worst records of nursery provision in the European Union and even 'lifelong education' plans propose the start at 3 years of age. The new Labour government's White Paper *Excellence in Schools* (DfEE, 1997) ostensibly devotes a whole chapter to 'A sound beginning' yet it fails to grasp the importance, in learning terms, of the years before three. The idea of babies and young children as people with the capacity to learn and the need to relate to others in meaningful ways, not as objects or possessions who should be mainly restricted to their own homes with only their own mothers for company, remains largely unrecognized. Parents need support and information to help them in their role as the primary educators of their very young children. Can we remedy or reduce the impact of all the negative factors in young children's lives and can early childhood education make a difference?

First, we need greater coherence, a more holistic view of what the services should be for as far as the children themselves are concerned (Penn, 1997). In many of our European partner countries what happens to the children, the kind of curriculum offered while in the services provided, is subject to evaluation and communal debate (Dahlberg and Asen, 1994). A recent EU Recommendation called for all member states to take measures to ensure the provision of childcare facilities for working parents and that those services should combine 'reliable care with a pedagogical approach' (Moss, 1996, p. 48). In the majority of our European partner countries, there is much more widespread support for parents in the form of childcare services, parental leave and recognition for public responsibility towards the children of working parents, so alleviating and sharing the challenges of bringing up small children in today's rapidly changing world. Despite the fact that almost all our 4- and 5-year olds are in school (not always the best solution for either children or parents) we come out badly in international comparisons because of our relative lack of provision for children aged three and under (Moss, 1996). The new government demands on local authorities to provide plans concerning future development of provision for all under fives is a good start and was stated as one of their first aims on coming into office (DfEE, 1997).

In the light of American and other evidence (Andersson, 1992; Barnett and Escobar, 1990; Sylva, 1994), such as that from the High/Scope longitudinal study (Schweinhart et al., 1993a), it seems that spending on the early years is an investment. Research has shown that if we want children's early experiences to have beneficial effects in terms of their emotional stability, present contentment and later achievements, we need to pay attention to certain key factors (Field, 1991). Those key ingredients include:

- the development of self-esteem in young children;
- investment in young children;
- stable childcare arrangements ensuring children interact with a limited number of familiar carers each day;
- low staff turn-over;
- good training;
- and low adult/child ratios. (Raban, 1995)

Together with other evidence about the importance of affective aspects related to learning (Roberts, 1995), 'emotional intelligence' (Goleman, 1996) has become a high priority. The foundations of robust emotional health and the ability to relate well to others seem to be laid during these very early years. Only recently has the powerful influence of the emotions on learning been acknowledged. The Age of Enlightenment split between body and mind, emotion and reason has not always served us well and it is especially limited for those who work with young children. Early childhood involves so much more overtly the imperatives of the emotions and bodily functions. This is not to say young children and their educators cannot be rational but that 'pure' rationalists have behaved as if the tip of the iceberg were the iceberg. We have reaped many benefits as a result of the scientific and industrial advances which have come in the wake of the Age of Enlightenment but it has also been responsible for the erosion of people's contact with the land and the rhythms of the cycles and seasons of nature. We are slowly realizing our responsibility to the earth and our need to live in harmony with nature rather than seeking domination. Perhaps, as a nation, we may have to undergo an equivalent realization with respect to babies and young children. Children can only develop the qualities listed by Bridie Raban (1995) and the emotional intelligence advocated by Goleman if the adults to whom we entrust them can engender those feelings of confidence and self-worth. The adults, whether parents or educators, can only undertake such a task if they have the necessary resources and feel valued in their turn.

Valuing What Young Children Can Do

Our beliefs about early childhood and the place of young children in society impacts upon policy and practice. Although we cannot know for certain what their lives in the twenty-first century will be like, we need to ask ourselves what, if anything, we hold as a vision of education which will equip these very young people for a post-industrial, 'high-tech' world, where environmental, health and other global concerns are likely to be even more acute than they are today (David, Curtis and Siraj-Blatchford, 1992). Decisions about curriculum reflect the values and the ideology underpinning a society. There are fears that the *Desirable Outcomes* (SCAA, 1996; QCA, 1999) and a narrow system of 'baseline' assessment at age five, which is also undergoing consultation, will result in an over-emphasis on literacy and numeracy at the expense of children's other powers.

Conclusion: Valuing Young Children

As a nation, the UK has signed up to the UN Convention on the Rights of the Child (United Nations, 1989). Furthermore, we have the Children Act 1989, which requires we act in the best interests of the child, heed the child's views, support parents in their role as responsible carers and, as professionals involved with children and their families, work together effectively to these ends. As Louise Sylwander, Children's Ombudsman for Sweden, has pointed out, 'the Convention is something which has to be lived'(Sylwander, 1996, p. 49). The way we think of and, as a result, treat children, especially those in their earliest years, has consequences. In the end, we get the children we deserve. *The Child as Citizen* (Council of Europe, 1996) reminds readers that children form one of the largest groups in society but they do not form a lobby and are rarely represented in decision-making processes.

Furthermore, we cannot disembed the economy from the polity. Valuing children, the inheritance of a 'civic covenant' which includes a moral responsibility for the generations which follow us, is John O'Neill's (1994) argument in *The Missing Child in Liberal Theory*. He suggests that the power of the global market must be restrained, that capitalism has always been dependent upon moral and political restraints to keep it from destroying itself.

The constant reminders that our education system is failing our children always seem to omit the fact that we do not, as a society, pay enough attention to the very earliest years. Perhaps our current malaise is in part due to our lack of attention to the 'needs' and rhythms of young children (David, 1996). And in an age when some parents may have plenty of time but no resources and others no time and a sufficiency of resources (Handy, 1994), we need to debate the issues of working hours and social justice as they impact upon children. Further, the African proverb 'It takes a village to raise a child' urges us to take stock of who is responsible for children — only parents or the whole of society, and what are the responsibilities?

Probably the most important debates to be joined concern our constructions of early childhood, the values exposed by those constructions. When we ask whether our society values young children, we would do well to remember it is these babies and young children now trying to make sense of their world who will be tomorrow's citizens.

References

ANDERSSON, B.E. (1992) 'Effects of daycare on cognitive and socio-emotional competence of thirteen-year-old Swedish school children', *Child Development*, **63**, pp. 20–36.

ARIES, P. (1962) *Centuries of Childhood*, London: Jonathan Cape.

BALL, C. (1994) *Start Right: The Importance of Early Learning*, London: Royal Society for the Encouragement of the Arts, Manufacturers and Commerce (RSA).

BARNETT, W.S. and ESCOBAR, C.M. (1990) 'Economic costs and benefits of early intervention', in MEISELS, S.J. and SHONKOFF, J.P. (eds) *Handbook of Early Childhood Intervention*, Cambridge: Cambridge University Press.

BERGER, P.L. and LUCKMANN, T. (1967) *The Social Construction of Reality: A Treatise in the Sociology of Knowledge*, London: Allen Lane.

BOWLBY, J. (1953) *Child Care and the Growth of Love*, Harmondsworth: Penguin.

BRINDLE, D. (1994) 'Poverty highlighted by school meals survey', *The Guardian*, 31 January.

BRONFENBRENNER, U. (1975) 'Reality and research in the ecology of human development', *Proceedings of the American Philosophical Society*, **119**, pp. 439–69.

BRONFENBRENNER, U. (1979) *The Ecology of Human Development*, Cambridge MA: Harvard University Press.

BRUNER, J. and HASTE, H. (eds) (1987) *Making Sense*, London: Methuen.

BUTLER, A.J.P. (1996) 'Review of children and violence', *Child Abuse Review*, **5**, 4, pp. 297–8.

COHEN, B. (1990) *Caring for Children: The 1990 Report*, London: FPSC/SCAFA.

COUNCIL OF EUROPE (1996) *The Child as Citizen*, Strasbourg: Council of Europe.

DAHLBERG, G. and ASEN, G. (1994) 'A question of empowerment', in MOSS, P. and PENCE, A. (eds) *Valuing Quality in Early Childhood Services*, London: Paul Chapman.

DAVID, T. (1996) 'Their right to play', in NUTBROWN, C. (ed.) *Children's Rights and Early Education*, London: Paul Chapman.

DAVID, T., CURTIS, A. and SIRAJ-BLATCHFORD, I. (1992) *Effective Teaching in the Early Years*, Stoke-on-Trent: Trentham Books.

DELOACHE, J.S. and BROWN, A.L. (1987) 'The early emergence of planning skills in children', in BRUNER, J. and HASTE, H. (eds) *Making Sense*, London: Cassell.

DfEE (1997) *Excellence in Schools*, Cm3681, London: HMSO.

FIELD, T. (1991) 'Quality infant daycare and grade school behaviour and performance', *Child Development*, **62**, pp. 863–70.

FOUCAULT, M. (1977) *Discipline and Punish*, London: Allen Lane.

GARDNER, H. (1983) *Frames of Mind: The Theory of Multiple Intelligences*, New York: Basic Books.

GARDNER, H. (1993) *The Unschooled Mind*, London: Fontana.

GIBRAN, K. (1926) *The Prophet*, London: William Heinemann.

GOLEMAN, D. (1996) *Emotional Intelligence*, London: Bloomsbury.

HANDY, C. (1994) *The Empty Raincoat*, London: Hutchinson.

HARRÉ, R. (1983) *Personal Being: A Theory for Individual Psychology*, Oxford: Blackwell.

HARRÉ, R. (1986) 'The steps to social constructionism', in RICHARDS, M. and LIGHT, P. (eds) *Children of Social Worlds*, Cambridge: Polity Press.

HAZAREESINGH, S., SIMMS, K. and ANDERSON, P. (1989) *Educating the Whole Child — A Holistic Approach to Education in the Early Years*, London: Building Blocks/ Save the Children.

INGLEBY, D. (1986) 'Development in context', in RICHARDS, M. and LIGHT, P. (eds) *Children of Social Worlds*, Cambridge: Polity Press.

KESSEN, W. (ed.) (1975) *Childhood in China*, New Haven CT: Yale University Press.

KESSEN, W. (1979) 'The American child and other cultural inventions', *American Psychologist*, **34**, 10, pp. 815–20.

KUMAR, V. (1993) *Poverty and Inequality in the UK. The Effects on Children*, London: NCB.

LAMBERT, J.-F. (1996) Des règles et du jeu. Paper presented at the European Seminar of OMEP, UNESCO Paris 24–27 October.

MILES, R. (1994) *The Children We Deserve*, London: Harper Collins.

MILLER, S. (1973) 'Ends, means and galumphing: Some leitmotifs of play', *American Anthropologist*, **75**, pp. 87–98.

MORSS, J. (1990) *The Biologising of Childhood: Developmental Psychology and the Darwinian Myth*, Hove: Lawrence Erlbaum Associates.

MORSS, J. (1996) *Growing Critical: Alternatives to Developmental Psychology*, London: Routledge.

MOSS, P. (1996) 'Perspectives from Europe', in PUGH, G. (ed.) *Contemporary Issues in the Early Years*, London: Paul Chapman, pp. 30–50.

NEWSON, J. and NEWSON, E. (1963) *Patterns of Infant Care*, Harmondsworth: Penguin.

NEWSON, J. and NEWSON, E. (1967) *Four Years Old in an Urban Community*, Harmondsworth: Penguin.

NUNES, T. (1994) 'The relationship between childhood and society', *Van Leer Foundation Newsletter*, Spring, pp. 16–17.

NUTBROWN, C. (ed.) (1996) *Children's Rights and Early Education*, London: Paul Chapman.

O'NEILL, J. (1994) *The Missing Child in Liberal Theory*, Toronto: University of Toronto Press.

PENN, H. (1997) *Comparing Nurseries*, London: Paul Chapman.

POSTMAN, N. (1985) *The Disappearance of Childhood*, London: Comet/W.H.Allen.

QCA (1999) *Consultation on the Review of the Desirable Learning Outcomes*, London: QCA.

RABAN, B. (1995) 'Early childhood years — problem or resource', inaugural lecture, Melbourne University, Australia, 27 July.

ROBERTS, R. (1995) *Self-esteem and Successful Early Learning*, London: Hodder and Stoughton.

SCAA (1996) *Nursery Education Desirable Outcomes for Children's Learning on Entering Compulsory Schooling*, London: SCAA.

SCHWEINHART, L.J. and WEIKART, D.P. (1993a) *A Summary of Significant Benefits: The High/ Scope Perry Preschool Study Through Age 27*, Ypsilanti MI: High/Scope Foundation.

SCHWEINHART, L.J., WEIKART, D.P. and TODERAN, R. (1993b) *High Quality Preschool Programs Found to Improve Adult Status*, Ypsilanti MT: High/Scope Foundation.

SHORROCKS, D. (1992) 'Evaluating Key Stage 1 Assessments: The testing time of May 1991', *Early Years*, **13**, 1, pp. 16–20.

SINGER, E. (1992) *Child Development and Daycare*, London: Routledge.

SYLVA, K. (1994) 'The impact of early learning on children's later development', in BALL, C. *Start Right: The Importance of Early Learning*, London: RSA.

SYLWANDER, L. (1996) *Why We Need an Ombudsman for Children*, in Council of Europe *The Child as Citizen*, Strasbourg: Council of Europe.

THE TIMES (1995) 'Three kind mice', (Editorial) *The Times*, 12 September.

TOBIN, D., WU, D. and DAVIDSON, D. (1989) *Preschool in Three Cultures: Japan, China and the United States*, London: Yale University Press.

TREVARTHEN, C. (1992) 'An infant's motives for speaking and thinking in the culture', in WOLD, A.H. (ed.) *The Dialogical Alternative*, Oxford: Oxford University Press, pp. 99–137.

UNITED NATIONS (1989) *The Convention on the Rights of the Child*, New York: United Nations.

UTTING, D. (1995) *Family and Parenthood: Supporting Families, Preventing Breakdown*, York: Joseph Rowntree Foundation.

WILKINSON, R.G. (1994) *Unfair Shares*, London: Barnardos.

9   Accounting Early for Lifelong Learning

Christine Pascal and Tony Bertram

This chapter explores 'outcomes' in early learning. It is an area that urgently needs attention at a time when there are renewed pressures to formalize aspects of provision for our youngest children. A number of current initiatives including Baseline Assessment, increasing early admission, notions of a 'core curriculum' and 'value added' tests, and top down institutional pressures are making many early years workers concerned about what they are being asked to do. What constitutes an 'appropriate' curriculum for young children is still hotly disputed but it is increasingly apparent that simplistic outcome measures, which only look to knowledge and skill competence in the short term, are seriously underestimating the issue. We wish to raise awareness of the deeper, latent, long-term effects of the curriculum processes. A similar concern underpins some of the affective outcomes recently identified by policy makers (DfEE, 1997), researchers (Wiltshire and Sylva, 1993) and the business community (Abbott, 1994; Handy, 1994). The evidence shows that lasting and important attitudes to learning are shaped early, crucially before the age of 6. Research, from a variety of disciplines, is providing us with rich and powerful evidence about how children learn; the nature of such learning; and the ways in which early experiences shape the pattern of progress, achievement and fulfilment, throughout an individual's life. The research highlights the importance of, for example, dispositions to learning (Katz, 1995); mastery orientation (Heyman, et al., 1992); conflict resolution (Lantieri, 1990); multiple intelligences (Gardner, 1983); involvement, linkedness, emotional well being and emotional literacy (Laevers and van Sandon, 1995; Laevers, 1996; Goleman, 1996).

National reports (National Commission, 1993; Ball, 1994) have indicated the importance of positive attributes towards early learning for lifelong achievement. They suggest that important learning characteristics associated with later achievement, such as aspiration, pro-socialization, self-esteem, motivation and confidence, are established in the early years. These enabling attitudes have been called the 'super skills' of learning (Ball, 1994).

These ideas about what is fundamental in developing lasting, positive attitudes to learning are to be the focus of a new national investigation by the authors of this chapter. We are interested in linking the implications of this new knowledge to our on-going work; that is, in supporting practitioners in rigorously and systematically self-evaluating their practice. The main vehicle for our work to date has been the Effective Early Learning (EEL) Project (Pascal and Bertram, 1997) which has had a significant impact on the quality of provision in early childhood settings throughout the UK and abroad (Pascal, Bertram and Ramsden, 1997). The EEL Project identifies, within its conceptual framework, effectiveness in early childhood settings through three domains: context variables, process variables and outcome variables (see Figure 9.1). Much of our research work has so far focused on the first two domains; the setting context, variables, which we delineated as 'ten dimensions of quality' (Pascal et al., 1996), and the interactive processes, which we identified and measured by using two key observation instruments, 'Child Involvement' (Laevers, 1994) and 'Adult Engagement' (Bertram, 1996). Our current work continues the search for 'effectiveness' in early childhood settings by focusing on the outcome variables. To this end, we are pleased to have been successful in obtaining funding for a major new research project entitled 'Accounting Early for Life Long Learning, (the AcE Project). This chapter investigates some of these issues and aims to lay out some of the emerging evidence for taking a wider view of effectiveness in measuring outcomes.

We are very aware that there are already a number of national initiatives focusing on outcomes in early years provision. These include the Desirable Outcomes Framework (QCA, 1998), the Nursery Inspection Schedule (DfEE, 1996), and the developing Baseline Assessment Schemes (DfEE, 1997). These policy developments are the result of government policy which is attempting to put into place outcome measures in early childhood education, as a means of quality control and quality improvement. At present, these outcome measures are focused mainly on the acquisition of skills and knowledge in academic areas, as, for example, detailed in the *Desirable Outcomes* (QCA 1998) for nursery-aged children. Concurrently, another concern has been to develop measurements of children's performance over time in respect of the delineated outcomes, the so called 'value added' approach. This has led to a burgeoning of interest in Baseline Assessment which focuses on children's competencies on admission (Wolfendale, 1993; Tymms, 1996). LEAs are now required to implement such schemes, but many appear to focus predominantly on language and mathematics. DfEE requirements for Baseline Assessment schemes (DfEE, 1997) have meant some aspects of 'personal and social' development are now being included, but very few schemes have any reference to attitudes, dispositions or emotional well being and emotional literacy. We feel that this is a major omission and one which should be addressed if schemes are to provide an effective indicator of children's long term educational progress. Whilst we recognize the importance of skills and knowledge, we believe that such a simplistic focus should not be the sole view of achievement. We need to widen our perspective on 'outcomes' and strengthen the practitioners' ability to support and assess those other areas of children's development which may be equally crucial to long-term success. These aspects of children's development and learning we summarize in our conceptual framework as dispositions to learn; respect for self and for others; and emotional well being. It may be helpful to set out some of the supporting evidence for our perspective.

A report by the influential US National Centre for Clinical Infant Programs (Brazelton, 1992) suggests that academic success rests predominantly on a child's early knowledge of how to learn, as well as what is learned. Goleman (1996) claims,

> that school success is not predicted by a child's fund of facts or a precocious abil-
> ity to read so much as by emotional and social measures; being self assured and
> interested; knowing what kind of behaviour is expected and how to rein in impulse
> to misbehave; being able to wait, to follow directions, and to turn to adults and
> peers for help; expressing needs whilst getting along with other children. (p. 193)

Our interest is targeted at 3- to 6-year-olds because there is evidence to show that this is the critically important phase for establishing learning attitudes. Gender and race studies (Siraj-Blatchford, 1996) show that lifelong attitudes are set early. Attitudes to 'self as a learner' follow the same pattern. Goleman (1996) talks of a 'window of opportunity' analogous to Lorenz's (1946) notion of 'imprinting'. These studies show that there is a biologically determined period when it is crucial to establish certain semi-permanent attitudes about learning. The stronger these are embedded, the greater their resilience to inevitable, climatic periods of poor stimu-lation, and the more likely that they will persist. The importance of this early period of social consciousness to lifelong achievement is recognized by Donaldson et al. (1983),

> Early childhood is . . . a period of momentous significance for all people growing
> up in our culture. . . . By the time this period is over, children will have formed
> conceptions of themselves as social beings, as thinkers, and as language users, and
> they will have reached certain important decisions about their own abilities and
> their own worth. (p. 1)

We live in an audited society where that which is measurable is seen as significant. We need to ensure that what we are measuring is significant and that we are not simply focusing on those things which are easily measured. The identification, development and measurement of young children's aptitudes, disposi-tions and inclinations are to be the subject of our new work. They are part of the intrinsic motivation which sustains a child's learning and, when strongly established, are carried forward to develop lifelong learning. We shall call these attitudes, dis-positions and inclinations 'Advancement Attributes'.

Conceptual Framework

The conceptual framework on which our project rests developed from The Effective Early Learning project. The EEL project postulated three sets of variables in evalu-ating 'quality' in early childhood settings; context, process and outcome variables (Pascal et al., 1996; Pascal and Bertram, 1997).

The **Context** variables describe the environmental characteristics of the set-ting. The EEL project defined the context variables as a list of 'Ten Dimensions of Quality', containing characteristics very similar to those outlined in the Rumbold

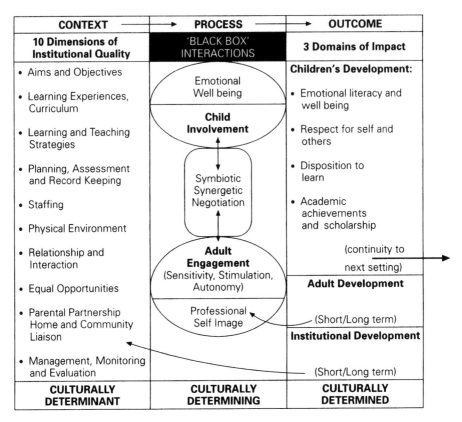

Figure 9.1: A conceptual framework for evaluating effectiveness in early childhood settings

Report (DES, 1990), the Royal Society of Arts (RSA) Report (Ball, 1994) and in the OFSTED inspection framework (DfEE, 1996). These include aims and objectives; learning experiences; learning and teaching strategies; planning, assessment and record keeping; staffing; physical environment; relationships and interactions; equal opportunities; parental partnership, home and community liaison; management, monitoring and evaluation.

The **Process** variables are generally taken by educational researchers (Kryiacou, 1994) to be the interactive processes, within the context of the setting, which facilitate learning. In the EEL project these were observed and measured by two instruments; the Child Involvement Scale and the Adult Engagement Scale.

The **Outcome** variables describe the results of the educational process. These would include attainments for the child and attainments for the practitioners.

The EEL project focused particularly on context and process variables in its aim to improve the quality and effectiveness of early learning. The new AcE project will focus specifically on the outcome variables. Figure 9.1 gives a summary of the conceptual framework which has framed our thinking. In this chapter we focus on the outcome domains associated with the child.

Child Outcome Domains

The outcomes of effective early learning can be seen in children's (i) academic achievements; (ii) in their dispositions to learn; (iii) in their respect for themselves and others; and (iv) in their well being. These four outcome domains offer a framework for analysis but are clearly not discrete and separate. Each of these domains will have a cluster of 'Advancement Attributes', which children, who have potential to be successful learners, will display. Let us consider each in turn.

Academic Achievements

Academic achievements is the first outcome domain and has been the focus of much recent policy. The introduction of Desirable Outcomes for 4-year-olds (QCA, 1998) exemplifies the official approach to academic achievements which is currently promoted. This, perhaps, has brought some much needed rigour to judgments about the effectiveness of the curriculum in some early childhood settings. The 'Desirable Outcomes' are 'goals for learning for children by the time they enter compulsory education' (QCA, 1998) and emphasize six areas of learning; language and literacy, mathematics, knowledge and understanding of the world, physical development, creative development, and personal and social development. Each of these areas of learning will have a cluster of 'Advancement Attributes'. For language, for example, these might be such things as the ability to listen attentively, to talk with fluency, to have an enjoyment of books and to be confident in role play.

There is a wealth of research evidence to show that children who have enhanced 'academic' abilities e.g. in language and literacy, and particularly, phonological awareness, on entry to compulsory schooling, are at an advantage throughout their schooling career and beyond (Tizard et al., 1988; Goswami and Bryant, 1990; Britton, 1992). The US-based High Scope programme, which has provided extensive empirical evidence on the long-term effects of certain types of pre-school interventions (Schweinhart and Weikart, 1993), demonstrates the long term benefits of providing young children with a cognitively based early learning curriculum. A recent UK report by Tymms (1996) shows that children who perform better on Baseline Assessment Schemes in respect of English and mathematics, continue to outperform other children from similar settings on the SAT's results at 7. In addition, a study by Shorrocks et al. (1992) shows that attendance at nursery school, which provides a cognitive and academically focused curriculum for young children, leads to enhanced performance in English, science and mathematics in the SAT's (Standard Assessment Tasks) at 7 years.

Assessment on entry to school is rapidly becoming the norm and we follow Tymms (1996) in recognizing the potential of Baseline Assessments, contextualized to local need, to offer important data about 'value added'. However, concern has been expressed that current developments may be based on very limited ideas about outcomes in this domain and convey a simplistic view that the tested reproduction of knowledge is the total objective (Olsen and Zigler, 1989). If Baseline Assessment is to be universal, it is argued that some items within this domain should capture broader curriculum objectives and include other areas of learning than literacy and numeracy. Gardner's (1983) ideas on 'multiple intelligence', for example, cast doubt on notions of a 'core curriculum' and suggest that other areas of learning may be just as important, for example, musical intelligence or spatial intelligence. However, the evidence of Tymms (1996) suggests that very few providers who are currently developing assessment schemes for young children are focusing on these other areas of learning. Indeed, even the 'personal and social development' of young children is neglected. The cluster of 'Advancement Attributes' which are associated with a broad range of academic learning need to be identified and explored in more depth.

We are particularly concerned to raise the expectation of academic achievement to include notions of 'scholarship'. By this we mean that knowledge of a subject should amount to more than mere competence but should also aspire to interest and enjoyment, or perhaps a love, of the area studied. A reader should not only be competent but have a desire to read. It is this deeper understanding and commitment to a subject which we are implying in the use of the word 'scholarship'. But our real concerns are to widen the outcome measures in this domain to reach beyond knowledge, skills and competencies.

Dispositions to Learn

Dispositions to learn is the second outcome domain and also has a cluster of 'Advancement Attributes' which we will need to consider. This notion arises from the work of Katz (1995) and others in the United States. Katz defines a 'disposition to learn' as,

> a pattern of behaviour exhibited frequently and in the absence of coercion, and constituting a habit of mind under a conscious and voluntary control, and that is intentional and oriented to broader goals.

Dispositions are different from predispositions, which are the genetic biological determinants. Resnick (1987) suggests dispositions can be cultivated and acquired through habit and through learning. They are part of intrinsic motivation and relatively lasting but they are not didactically acquired. They are not skill or knowledge acquisition but something else. Dispositions require another level of involvement and, we believe, are very strongly linked to lifelong learning.

Research in this area is developing fast and there is increasing evidence from US and cross national empirical studies that these learning orientations and abilities, or dispositions, are evident in very young learners (aged 3 and 4 years) and continue to shape a child's progress and attitudes towards learning throughout their schooling and beyond. For the past 15 years a group of American psychologists — Heyman, Dweck, Elliot, Leggett and Cain (Leggett and Dweck, 1986; Dweck and Leggett, 1988; Elliott and Dweck, 1988; Heyman, Dweck and Cain, 1992) — has been exploring academic motivation, learning characteristics and attitudes in children from the age of 3 and 4. They have carried out scores of experiments which have demonstrated that most children fall somewhere on a continuum of 'helplessness' or 'mastery' in their approach to learning, and that these behavioural patterns go hand in hand with differing goal structures. They found that children with a 'mastery' orientation to learning manage to coordinate their performance and learning goals successfully and set in motion cognitive and social processes which facilitate educational and social progress in the long term. Their most recent work has focused on young children aged 3 and 4 (Heyman et al., 1992) and has shown that such characteristics are already well established and affecting the child's approach to learning and exploration of the world. Another major US report on infant development (Brazelton, 1992), worryingly, finds such characteristics already established in very young babies, whose,

> demeanour is 'hang dog', a look that says, 'I'm no good. See, I've failed'. Such children are likely to go through life with a defeatist outlook, expecting no encouragement or interest from teachers and finding school joyless, perhaps eventually dropping out.

Major longitudinal studies of achievement further support this evidence. The High Scope Programme (Schweinhart and Weikart, 1993) has followed children through from the age of 5 to adulthood and found that children with high aspirations, independence and who experience an early education curriculum (at the age of 5 to 7) that encourages a mastery orientation are significantly more effective learners and achievers in the long term.

Dispositions can become more robust when supported by a scaffolding adult. They can be influenced, also, by curriculum process, negatively or positively (Rogoff et al., 1993). Creating a taxonomy of positive dispositions is an urgent task and might contain, for example, such elements as 'mastery orientation' (Leggett and Dweck, 1986), resilience (Walkerdine, 1985; Rutter, 1997), organizational skills, curiosity, concentration, inventiveness, self management and openness (Laevers, 1996). Clearly, not all dispositions are educationally positive ones; a disposition to be quarrelsome or be undisciplined, for example, might be an impediment to learning. Part of our future work will be identifying and developing with practitioners those characteristics in young children which seem to be associated with positive dispositions towards learning.

Respect for Self and Others

Respect for self and others is the third outcome domain and is located conceptually in the field of social psychology. It is now a well established tenet in the field of cultural, social and neural psychology that, from birth, learning is a process which occurs in a social context. Even as helpless neonates, young humans have the ability to reach out to others to help them make sense of their world (Vygotsky,

1962; Trevarthan, 1992; Bruner, 1996; Caxton, 1997). The burgeoning of work in the field of brain science and social cognition is underlining the importance of the social and affective domain in learning, and revealing the extent to which educational progress is affected by a child's view of herself in her world and her ability to reach out and connect to others within her world. As Ball (1994) has pointed out in his review of the importance of early learning,

> The most important learning in pre-school education has to do with aspiration, socialization and self-esteem . . . no-one learns effectively without motivation, social skills and confidence. (para. 2.16)

The experiences and interactions of a child with others create internalized perceptions of self which then become predictors of their future behaviour. The child's main carer has a particularly strong influence in establishing respect for self and in 'empowering' children to be strong (Whalley, 1996). With the increasing institutionalization of young children's upbringing, early childhood practitioners need to be more aware of the dangers of undermining and deskilling parents by offering one 'best' model of practice. Paradoxically, at the same time, they need to be able to offer guidance and support which, whilst acknowledging parents' capabilities, needs and cultural differences allows parents to fully support their child's social psychological development (Dahlberg and Åsén, 1994; Moss and Pence, 1994). Practitioners need to work with parents to create the development of children's self respect and a strong self-esteem (Roberts, 1996). The 'Advancement Attributes' that cluster around a strong sense of worth and a feeling of self-esteem need to be explored. Children with high levels of respect for self have the courage to stand up for themselves, to express their needs self confidently, and know how to handle life. There is a need for child, parents and practitioners to recognize these attributes and to develop the 'emotional literacy' to discuss them (Goleman, 1996).

As with respect for self, young children also need to develop a respect for others. Again, there is a growing body of empirical evidence which demonstrates the influence such personal and social 'Attributes' have on a child's educational progress. For example, Lipman's (1989) pioneering work in the US on the importance of respect for self and respect for others in young children aged 6 has demonstrated how programmes which develop these 'Attributes' directly benefit a child's cognitive and social development and educational progress. Lipman shows that young children can be encouraged to express preferences and opinions, to articulate their viewpoint and to have it acknowledged and given credence by peers and by their educators and significant carers. Such children are more likely to be able to acknowledge that there are other alternative views held by others which are equally valid and should be given respect. This understanding of multiple perspectives has been shown to reduce classroom tensions and advance learning achievements.

Laevers' (1996) recent work on the notion of 'linkedness' and the dangers inherent in feeling unconnected to the world is relevant here. Those who are, or become, delinquents lose their ability to connect to their inner self or to others. They become 'de-linked' delinquents. But this issue is wider than self connection.

It is about societal cohesiveness. We live in an increasingly plural society and if we are to do this harmoniously then we need to be able to respect each other and to acknowledge and celebrate difference. Paradoxically, this celebration of difference makes us have a great sense of belonging and community. The origins of these attitudes and their development are in early childhood (Siraj-Blatchford, 1996). We need to sensitize children, parents and practitioners to these issues and define and measure the attributes which create them.

Well Being

Well being is the fourth outcome domain we delineate. The 'Attributes' we are looking at in this domain include an openness and receptiveness to the environment; a flexible attitude; self confidence; the ability to initiate and assert; vitality and energy; an ease and inner peace which allows the child, even very young neonates, to take pleasure, reach out and enjoy learning (Trevarthan, 1992; Laevers, 1996). Such qualities are seen to be critical in sustaining learning in the long term and through difficulties and learning challenges. Rutter's (1997) recent overview of the link between 'resilience' attributes and achievement further underlines the importance of 'well being' to educational achievement.

Laevers (1996) describes young children as readily displaying the level of their 'well being' in eight observable signals. Children with high levels of well being are, he says, 'like fish in water' in their educational environments and maximize their learning potential. Laevers has developed a five point scale to be used by practitioners to assess children's 'well being'. The New Zealand Early Childhood Curriculum (New Zealand Ministry of Education, 1996) Te Whāriki uses the strand of 'well being' as a permeation issue which interweaves with their curriculum principles. Health, safety and nurture and sensitively handled transitions develop consistency, trust and security. 'Well being' leads to the establishment of the confidence to explore, and the foundation of remembered and anticipated places and experiences. It encourages the positive development of that innate exploratory drive that characterizes humans. Above all, children who display the quality of 'well being' have learnt the joy of empowering contact with responsive people. The identification of the 'Advancement Attributes' associated with 'well being' is the final element in the creation of a comprehensive typology of the outcomes of young children's learning which we are developing as part of the AcE Project.

In Conclusion

As Ball (1994, para. 2.17) points out, 'major educational research is on the threshold of a revolution', a view echoed by Bruner (1996), who talks of a 'cognitive revolution' which is changing the way we think about learning. The knowledge base which supports our understanding of early learning is developing fast, and clearly showing that a focus on education as the injection of facts, subjects and disciplines of knowledge alone, particularly in the early years, provides only a partial explanation of what makes for effective and lifelong learning. Our focus on 'Advancement Attributes' has two main thrusts. Firstly, we are attempting to encourage those who work with young children to apply this new knowledge to their practice and ensure their work is at the forefront of professional knowledge. Secondly, we are aiming to communicate this newly acquired professional knowledge to those who create policy so that they also may act from an informed base. The need to review and evaluate both practice and policy in relation to current educational research is a priority as we approach a new millennium. We should aim for the knowledge revolution in early learning to come off the shelves and feed directly into the actions of those who shape young children's early educational lives.

References

ABBOTT, J. (1994) *Learning Makes Sense: Recreating Education for a Changing Future*, Hertfordshire: Education 2000.

BALL, C. (1994) *Start Right: The Importance of Early Learning*, London: Royal Society for the Encouragement of the Arts, Manufacturers and Commerce (RSA).

BERTRAM, A.D. (1996) 'Effective early educators: A methodology for assessment and development', PhD Thesis: Coventry University.

BRAZELTON, T.B. (1992) *Heart Start: The Emotional Foundations of School Readiness*, Arlington, VA: National Center for Clinical Infant Programmes.

BRITTON, J. (1992) *Language and Learning: The Importance of Speech in Children's Development*, Harmondsworth: Penguin.

BRUNER, J. (1996) *The Culture of Education*, London: Harvard University Press.

CAXTON, G. (1997) *HARE BRAIN, TORTOISE MIND*, London: Fourth Estate.

DAHLBERG, G. and ÅSÉN, G. (1994) 'Evaluation and regulation: A question of empowerment', in MOSS, P. and PENCE, A. [eds] *Valuing Quality in Early Childhood Services: New Approaches to Defining Quality*, London: Paul Chapman Publishing.

DEPARTMENT OF EDUCATION AND SCIENCE (1990) *Starting with Quality* (The Rumbold Report of the Committee of Inquiry into the Quality of the Educational Experience offered to 3- and 4-year olds), London: HMSO.

DfEE (1996) *OFSTED Inspection Framework for Nursery Education*, London: HMSO.

DfEE (1997) *Baseline Assessment Schemes: Submission Guidelines*, London: HMSO.

DONALDSON, M., GRIEVE, R. and PRATT, C. (1983) *Early Childhood Development and Education: Readings in Psychology*, Oxford: Basil Blackwell.

DWECK, C.S. and LEGGETT, E. (1988) 'A socio-cognitive approach to motivation and achievement', *Psychological Review*, **95**, 2, pp. 256–73.

ELLIOTT, E. and DWECK, C.S. (1988) 'Goals: An approach to motivation and achievement', *Journal of Personality and Social Psychology*, **54**, 1, pp. 5–12.

GARDNER, H. (1983) *Frames of Mind: The Theory of Multiple Intelligences*, London: Fontana Press.

GOLEMAN, D. (1996) *Emotional Intelligence: Why It Can Matter More Than IQ*, London: Bloomsbury.

GOSWAMI, U. and BRYANT, P.E. (1990) *Phonological Skills and Learning to Read*, Hove: Lawrence Erlbaum.

HANDY, C. (1994) *The Empty Raincoat: Making Sense of the Future*, Hutchinson: London.

HEYMAN, G., DWECK, C.S. and CAIN, K. (1992) 'Young children's vulnerability to self blame and helplessness: Relationship to beliefs about goodness', *Child Development*, **63**, pp. 401–15.

KATZ, L.J. (1995) *Talks with Teachers of Young Children: A Collection*, NJ: Ablex Publishing Corporation.

KRYIACOU, C. (1994) *Effective Teaching in Schools*, Hemel Hampstead: Simon and Schuster Education.

LAEVERS, F. (1989) *Ervoringsgericht Werken in der Basisschool*, Leuven: Leuven Projectgroep EGO.

LAEVERS, F. (1994) *The Leuven Involvement Scale for Young Children*, LIS-YC, Manual and Video Tape, Experiential Education and Series No. 1, Leuven: Centre for Experiential Education.

LAEVERS, F. and VAN SANDEN (1995) *Basic Book for an Experiential Pre-primary Education*, Leuven: Centre for Experiential Education.

LAEVERS, F. (1996) 'Social competence, self organisation and exploratory drive, and creativity: Definition and assessment', Paper presented at the 6th European Early Childhood Education Research Association Conference on the Quality of Early Childhood Education, Lisbon, Portugal, September.

LANTIERI, L. (1990) *The Resolving Conflict Creativity Problem 1989: Summary of Significant Findings of RCCP*, NJ: Metis Associates.

LEGGETT, E.L. and DWECK, C.S. (1986) 'Goals and inference rules: Sources of causal judgments', *Psychological Review*, **95**, 2, pp. 256–73.

LIPMAN, M. (1989) *Philosophy Goes to School*, NJ: Temple University Press.

LORENZ, C. (1946) *Studies in Animal and Human Behaviour, Vol. 1.*, Cambridge, MA: Harvard University Press.

MOSS, P. and PENCE, A. (eds) (1994) *Valuing Quality in Early Childhood Services*, London: Paul Chapman.

NATIONAL COMMISSION ON EDUCATION (1993) *Learning to Succeed: A Radical Look at Education Today and a Strategy for the Future*, Report of the Paul Hamlyn Foundation National Commission on Education, London: Heinemann.

NEW ZEALAND MINISTRY OF EDUCATION (1996) *Te Whariki, Early Childhood Curriculum*, Wellington: Learning Media.

OLSEN, P. and ZIGLER, E. (1989) 'An assessment of the all day kindergarten movement, *Early Childhood Research Quarterly*, **4**, pp. 167–87.

PASCAL, C., BERTRAM, A.D., RAMSDEN, F., GEORGSON, J., SAUNDERS, M. and MOULD, C. (1996) *Evaluating and Developing Quality in Early Childhood Settings*, Worcester: Amber Publications.

PASCAL, C. and BERTRAM, A.D. (1997) *Effective Early Learning: Case Studies in Improvement*, London: Hodder and Stoughton.

PASCAL, C., BERTRAM, A.D. and RAMSDEN, F. (1997) *Effective Early Learning: Phase 3 Final Report*, Worcester: Amber Publications.

PHILLIPS, D. (1995) 'Giving voice to young children', *European Early Childhood Education Research Journal*, **3**, 2.

QCA (1998) *An Introduction to Curriculum Planning for Under Fives*, London: QCA.

QCA (1998) *Desirable Outcomes for Children's Learning on Entering Compulsory Education*, London: HMSO.

RESNICK, L.B. (1987) *Education and Learning to Think*, Washington DC: National Academy Press.

ROBERTS, R. (1996) *Self-esteem and Successful Early Learning*, London: Hodder and Stoughton.

ROGOFF, B., MISTRY, J., GONCU, A. and MOSIER, C. (1993) 'Guided participation in cultural activity by toddlers and care givers', *Monographs of the Society for Research in Child Development*, **58**, 8, (Serial No. 236).

RUTTER, M. (1997) 'Resilience and recovery in young children', Paper delivered at the Seventh Conference on the Quality of Early Childhood Education, EECERA: Munich, September 1997.

SCHWEINHART, L.J. and WEIKART, D. (1993) *A Summary of Significant Benefit: The High Scope Perry Pre-school Study through Age 27*, Ypsilanti, MI: High Scope UK.

SHORROCKS, D., DANIELS, S., FROBISHER, L., NELSON, N., WATERSON, A. and BELL, J. (1992) *Enca 1 Project: The Evaluation of National Curriculum Assessment at Key Stage 1*, Leeds: University of Leeds.

SIRAJ-BLATCHFORD, I. (1996) *The Early Years: Laying the Foundation for Racial Equity*, Stoke on Trent: Trentham Books.

TIZARD, B., BLATCHFORD, P., BURKE, J., FARQUHAR, C. and PLEWIS, I. (1988) *Young Children at School in the Inner City*, Hove: Lawrence Erlbaum.

TREVARTHAN, C. (1992) 'An infants motives for thinking and speaking', in WOLD, A.H. (ed.) *The Dialogical Alternative*, Oxford: Oxford University Press.

TYMMS, P. (1996) *Baseline Assessment and Value Added, A Report to the School Curriculum and Assessment Authority*, Middlesex: SCAA.

WALKERDINE, V. (1985) 'Child development and gender: The making of teachers and learners in nursery classrooms', in ADELMAN, C. et al., *Early Childhood Education, History, Policy and Practice*, Reading: Bulmershe.

WHALLEY, M. (1996) *Learning to Be Strong*, London: Hodder and Stoughton.

WILTSHIRE, J. and SYLVA, K. (1993) 'The impact of early learning on children's later development', *European Early Childhood Education Research Journal*, **1**, 1, pp. 17–40.

WOLFENDALE, S. (1993) *Baseline Assessment: A Review of Current Practice, Issues and Strategies for Effective Implementation*, Paris: OMEP.

VYGOTSKY, L.S. (1962) *Thought and Language*, Cambridge, MA: MIT Press.

10　Musings from a Nursery Inspector and Letters from a Pupil 1990–98

Margaret Stevens

Following a long career as an early years teacher in north west England and eight years as a tutor working on teacher training courses at the Manchester Metropolitan University (MMU), two years ago I decided to take early retirement and train as a nursery inspector. The publication by the Labour Party, of their pre-election document *Early Excellence — A Head Start For Every Child* (1996) was a heartening indication that the early years were firmly on the political agenda. My decision was also influenced by my involvement, whilst at the university, in the production of the professional development pack — *Firm Foundations: Quality Education in the Early Years* (1996), developed to support early years staff in the 'delivery' of the *Desirable Outcomes for Young Children's Learning on Entering Compulsory Schooling*, SCAA (1996). The snippets of video, filmed in a variety of preschool settings, showed how the requirements of the 'Desirable Outcomes' could be met in many different ways whilst safeguarding the autonomy of the child and recognizing that learning is not compartmentalized.

It was interesting to discover that some of the video sequences from 'Firm Foundations' had been selected by OFSTED for use in Nursery Inspection training, and I felt proud to have played a part in their production. I enjoyed the debate which took place during the training sessions and was grateful for the opportunities afforded to me during my time at the university to visit a wide range of the preschool settings as a supervisor of students during their school experience. My involvement in nursery schools, classes, combined nursery centres, reception classes and other types of provision visited, which included playgroups, day nurseries and private and voluntary sector provision, had given me an appreciation and understanding of the variety of factors influencing a child's experience in any one of those settings. At the university I had also been responsible for coordinating 'The Four Year Old in School' course for a number of local authorities, in the heady days when teachers were supported in order to come out of school during the day time in order to retrain for that age group or renew their contact with the under 5s! As a result of that challenging experience, I was all too aware of the differences encountered by 4-year-olds in many reception classes, as distinct from the experiences they would have in a nursery school or class.

I felt privileged to be involved in a process which I considered an important quality assurance mechanism and provided parents with some assurance that the standard of care and education received by their children had been subject to external scrutiny and had, at least, met the minimum standards required of all early years settings. I was also conscious, during the training, that all those undergoing nursery inspection training had been involved to a greater or lesser degree with young children of this age. I was less convinced that this was the case with regard to nursery inspection under the requirements of section 10 of the 1992 Education Act. My discussions with nursery and reception class teachers in primary schools, who had been inspected as part of the general OFSTED primary inspection, led me to believe that for some of them it was a less than positive experience. The lack of an early years specialist on some teams led teachers to feel that the understanding of young children's needs and of some of the difficulties they were facing, was not always evident.

The differences between the two inspection processes, in terms of requirements and emphasis, are discussed particularly in relation to the under 3s, by Barnes and Rodger (1997). The former outlines the registration and inspection requirements of the Children Act (DoH 1989) and her role as an inspector, whilst the latter considers the requirements of section 10 inspections. They write:

> These inspections use a different quality framework although their aims and outcomes are in some ways similar. Both registration and inspection procedures are aimed at enabling providers to meet acceptable standards.

However, both writers feel that it is very important that all parties are involved in the process and that inspection is not seen as something that is 'done to you' but as something 'done with you'. This is not easy to achieve given the anxieties and tensions surrounding the word 'inspection' and the history of 'OFSTED-related' stress which seems to have spread through primary and secondary schools.

Rodger (1997) says, that although clear guidance is provided in the OFSTED (1996) primary subject guidance in relation to the inspection of under 5s in primary school:

> There are dangers within the inspection process if inexperienced practitioners are given responsibility for making judgments about the quality of teaching without being able to understand how, for example, high expectations manifest themselves in a teaching situation with young children . . . the research findings of Sylva et al. (1980), Meadows and Cashdan (1988) and Munn and Schaffer (1993) all highlight the importance of the adult role in children's learning. Understanding the subtleties of that role takes experience and objectivity.

The importance of each inspector, whether those inspecting under section 10 arrangements or those appointed to inspect within private, voluntary and independent sectors having a sound knowledge of child development and early learning, cannot be overestimated.

It has been argued that inspection should lead to improvement. One of the strengths of the OFSTED inspections of establishments where there are children under 3 i.e. LEA Nursery Schools, is that 'the youngest children receive an entitlement to an inspection process that looks at standards of achievement, quality of education, the efficiency of the school and the children's spiritual, moral, social and cultural development' (Ensing, 1996).

A 'top-down' model of inspection which concentrates on 'academic' achievements and fails to acknowledge the importance of cultural, moral, spiritual, creative and emotional development is inappropriate for our youngest children. But Ensing (1996), drawing on her previous experience as HMI responsible for the early years sounds a note of caution with regard to the new 'light touch' inspections (DfEE, 1995): 'Too light a touch, that is of minimal requirements, may lead to minimal quality provision and would reduce children's rights.' There is clearly a need for a rationalization of the inspection procedures and an evaluation of the purpose, value and effects of the whole process on staff, children, parents and the future of early years education.

It is encouraging that the Consultation document — *Early Education and Day Care* (DfEE/DoH, 1998) invited responses to a series of important questions with regard to the whole process of inspection. Perhaps a more radical question, as we approach the millennium, is whether inspection in its present form is necessary at all — given the amount of time, money, anxiety and stress it involves. Should a concentration on team and self evaluation be introduced, once minimum standards and criteria have been met in terms of such things as provision, space, staffing, training and admissions policies?

Given the vast differences between settings surely it would be more appropriate, given that all staff are appropriately trained, and this would be the major requirement, that they are then trusted to undertake a rigorous process of context-related evaluation under the guidance of a mentor, who may well be one of the new breed of 'specialist early years teachers' assigned to the setting. This way there would be a degree of autonomy and a guarantee that regular support would be available, something which is sadly missing under the present system. My own experience of having been responsible for the inspection of over fifty very different pre-school settings is that many feel isolated and unsupported. Having responded to the inspection feedback and report, prepared an action plan and often gained fresh impetus in the process, there is then no one who can take an objective view of developments and share with them successes or concerns in a non-threatening way.

My response to the future of the inspection process would be to see it in the context of all the exciting and challenging developments which are taking place in the field of early childhood care and education. Given that children's entitlement to well trained adults who are continuing their professional development by means of an accessible 'climbing frame' of training opportunity is met, Abbott and Pugh (1998) I would move towards a programme of monitoring and evaluation. There would still be criteria to be met, information to be detailed and shared with parents and open to local and national scrutiny if necessary, but I would take away the anxiety generated by the word inspection. The process would be no less rigorous or demanding, but there would be a feeling of mutuality, of partnership, about the whole procedure. Similar to the Danish model, parents would be fully involved in both planning and monitoring, and staff would have an entitlement to support, not only from their mentor but from their local Early Excellence Centre, where both training and a wide range of resources and services would be available.

The whole process would be monitored at local level by the Early Years Development and Childcare Partnership, of which the mentor, with responsibility for a range of different settings, would be a member. This would remove the bureaucracy which the present system generates and would be a much more user friendly process for all concerned. Tick lists and clipboards would be banned and instead video, digital cameras, close observation of play sequences and children's activities by staff and parents trained in observation techniques would be used to feed information into computers, folders and portfolios, to be shared at open meetings.

There is already evidence that this kind of shared, but nonetheless rigorous, system of monitoring centres, staff, children and curriculum progress is happening successfully, not only in Scandinavia but in centres in the UK. At Pen Green Early Excellence centre parents and staff are involved in planning, monitoring and evaluation. Records of achievement employing innovative approaches and new technology trace progress and development of all concerned which is then made available in a number of interesting formats. There is much enjoyment but also a great deal of commitment. Like the Finnish Centres, where meetings with parents take place anywhere but in the school or centre, including the pub, bowling alley or sauna, parents and staff and children take part in social activities which are just as much a part of the monitoring, evaluation and development process as any formal session.

I have enjoyed immensely my involvement with the many settings I have inspected during the past two years and feel very privileged to have been part of their process of development. Each one was different, ranging from small playgroups in sleepy Cotswold villages to inner city nurseries on busy main roads and independent schools in leafy suburbs. The individuality of each context, in terms of building, physical environment, space, provision, resources, staffing, numbers, outdoor facilities, curriculum, size, relationship with parents, ethos and location makes comparison between settings almost impossible, which is why I found some of the findings in the recently published inspection report — *The Quality of Education in Institutions Inspected Under The Nursery Education Funding Arrangements*, (OFSTED, 1998), a cause for concern. Whilst accepting that agreed criteria are important in making judgments about individual centres, the almost exclusive concentration on the areas of learning under the headings of 'Desirable Outcomes', and the overly formal and restrictive nature of the inspection notebook, leaves little scope for the recording of some of the unexpected outcomes, particularly illuminating moments, demonstrations of competence and moments of discovery which all inspectors must witness on a regular basis.

I, along with other colleagues, have recorded many, what can only be termed 'magic moments', which do not fit neatly into the compartments labelled 'language and literacy', personal and social development or 'knowledge and understanding of the world'.

One such moment was recorded in a village playgroup in the Cotswolds during play in the 'Pirate Ship'. A corner of the room had been made into a pirate ship, where a band of happy pirates, sporting headscarves and eye-patches were playing happily. Overhead, the sails of the ship were blowing in the wind, powered by a high-mounted electric fan on the wall. Planning showed that these children had learned about ships and boats and the influence of wind as a source of power for sailing. Observation showed children using their developing skills of imagination, investigation, language, decision making, making choices, negotiating and socializing during play. In a suburban nursery, following a visit to the local library, the home-corner had become a 'library', for the children to enjoy. This was a print-rich environment offering many opportunities for young children to develop language and literacy skills. A young 'librarian' sat in front of a computer keyboard issuing library tickets to a small group of children. The children were able to choose not only real books, but little books which they had made themselves. There was a list of library 'rules' and 'times of opening' on the wall. A parent had made the wooden structure of the library, fostering a partnership in learning. Further activities, involved children in sorting and classifying the books into different categories, discussing how a book 'works' and selecting the rhyming words in a poem.

Another example of the level of understanding and sensitivity displayed by young children was witnessed by a colleague in an early excellence centre:

> A four-year-old boy; having studied the life cycle of the caterpillar with his teacher using carefully chosen reference books, microscopes to study caterpillars at close quarters, observing butterflies as they settled on carefully chosen plants to which they would be attracted, having discussed his observations with interested adults and painted, drawn, written and talked, was observed in a quiet moment holding the reference book open at the butterfly page and 'showing it' to the caterpillars hanging from the netting covering their tank.
>
> 'Look', he explained, 'this is what you will look like soon. Won't you be beautiful?'

How disappointed the staff and parents of these two very different centres must have been to read the headline which appeared in the paper the same week as these two observations took place.

> Children 'get best start' at private nursery schools . . . children aged four are receiving the best education at independent schools and Montessori nurseries say a report by OFSTED. (*Daily Telegraph*, 13 June 1998)

The list of findings in Figure 10.1 from the review undertaken by OFSTED during 1997–98 will no doubt be used to inform those responsible for providing training but it serves to reinforce a compartmentalized view of early learning and to perpetuate the notion that any form of literacy behaviour before 5 is simply pre-reading, rather than appropriate reading activity for that age and stage of development. Like preschool it is still seen as preparation for the next stage when 'real learning' will take place.

	Overall	Playgroup	Private Nursery School	Independent School	LA Day Nursery	Private Day Nursery
Personal and Social Development						
Response to cultural or religious events	*	*	**	**	***	**
Language and Literacy						
Recognize own names and some familiar words	**	**	***	***	**	**
Recognize letters of the alphabet by shape and sound	**	*	***	***	*	**
Associate sounds with patterns and rhymes, with syllables, and with words and letters	*	*	**	***	*	**
Use pictures, symbols, familiar words and letters in their writing to communicate meaning	*	*	**	**	*	**
Write their names with appropriate use of upper and lower case capitals	**	**	**	***	*	**
Mathematics						
Recognize and use numbers to ten	**	*	**	***	**	**
Through practical activities, begin to solve problems, record numbers and show an awareness of number operations	*	*	**	**	*	*
Knowledge and Understanding of the World						
Look at similarities, differences, patterns and change	**	**	**	***	**	**
Talk about and sometimes record their observations	**	*	**	***	**	**
Question why things happen and how they work	*	*	**	**	*	*
Physical Development						
Use balancing and climbing apparatus, with increasing skill	**	**	*	**	**	*
Creative Development						
Explore sound	**	**	**	***	**	**

Figure 10.1: Quality of provision in some aspects of the desirable outcomes
Source: OFSTED, 1998.

What is missing from this list, and from the report, is the child and the vignettes such as those cited which enliven and enrich the day and make the job of nursery inspection worthwhile. These activities had meaning and relevance for the children concerned, adults were of central importance in supporting children's learning, and by working together in a partnership children's individual needs were met. In contrast with these rich experiences, few of the independent schools or Montessori nurseries inspected had the space, resources or inclination to support children's play experiences such as these. Whilst delivering an excellent structured curriculum, I felt strongly that some children in such settings were not receiving the education they deserved or the freedom to develop their own potential. As one headteacher explained whilst serving tea in her study, 'our parents are professionals, they expect to see their children reading and writing and taking the next reading book home each evening. They do not want to think that they are wasting their money on children spending the day playing.' Discussion with parents and carers at the start and end of the day backed this up, they were obviously more interested in comparing the reading levels of their offspring than discussing the importance of play! If we accept that children learn best through first-hand experiences, which kind of activity provides the best learning opportunities for our children? How do the opportunities for learning for a child sitting at a desk, copying numbers and letters into a workbook or completing a worksheet, compare with a child in a playgroup or nursery playing in the 'post office', sorting letters and parcels, making and writing envelopes, writing cards, letters and invitations, using a till with real money, using the telephone, posting and delivering letters to children playing in the home-corner? Sensitive planning for rich play experiences can ensure that the curriculum provides for progression in the acquisition of knowledge, understanding and skills for individual children.

Some of the learning moments I have witnessed and recorded bear similarities to those recorded by Mary-Jane Drummond (1997) in her description of the approach to young children's early learning adopted in Reggio Emilia, Italy.

For the Italians, children's acts of representation and expression are the foundations for all subsequent learning. So, for example, their approach to literacy starts from the concept of exchange — 'lo scambio'; not with the book, or the story, or the printed word, but with the early capacity of the baby and the toddler to communicate in a give-and-take process of exchange. The exchange of a look, a smile, a touch, between the baby and the primary care-givers is, for the Italian educators, the beginning of all one hundred of children's symbolic languages, including the language of books and the world of print. Their earliest provision for this foundation stone of learning, again, not the book, as it is here, but a structure of tiny pigeon holes, one for each child and adult educator, labelled with names and photographs, for the exchange of meaningful messages between children and adults. The youngest children post each other stones, flowers, biscuits, fetishes and tiny treasures; the older ones exchange marks, drawings, letters, notes and news bulletins. These children are not only learning to read and write, they are learning to give and to receive. Carla Rinaldi, a pedagogical coordinator who works to support curriculum development in a group of preschools and nurseries summarizes their approach:

> The cornerstone of our experience, based on practice, theory and research, is the image of children as rich, strong and powerful . . . They have . . . the desire to grow, curiosity, the ability to be amazed and the desire to relate to other people and to communicate . . . Children are eager to express themselves within the context of a plurality of symbolic languages . . . Children are open to exchanges and reciprocity as deeds and acts of love which they not only want to receive but also want to offer. (Edwards et al., 1993)

Comparing the very different approaches to the early years curriculum exemplified by the 'Desirable Outcomes' and the OFSTED report and that adopted in Reggio Emilia, I found myself thinking about an 'early learner' with whom I worked some ten years ago and whose career I have followed with interest, and wondering how he might have responded to these very different approaches and, indeed, different views and expectations of young children.

Mark first came into my classroom more than ten years ago, a slightly built 6-year-old with an antipathy towards PE and time wasting of any kind. He appeared uncoordinated and his writing was, and by his own admission still is, barely legible, but he had a curiosity and maturity unmatched amongst his peers. Life was for living and discovering new things and, much to his parent's surprise, I soon realized that I had the privilege of teaching a gifted child. Although we celebrate the uniqueness of every child in our care I was delighted to be challenged by Mark and enjoyed the pleasure of his company for the following twelve months.

After nearly twenty years teaching the full range of primary age children in a wide variety of settings, I had developed my own method of teaching young children, which seemed to appeal to Mark. I hoped to provide relevant, rich experiences for these children whilst involving them in making choices and taking responsibility for their own learning. My system was quite simple but involved careful planning and I discovered that it worked as well with older junior pupils as with much younger infant children. After timetabling whole-class periods of teaching for activities such as, story, music, discussion, games and PE, I planned programmes of work for small groups of children or individuals. The activities were carefully matched to their individual needs. Children were sometimes involved in the planning and decision making, at other times I made the decision. I felt we were becoming partners in learning and children appeared to become self-motivated. The activities could be completed in any order and at any time of the day, but they had to be finished. This meant that those children who decided to take a break early to select their own play activity soon realized that they had insufficient time to finish the programme! Mark always chose to complete his 'work' first in order to enjoy the many other learning experiences on offer.

During a topic on Space, we decided to build a spaceship in the corridor, as space was at a premium in the classroom. The children helped to design and build it and because they owned it, respected and enjoyed it. It soon became the centre of attraction and the teacher in the adjacent class requested that her children be allowed to play in it also. The following morning, much to Mark's disbelief as chief designer, the spaceship appeared rather worse for wear. He later disappeared, and I was very amused to find him pinning up lists of rules and regulations on every corner of the spaceship signed by himself!

In a recent frenzy of activity in which I was clearing out an attic where I had stored a lot of material from my days as an early years teacher, I came across this letter 'typed' by Mark and his friend Thomas aged 6 and I realized to my chagrin that it was a 'space station' and not a spaceship as I had thought.

---

26 Glenwood Grove
Woodsmoor
Stockport

Dear Mrs Steavons,

The bay is a big reck area and all the roof bit is riped and damiged and is VERY poped it is damiged so much that we (if we cared about it so much that we band children from playing in it) and if necersery us we would have to put a new roof on it. The celfain on the ailon detecter on the front of the space staion is quite riped we need a new piesce of celafain and stick it on and put some kind of ruber pretecting surfice to fit on it and only take it off when the children were playing in the bay (Top infants). We are developing a new defise tht wires up from a battry oprated light to all the things that might be brocken and then if any movement or obstrucking the wires the light will flicker or go (automaticly switch off.)

Yours sencerly
Thomas and Mark

So the school year passed by quickly and eventfully, and the children left my class to enter the big new world of the Junior School. I discovered years later that Mark had been very upset on leaving my class and told his parents that he couldn't understand why I did not go too, as he felt quite sure that I was clever enough to teach in the Juniors!

It was quite usual for some of the children to return to see me during the first weeks of their new term in the Junior School. I was not surprised therefore to receive a visit from Mark after school on the first day of the new term. However, he took one look at the state of my classroom after the first day of the new intake and was visibly horrified. He gave me a pitying look and was soon on his way home! Obviously standards had dropped since he was in my class. A few months later I received the following letter from Mark, dated 2nd March 1990 together with *The HC Book of the Body*, to help me with my teaching!!

26 Glenwood Grove
Woodsmoor
Stockport SK2 7EF
2nd March 1990

Dear Mrs Stevens

I enclose a copy of *The HC Book of the Body*, that you asked for earlyer today, that I hope you will enjoy reading. Although the book is marked Copywrite 1989–90 HC Publications Let, as you have been so kind to me from being at the age 6 and a half, I shall let you photocopy it. I also enclose a few copys of a work sheet, for children of infant schools, and the answers. Both of thease, I allaw only you, and my family to photocopy, and it may be used in the classroom.

I hope your class have got better since the first day, what a mess it was then.

One day, I must bring my clarinet, after school and play it to you, that is when my ximer on my lip is better, as at the moment it is a right newscence.

Your old pupil
Mark Vandevelde

THE HC CHILDRENS BOOK OF
YOUR BODDY
BY MARK VANDEVELDE

CHAPTER 1
TEACHER/PARENTS NOTES

This book is a guide to young children how your boddy works and how there's works. It is really an educationel book and is probebly best used at home. There are not many illustrations so keep a pencil and papper handy just incase. Allso another problam with this book is that there are some difficult words in it so if your child does not understand it explain what that word meens. This book is probebly best used with infants. After reading this book to children it is best (in schools) to start a topic (if not allready started) there are a few THE HC CHILDRENS BOOK OF out now all to do with how different parts of the boddy work. This one is probebly the best one to start with because it is mostly about the blood in the boddy and explains quite a few dificult words. This book allso showes how grims get into the boddy.

NOTE: READ TO CHILDREN FROM HERE
CHAPTER 2
WHO ARE WE?

All of the people in the world have a speachel name that name is Humans. The reason for this is because we are all animals, allthough it sounds the funniest thing to think that we are animals it is true. But a harder thing, what do we do? The answer is we do many things but one of those things, infact the most important thing is that we live. But how do we live? What go's on inside us? Read chapter 3 to find out.

CHAPTER 3
WHAT IS OUR HART?
WHAT DOES IT DO?

Realy what your heart is, is a pump but it is not like your centrel-heating pump it is a pump that pumps your blood round our boddy. Without blood we could'nt live, the reason for this is because it is the only way to pump air round the boddy. Without your heart you could'nt move any blood round the boddy so you could'nt move oxygen round the boddy. But there must be something behind everything to make your heart work what is it? There are to things the first one is energy and without that something els couldent work, your brain. Without your brain your heart could'nt work and without energy your brain could'nt work. So realy for your heart you need a mains supply (energy) and a junction box (your brain) and your heart of course well that is an electricel system working 24 hours per day. But what is blood? What does it do? Read chapter 4 to find out.

CHAPTER 4
WHAT IS BLOOD?

Blood is a liquid that has no colour but the BLOOD CELLS in it make it look a colour. You think all blood is red but it isent some is white, some red and some purple. The red cells carry oxygen, the purple cells carry food and the white cells kill girms. But blood is like a river there is no part of your boddy that is'nt covered in blood. So your boddy could'nt produce all this fluid that is because more than half your blood is water. However the below diagram shows how your cells work:

But some babies are not lukey they are born with parts of there boddy not working or missing. Or some are born to early and have to be kept on a speacel macheen.

This book is by Mark Vandevelde and coppywrite HC Publications LTD 1989–90.

THE BODY
WORKSHEET FOR INFANTS

1 Who are we?
2 Are we animals?
3 What keeps the brain going?
4 What pumps the blood round the body?
5 What works out your sums?
6 Is the heart working day and night?
7 Is the brain working day and night?
8 Does the brain work like a junction box or a sewing macheen?
9 What pumps oxygen round the boddy?
10 Draw a picture to do with the body ither on the back of this sheet, or on another sheet of paper.

THE HC BOOK OF THE BODY
WORKSHEET ANSWERS

1 Humans
2 Yes
3 Energy
4 The heart
5 Brain
6 Yes
7 Yes
8 Junction box
9 Blood
10 To be checked by teacher

Soon after receiving Mark's gift of the 'Boddy Book', I left the school to take up a post at the university and about this time Mark left the Stockport area to live in Bedford. I quickly became absorbed in my new life at the university contributing to all aspects of early years training, supervising students in school and establishing a resource base as a focal point for good practice in early years and primary education. During this time I kept in touch with Mark and was pleased to receive a hand-written letter in December 1991 from his new address (see Figure 10.2). It was written with his usual style, flair, imagination and knowledge. He was now 10 years old.

During my time at the university I have shared with colleagues and students many similar early letters, poems and stories sent to me by Mark.

16 Brockwell,
Oakley,
Bedfordshire.
MK43 7TD
14 December 1991

Dear Mrs Stevens,

Hi! I am having a mr mixture of a gun and a hectic time, as usual at Christmas! I've set up an organisation called 'The Environmental Research Centre'. We have done 5 checks on rivers so far and I am making an air checking device at the moment. My equipment is home made and works like this :-

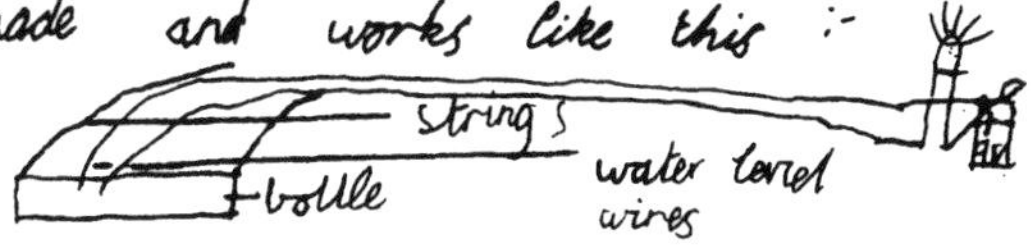

strings
bottle
water level
wires

When the water level reaches a certain height the L.E.D. illuminates. My design for air checker is:-

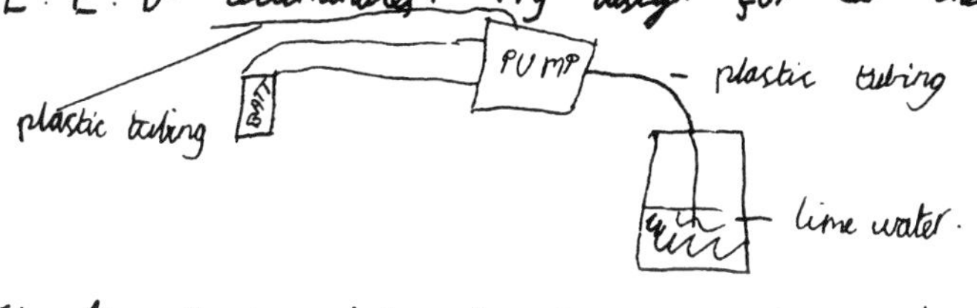

plastic tubing
PUMP
- plastic tubing
lime water.

The limewater is misty when CO_2 is added, therefore the pump will make CO_2 more direct — as it needs to be. However, I am writing round companies trying to obtain more sophisticated equipment.

We also have a warrent each, containing a passport photo, card no., issue date and expiry date. Dad hasn't got a photo yet, neither has ~~got~~ Gran. But Mum and I have - they ~~took~~ me ages to design this morning.

Something I'm hopefully going to do this week is to 'electroplate' a nail. ~~That~~ is done by connecting the nail by means of a wire to the - terminal (negative) of a 4.5 v battery. Some copper sulphate is added to water and dissolved. The water is connected to the + (possitive) terminal of the battery and is left for 20 minss with the nail in it.

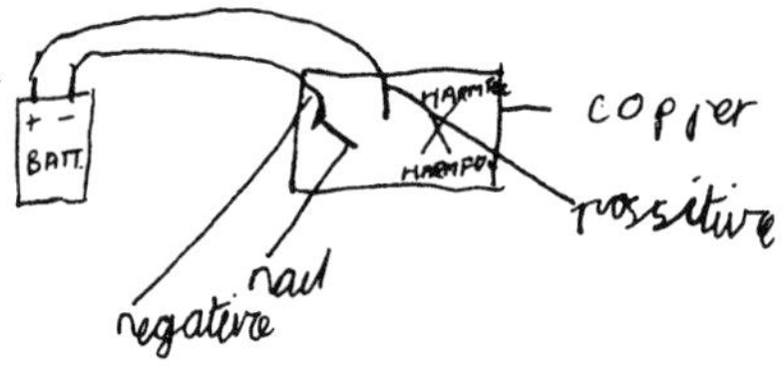

When the nail comes out it is copper plated.

Anyway! after 1¾+ pages of my science lark lets get onto 'something else'! On Wednesday, I am in a concert with the school choirs and orchestra. My clarinet had a few hitches in it so it was a dash to get it repaired. However, we got it done in the end!

Hope you are well.

Best wishes,

Mark.

Figure 10.2: *Letter from Mark Vandevelde December 1991*

Bedford
13th April 1996

Dear Mrs Stevens

I am sorry that I have not been able to write sooner — this term has been an extremely busy one!

November was quite a special time for me. The BBC's 'Newsround' programme runs a club called 'The Press Pack' for aspiring journalists — and since I last wrote I have become an aspiring journalist! Last October, an assignment on the future of transport was set, and I sent in an entry. The article had to be less than 200 words long, and could be anything at all to do with transport's future. In November, A Newsround researcher telephoned me to say that I had been shortlised, and asked me how I thought of my article and whether I would be too shy to talk to a camera. The next day someone else from the BBC telephoned Mum to say that I had an audition the following Monday! I had a great time, was mistaken for Jeremy Paxman and photographed with Newsround's presenter.

My alarm clock has recently developed a fault and now wakes me at 8.15 to the cacophony of radio jingles. One morning this January, it chose Radio 5 Live, where a phone-in debate on the Newbury bypass was taking place. Hours before a mock exam and against my own better judgment, I decided to participate. The enclosed tape is a recording of my contribution!

Mark's winning article written at 13 is as follows:

November 1995 Press Pack Assignment: The Future of Transport

CYBERSPACESHIPS DRIVE SCHOOL BUSES OFF THE ROAD

The 20th century has seen the most significant advances in transport since the invention of the wheel. But with the 21st century just a few stops away, digital communications technology is on the road to replacing transport altogether.

There will always be the need to move an object from one place to another. You can't get a bunch of bananas from one end of the world to the other using a computer and a satellite dish. And, no matter what the nerds say, you'll never jive with Windows 95. But imagine a 'virtual school', with teachers and students separated by hundreds — even thousands — of miles.

The technology isn't as sophisticated, or as cheap, as it needs to be. Providing each child in the country with a laptop computer, modem, videophone and telephone line isn't realistic. But as the information superhighway moves closer to home, it would be a TV monitor — not a bus — that transports the next generation of learners to their virtual classroom.

I happened to share Mark's letters and winning article with my head of department Professor Lesley Abbott who was interested in asking Mark about his memories and views on early education. He replied to my request as follows:

Bedford
29th April 1996

Dear Mrs Stevens
Wow! Your letter was an inspiration!
Thank you very much for your letter, and for sharing mine with your Head of Department, Lesley Abbott.
Enclosed is my paper — of about 1,800 words — entitled 'The Importance of Early Learning'. I found your letter very thought provoking and hope that you enjoy reading my article.

The following extract, from Mark's article written when he was age 15 years, on 'The Importance of Early Learning', reflects his views on teaching methods.

'Independent Learning' . . . an advantage of the fact that Primary teachers are 'generalists', is that they are not bound to a rigid timetable. Primary teachers can use this freedom to give pupils the opportunity to take control of their study time. I remember how mature I felt when a teacher set several pieces of work to be completed in an afternoon, and left us to organise ourselves as we please. As an incentive we were told we could play in any spare time. This scheme encouraged the development of time management skills, and allowed us to work at our own pace, speeding through the exercise that we found easy while spending longer on areas of work in which we were less proficient, completed them thoroughly in the absence of pressure to answer questions quickly but superficially. At some point in Secondary Education this freedom is lost. Often, we are forced to work at the pace of the least able in the class, filling time by copying text or colouring pictures. The independence that is given to pupils during their first years of education prepares them better for the work organisation characteristics of the 1990s as opposed to the low-trust Taylorite principles of Secondary education. It often seems that the most important quality required of pupils during this period of education is obedience. Applying 'scientific management' to schools may damage pupils' education!

In the same article in a detailed review of the value of early learning Mark comments on *social* skills — 'until the beginning of early years education, a toddler has never been far from a trusted adult — a parent, close member of family or childminder. Now he must adapt to a new environment and become more independent where teachers facilitate the learning of social skills rather than teaching them.' He goes on to comment:

On *cognitive* development — 'It is possible for an individual to analyse the education he has received during the first years of his life in terms of the impact that it has had on his development. He may speculate, for example that he would not be as articulate as he is today had he not been encouraged to express his thoughts at such an early age.'

On *motivation* — 'Early education can have a more significant impact on children's motivation to learn than on any other learning outcome — Praise during the first years of a child's education represents the first acknowledgment by the adult world that he has value.'

On the *Economic Impact* of early learning Mark concludes — 'During early years education, pupils are encouraged to embrace the concepts of pride in their work and loyalty to the team, healthy living, citizenship, team skills and law and order. If they do maintain these principles throughout their life, then the NHS workload will be reduced, our workforce will be more dynamic, efficient and motivated and there will be less social unrest. If this is the case, then early years education represents a sound investment in social order, national prosperity and personal fulfilment.'

Further letters followed, each one charting some further achievement including winning a public speaking contest in which along with two other pupils from his school he gave a presentation on whether the NHS should remain free after the year 2000.

For his GCSE studies he produced a video on the early years, interviewing Lesley Abbott and other early years trainers by telephone and recording their comments. He was asked by the headteacher to produce a video about the school, impressing all concerned with his media skills.

He comments in his article on early education that 'nothing motivates a child more than feeling superior to his teacher. I taught one of them how to use a computer. This technique developed my language, mathematical and technical skills, motivating me with the belief that I could do something that they could not.' Given that his skills in this field were well developed even at age 6 and were far in advance of my own he would not find it difficult to feel that he had skills which were in advance of those of his teachers. It is not surprising then that a further article which subsequently came my way is one which deals with this issue and fits well with the theme of this book. It is one in which Mark presents his vision of the 'classroom' of the future.

Room with a Virtual View

The classroom of the future will not be a room, but an amoebic network, exploited through silicon technology. It is the nature of this technology and the way in which we interact with it as learners that will define the learning environment of the future, and determine its success at equipping its users with the skills and knowledge required for prosperity.

Advances in technology, coupled with changes in the world of work, are rendering obsolete many skills taught in schools today. As faster processors combine with network linkages to increase the power of computers, they develop the capacity to support software that, for example, corrects spelling, performs complex arithmetical functions and accesses new vistas of knowledge. As these lower order lexical and mathematical skills become less important, the significance of others, such as the ability to retrieve and analyse information from the Internet, expands exponentially.

The nature of the 'classroom' is destined to change as dramatically as the curriculum associated with it. Students able to access learning materials remotely through cellular links will attend school to enrich their experience with resources unavailable from home. These resources will be associated, not with the raw material of knowledge, but with specific applications of it through face-to-face interaction in real time. Lessons will mutate into embryonic teamwork collaborations, where the teacher assumes the role of team coach, negotiating and assessing assignments.

Teachers will abandon their didactic mode of delivery — as a source of knowledge, they will be unable to compete with the depth and diversity of the on-line environment. Rather, teachers will become personal learning assistants, promoting in students the application of knowledge gleaned from other sources.

The Internet is already home to virtual worlds defined in three dimensions. In these worlds, students learn through exploration and discovery based on the synthetic recreation of experience. These students will be better motivated to learn, and will accumulate intellectual capital more rapidly and effectively than at present.

Schools will serve as places of social interaction, while communities continue to be based at geographically definable locations. The ability to access educational opportunity electronically, regardless of location, will allow the growing number of children of internationally mobile parents, to remain part of a single, albeit virtual, community, and therefore to maintain their cultural affinities, irrespective of their movement.

Although it is certain that the advanced technology required to support these revolutions will be available at prices affordable to the public sector, the learning revolution envisaged above is not inevitable. Computers could instead replace teachers with electronic drill sergeants, maintaining discipline among halls full of children, perfecting outmoded spelling and arithmetical skills with (literally) mindless computer-generated tests.

It is in the way in which we apply technology that we will choose between a physical classroom which symbolises enslavement to mechanistic drudgery, and a virtual classroom which connects learners to spheres of learning which operate beyond the constraint of time and place.

I have followed Mark's progress with great interest and will continue to do so. There is much to be said for the Jesuit maxim 'Give me a child until he is seven, and I will show you the man.' But I am also reminded of the explanation given by Mabel Lucie Attwell of her idiosyncratic and well loved drawings: 'I see the child in the adult . . . then draw the adult as a child.'

To return then to where I began — my musings on my experiences as a nursery inspector. I have gained a great deal from the experience. I consider that the best provision for young children, is not always found in purpose-built, highly-resourced settings, but depends on the commitment to children and the quality of teaching and training of the dedicated professionals who work with them. This early and important stage of the under 5s should be given a much higher priority in terms of status, staffing, resources, funding and inspection procedures. My hope for the millennium is that teaching in the early years is seen by everyone to be more important than teaching any other age group. It is encouraging that this government has put the early years high on its agenda. Only by providing the prestige, opportunities and resources to extend the provision of quality early years education, will every child be able to achieve his true potential. I have followed the progress of one such child with keen interest. He is now 16 years of age and during this time he has already achieved a great deal. He started his formal education in a playgroup similar to those I have described and I had the pleasure of his company in the final year in the infant school. Since then he has progressed through the junior and secondary school where his work continues to show outstanding promise. He has been interviewed on radio, won a public speaking award, and scooped a national award for young journalists. More recently, he has described his work experience in *The Times Educational Supplement*, become a computer buff and has even interviewed the Chief Inspector of Schools!

What more can I say? Except that I think we shall hear much more from this young man in the new millennium. The following chapter is his contribution to this publication!

References

ABBOTT, L. et al. (1996) *Firm Foundations — Quality Education in the Early Years*, MET: The Manchester Metropolitan University.

ABBOTT, L. and PUGH, G. (eds) (1998) *Training to Work in the Early Years — Developing the Climbing Frame*, Buckingham: Open University Press.

BARNES, S. and RODGER, R. (1997) 'Registration and inspection', in ABBOTT, L. and MOYLETT, H. (eds) *Early Interactions Working with the Under 3s — Training and Professional Development*, Buckingham: Open University Press.

DEPARTMENT for EDUCATION and EMPLOYMENT (DfEE) (1995) *Framework for Inspection of the Educational Provision for Four Years Old Children*, London: HMSO.

DEPARTMENT for EDUCATION and EMPLOYMENT and DEPARTMENT of HEALTH (DfEE/DoH) (1998) *Consultative Paper on the Regulation of Early Education and Day Care*, London: DfEE/DoH.

DEPARTMENT OF HEALTH (DoH) (1989) *The Children Act*, London: HMSO.

DRUMMOND, M.-J. (1997) 'Starting with children — Towards an early years curriculum', in DAINTON, S. (ed.) *Broader Thinking about the School Curriculum*, London: Association of Teachers and Lecturers.

EDWARDS, C., GANDINI, L. and FOREMAN, G. (eds) (1993) *The Hundred Languages of Children*, Norwood NJ: Ablex Publishing.

ENSING, J. (1996) 'Inspection of early years in schools', in NUTBROWN, C. (ed.) *Respectful Educators – Capable Learners. Children's Rights and Early Education*, London: Paul Chapman Publishing.

LABOUR PARTY (1996) *Early Excellence — A Headstart for Every Child*, London: Labour Party.

MEADOWS, S. and CASHDAN, A. (1988) *Helping Children Learn: Contributions to a Cognitive Curriculum*, London: David Fulton.

MUNN, P. and SCHAFFER, H.R. (1993) 'Literacy and numeracy events in social interactive contexts', *International Journal of Early Years Education*, 1, 3, pp. 61–79.

OFFICE FOR STANDARDS IN EDUCATION (OfSTED) (1996) *Areas of Learning for the Under Fives in Primary Subject Guidance for Registered Inspectors*, London: HMSO.

OFFICE FOR STANDARDS IN EDUCATION (OfSTED) (1998) *The Quality of Education in Institutions Inspected Under the Nursery Education Funding Arrangements*, A report from the office of her Majesty's Chief Inspector of Schools, London: HMSO.

RODGER, R. and BARNES, S. (1997) '"Our Very Best Show" — Registration and inspection, implications for under 3s', in ABBOTT, L. and MOYLETT, H. (eds) *Early Interactions, Working with the Under 3s: Responding to Children's Needs*, Buckingham: Open University Press.

SCHOOL CURRICULUM and ASSESSMENT AUTHORITY (SCAA) (1996) *Desirable Outcomes for Young Children's Learning on Entering Compulsory Education*, London: SCAA.

SYLVA, K., ROY, C. and PAINTER, M. (1980) *Childwatching at Playgroup and Nursery School*, London: Grant McIntyre.

THE MANCHESTER METROPOLITAN UNIVERSITY (1966) *Firm Foundations — Quality Education in the Early Years — A Professional Package*, Manchester: M.M.U.

VANDEVELDE, M. (1998) 'FE Focus', *The Times Educational Supplement*, 27 June.

11 Planetary Influences

Mark Vandevelde

This paper assesses the implications of the information revolution and of human-kind's perception of this phenomenon for early years education. I examine how early childhood education can counter the global trend towards the exploitation of children. I explore how a stable platform for child development can be achieved after the breakdown of the patriarchal family and I analyse the benefits and dangers of information technology during the first years of a child's life. Finally, I set early childhood education in the context of lifelong learning by showing how the first years of education can prepare a child for independent learning throughout the rest of their lifetime.

Reading the Runes

As we approach a new millennium, our mental landscape is undergoing a trans-formation. The invention of hypertext has fused the alphabetical order with an audio visual system made up of symbols and sensory stimuli which are comple-mentary to the full expression of the human mind. This mode of communication symbolizes the wider, informational revolution we are experiencing, characterized by an economy centred on the generation and application of knowledge.

The information revolution differs from previous social and economic trans-formations in that we appreciate simultaneously with the events in question the revolutionary nature of the change that is taking place. Furthermore, while previous revolutions have spread through the world at different rates, the information revolu-tion is engulfing the entire planet.

A cognitive chasm will separate anybody old enough to have contributed to this book from the children born into the new millennium. Because it is now possible to make tentative predictions about the developmental needs of children in the informational society, early childhood education can begin to redefine its role for social, economic, cultural and political mutations which are now unfolding.

First Impressions

It has been argued that any advantage gained from early childhood education is short-lived, becoming undetectable within five years. New research and laboratory evidence, however, reinforces the opposite conclusion.

There is a strong scientific basis for the assertion that experience shapes personality. Neuroscientists have demonstrated that the brain develops by forming different pathways between its constituent neurons. During the first days of childhood, the brain produces billions more of these pathways, known as synapses, than it can use. Over the subsequent ten years, the synapses that are most used will be strengthened, while those which are rarely stimulated will be eliminated through synaptic pruning.

This evidence implies that experience during the first years of life has the most impact on a child's capacities and character. A child born with cataracts will become permanently blind in the affected eye unless the clouded lens is removed — not because of the eye defect, but because the sensory channel which links the eye to the brain falls into disuse, and disintegrates. Similarly, if a child is deprived of stimulation during the early years, they are condemned to a life of developmental impoverishment.

Most unsettling are the implications of this research for the child's emotional development. Psychologists are beginning to understand that the key to emotional well-being is the ability to recognize emotions, and thereby to control them. We are born with the rudiments of emotional awareness: a 3-month-old child will exhibit empathy on hearing another child cry. If, however, a child's feelings are not acknowledged by the adults who surround them, the child not only ceases to express those feelings, but loses the ability to recognize them in himself.

Research on child development confirms that early childhood education provides the key opportunity to harness the developmental capacity that individuals possess during the first years of childhood, and to exploit it for the benefit of the individual and society. To this end, early childhood education should allow children to sample an array of diverse activities in order to build upon children's relational, affective and cognitive skills. The emphasis should be on interaction — with other children and with the world. By developing children's cognitive ability, early childhood education can enhance their potential as individuals, and add value to society as a whole.

There are, however, social, technological and economic developments which require more imaginative childhood education strategies. I now examine how these developments will impact on children.

Growing Apart

Most of a child's early years are spent at home, so it is a prerequisite of sound child development that parents know how to stimulate their children. Yet studies in the US show that nearly half of all infants and toddlers face one or more risk factors at home which threaten to impede their development.

Until recently, western cultures based upon a patriarchal society provided the stability of a family unit for most children's development. However, the mass intake of women into the workforce, together with technological advances related to human reproduction, have led women to challenge their domination by men. The result is the collapse of the patriarchal family and, for children, this can mean growing up within a haphazard parental structure, often in an unstable family environment which engenders a confused identity.

At the same time, the integration of global economies has deprived governments of the ability to control their own fiscal and redistributive policies. Threatened with exclusion from the global market if labour costs rise too high, governments have been forced to rein back the welfare state which once provided security for those unable to work. Even when the child has only one parent, the state no longer bestows an income that can provide basic necessities, and the result is that many parents are absent for a substantial proportion of their children's early (and teenage) years. More than half of all women with children younger than 4 years now work (Office for National Statistics, 1998).

This trend should not necessarily be discouraged — studies suggest that children benefit from the pride a parent derives from earning income rather than receiving a state handout. Nevertheless, this development makes it even more important that the time the child does share with their parent is enjoyed as a positive developmental experience.

Some American states provide education programmes for parents on how to stimulate their children. In Oregon, for example, a child development consultant visits a newborn's parents within two weeks of birth. The visits continue for up to three years. The State of Oregon funds the scheme because it believes that appropriately stimulated children are likely to be more employable and are less likely to resort to crime. The aim is to use early childhood education to promote social cohesion and so reduce spending on remedial measures — like social welfare and law and order.

Parents and educators face a new challenge: the need to exploit in the home the developmental opportunity which early childhood represents. If children are to be prepared for life in the informational society, parents must be educated on how to provide learning opportunities for their children. For the child, this represents an early start to the learning process; for the parent, it is another step in the pursuit of lifelong learning. Potentially, it is the foundation of a new form of partnership between the child, the parent and the educator.

The learning trajectories of parent and child will be affected by a critical element of the informational society: the revolution in information and communications technology. Does this open up new opportunities for early childhood development, or is it a sinister source of child exploitation?

Soft Wiring

The debate about how early to introduce information technology to children has been raging since the introduction of its most primitive audiovisual form — television. Television provides children with a window on the world. It can perform a specialist teaching role that few parents would be able to fulfil, but research has shown that television also introduces the average schoolchild to 100,000 acts of violence before the age of 11. While some parents cling uncritically to the anaesthetizing rectangle as analogue childminder, others have become wary of the potential harm which might arise from their children's exposure to the medium.

Although regulation can help to ensure that broadcasters provide learning opportunities for children, state intervention is only partly effective in shielding children from potentially harmful content. It is impossible to prevent parents from using media entertainment as Prozac substitutes for their children. Early years education has a significant role in stimulating children who succumb to Pied Piper passivity and in reconnecting them to authentic reality. Children can only be protected from the more harmful influences of the media by parents who understand how to use ICT constructively.

Computers pose an even greater dilemma for those involved in the upbringing of children. Used imaginatively, computers provide an interactive and engaging learning interface and allow children to learn more effectively. Like TV, however, they have an enormous capacity to entrap their users within a mind-wasting gulag at best, and a sinister swamp of exploitation at worst.

The first step towards maximizing the potential of computers to add value to learning, is to combat their destructive potential. Video games, for example, have no educational value beyond skills related to hand–eye coordination, and have a negative psychological and physiological effect upon children. Even in educational institutions, cost-cutting drives or sheer laziness can turn computers into automated drill sergeants — millennial technology imposing low level skills upon children and undermining creativity. Computers shouldn't be seen as a cheaper or more convenient means of achieving the goals of today's education system. Rather, digital literacy (and in particular the ability to reprogram the mind to perform different tasks) is as significant a part of the fabric of the informational society, as alphabetical literacy has been for the industrial society.

The capacity of computers to enhance learning potential is maximized when they are connected to networks like the Internet. The hypertext of the World Wide Web fuses reflective thought with the audiovisual system of information exchange that is natural to humans. It offers a three-dimensional mesh of articulation, in which multiple layers of complexity can be viewed selectively. This medium promises to revolutionize human expression, but its full exploitation requires new skills of interpretation and expression.

Growth in the informational economy will be based upon mind working with machine to add value to economic endeavour. ICT will be an essential part of activity for workers of the future, so it should be introduced early. Today's parents, however, grew up in a society in which ICT was a specialist occupation. They need to be educated on how to use computers effectively — to further their own potential for income generation as well as for the benefit of their children.

If ICT symbolizes the empowerment of children to take control over their own learning, it also incubates a malignant form of child exploitation. We take a look at this developmental hazard now.

Marketing Innocents

Children's increasing exposure to the media subjects them to the further threat of commercial exploitation. Although children in the UK spend on average only £225 in pocket money each year, they influence a large proportion of the family budget. Witness the Teletubbies and the Spice Girls — two products with multimillion pound sales based upon their popularity with children. Children's advertising has become so lucrative that some advertisers have begun to specialize in the field — Saatchi and Saatchi, for example, recently established 'Kid Connection', an off-shoot specializing in marketing to children. Advertising is the latest industry to colonize the open-eyed receptiveness of children.

A more oppressive form of child exploitation is also spreading through the world. Child labour is on the rise. In developing countries, which have had the highest incidence of child labour this century, 250 million children between the ages of 5 and 14 were working for pay in 1996 (ILO, 1996). In the western world, too, the exploitation of children is becoming more common. In Britain, almost 44 per cent of 10–16-year-olds are employed, or have had a job in the recent past (Lavalette, 1994). Child labour doesn't just threaten the education of the next generation — it imperils its existence. In the US alone, it's estimated that 300 children are killed and 70,000 injured at work annually. 'The National Safe Workplace Institute estimates that 300 children are killed and 70,000 injured at work annually in the US alone.'

The exploitation of children is here to stay. Many child labourers are forced into work by their poverty. Stricken families, desperate for extra sources of income, undermine their children's education and with it all hope of economic emancipation for the future.

The informational society has empowered some children to take control of their learning, and ultimately their destiny. Globalization, deregulation and poverty have, however, subjected children at the opposite extreme to a life of slavery. The spectrum of experience between learning opportunity and learning inaccessibility has never been wider. There is a vibrant future for those who experience a stimulating early childhood education. Those who are shackled by the economics of child labour, who are deprived of stimulation and lack the means to connect themselves to the informational society, are unlikely to break free.

Child Benefit

The most recent economic and social upheaval comparable to that which we are witnessing today was the industrial revolution. Those who lost out then, were the manual labourers whose muscular energy had previously sustained the economy. Their strength did not match that of the machines which replaced them — their role in the new order moved from marginalization to obsolescence.

Today, elements of human skill upon which society has relied are once again becoming redundant. No human brain can match the arithmetical aptitude of a computer; demand for lower order mathematical and lexical skills in humans is falling. In this context, the current drive towards imposing these skills upon young children would appear misguided.

The realignment of economic activity towards the generation and processing of information requires a change in the education system that was designed to provide for the needs of an industrial economy. To this end, I propose that early childhood education should:

- **focus upon higher skills of communication and collaboration.** Promoting the skills that enable an individual to work with others is more important than developing academic potential. Children who enter adolescence in an emotionally unstable state, or without the skills of social interaction, will lack the basis for further education and are unlikely to escape from a trajectory towards exclusion. In any event, there is strong evidence to suggest that children learn academic skills most effectively later in their education.
- **be set in an international and multicultural context.** In the UK, young people's international experience is usually limited to Europe, in the form of a brief exchange visit at the age of 14 or 15. With the spread of technologies like the Internet and videoconferencing, however, international experience can begin in the nursery. Children, for whom international collaboration has been a part of school life, will be best placed to connect to the global networks of wealth creation that will be characteristic of the next century.
- **develop digital literacy in context.** The use of ICT to facilitate learning should begin at an early age, both to accelerate progress in the wider curriculum, and to prepare an individual for a lifetime of working with ICT. Children should be encouraged to use resources like the Internet to take control of their own learning. Computers will take over from teachers as a child's principal source of knowledge; teachers should instead promote the kinds of learning activity which can't be accessed through a computer.
- **generate a tripartite network of exchange for lifelong learning.** Early childhood education should aim to develop the skills of independent learning, and to provide the antidote to digitally mediated substitutes for experience in order to motivate individuals to continue learning throughout their lives. Fundamental to this is the negotiation of an interactive learning relationship between the early years educator, the parent and the child, in which each contributes to the learning of the other two parties. The ultimate goal is the achievement of equitable exchanges in this network relationship.

The importance of early learning has never been greater. Those who do not develop the personal, social and intellectual foundations to engage with others within a cauldron of change, will face social exclusion and be the victims of the corrosive divide between those with the ability to generate wealth and those without.

The provision of early childhood education has also become more challenging. In the post-patriarchal society, educators face intense social and behavioural problems associated with the growing fluidity of parental relationships. For the first time, children are being prepared for accelerating change both inside and outside the classroom, which will affect their lives well before they reach adulthood. Only if early childhood education rises to these challenges, can it lay the foundations for insulating individuals from the prospect of becoming the downtrodden serfs of the information age.

References

INTERNATIONAL LABOUR OFFICE (ILO) (1996) *Child Labour: Targeting the Intolerable*, Geneva: ILO.

LAVALETTE, M. (1994) *Child Employment in the Capitalist Labour Market*, Aldershot: Avebury.

OFFICE FOR NATIONAL STATISTICS (ONS) (1998) *Social Trends 28*, London: Office for National Statistics.

TIME (1997) 'TV or not TV', 8 September.

Web Site:
http://cgi.pathfinder.com/time/magazine/1997/dom/970908/fam.tv-or-no-tv-.html

12 'If this was on the computer we could hear the lion go roar' — Information and Communications Technology in Early Years Education

Paul Baker

Rationale for ICT in Early Years

It is hard to write about Information and Communication Technology (ICT) in the context of early years education without wondering where its relevance lies. Why should very young children engage in work on machines? The two little girls in the title discussing the difference between an interactive book on the computer and its traditional counterpart put their finger on an important point. Computers do things that other educational tools can't.[1] It isn't simply the obvious issues such as making sounds and presenting attractive graphic displays; computers can motivate, reward and facilitate in ways that makes learning exciting and attractive for pupils. It may also provide access to areas of the curriculum or education for pupils who would previously have been excluded.

The relevance of ICT also lies in the future. The children who are in their first years of education now will inhabit, not only a new millennium, but a different technological world. That world will make huge demands on the knowledge and skills the education system has equipped them with. They will need to be able to learn new skills and work patterns with flexibility never before demanded from a workforce. The assumption may well be that they will have to take responsibility for re-skilling themselves a number of times in their work careers. To do this they will have access to a vast array of information through communications technology. These children will be the first generation to have been born since the Internet and e-mail revolutionized both the provision of information and the way we see the world.

In the past, it is fair to say that some professionals questioned whether young children can benefit from using ICT, and whether there is a danger that they will be damaged educationally, physically or socially by their use of ICT. It is perhaps important that few professionals give credence to such questions now. The recognition now is that ICT needs to be part of a well thought out curriculum that offers pupils a wide variety of rich educational activities. As Johnston (1997) makes clear, the potential offered by ICT makes it an essential part of early years education.

The curriculum for ICT needs to address not only how we use technology, but also the deeper ethical questions of why we use it and for what purpose. The professionals working in the field of early years education have the challenge of helping pupils begin to see beyond the technical skills to the moral and ethical dimensions of ICT. It is their responsibility to educate their pupils rather than to teach. In this way we will have a generation of thinkers rather than a generation of consumers.

It is of course a truism that the best education flows from children seeing good models. Teachers and other professionals need to exploit ICT in their own professional domains. This means moving beyond the use of ICT for administration, to using it as a supportive educational tool when working with parents and colleagues. Accessing information and participating in the development of policy and ideas can be facilitated through the use of ICT. It is possible that the move from multi-disciplinary work to interdisciplinary working, which has proved so difficult in the past, may be facilitated through the immediacy of communication provided by ICT.

Desirable Outcomes, NC and the Curriculum

The two documents that provide guidance on the content of children's early education, *Desirable Outcomes for Children's Learning on Entering Compulsory Education* (SCAA, 1996) and The National Curriculum Level 1 provide us with very little material on which to base our teaching. Rather they act as signposts for the direction our teaching should take. The emphasis in both documents is on children 'using' technology to do things. Whether they use it to write stories, to listen to stories or to paint pictures is immaterial; the point is that they use technology to support their learning experiences.

Additional guidance can be found in the Review of Inspection Findings produced by OFSTED (1995). In the latest review for 1995–96, early years education is singled out for praise. OFSTED welcome the interesting and constructive work being done with pupils being motivated and challenged through the use of ICT. The curriculum opportunities offered by ICT are varied, as any glance at the developing literature will bear out. There is increasing evidence of ICT moving beyond the support of Literacy and Numeracy into a wider variety of subject areas (Betts, 1996; Burns, 1996). The challenge for any early years professional is to consider how the ICT resources at their disposal may be used to extend children's learning and experience in not only other subject areas such as geography as illustrated by Betts; but also in more fundamental areas of their personal development. In her article on using 'roamers' in early years settings, Bilton (1995) points out that suddenly the children are given the opportunity to act as teachers to others, to explore spatial awareness and to develop their personal confidence. I am not claiming that only ICT offers such opportunities, that would be ridiculous; but to miss out on the possibilities offered by ICT would also be professionally ridiculous.

It is also important to place ICT firmly within the current government policy initiatives such as the national literacy strategy. Keeling (1995) is one of a long list of writers who record the enthusiasm and progress of early years pupils when computers are used to deliver not only text or pictures, but both of these combined with speech. The addition of high quality speech now possible with multi-media machines means that pupils can work independently from the teacher whilst still accessing literature and practising reading skills (Taylor, 1996). The more active side of literacy, illustrated by Pescod's (1995) report of children creating their own books for personal and class use would seem to bring the area up to date. Yet ICT moves on, and already there is evidence that professionals in the field are utilizing the latest development of voice recognition software to allow pupils who are not at the stage of writing to commit their ideas to text. This development, long seen as a vehicle for giving curriculum access to pupils with motor disabilities is the latest in a long line of developments that have proved far wider in their application than was imagined by their developers. A literacy project where pupils are writing and illustrating their own books before they have mastered the physical mechanics of handwriting puts a very different spin on the national literacy project.

Software

When faced with the question of which software to use in the early years setting, the answer lies in two different but significant directions. The first question is less about software and more about the curriculum. Technology is there to support the curriculum rather than to lead it and the mistakes of the past, when a new piece of software could decide the curriculum direction of teaching is happily a very rare event. The first question when contemplating ICT should be what software do I have that will support this theme or area. If schools have built up a collection of software that is related to curriculum areas it is important to relate the skills that pupils have to employ when using it. Software can make skill practice interesting when it may otherwise be tedious; equally, it can allow sufficient variation in a task to allow a pupil to develop competence without becoming bored.

The other direction that we can look at when considering software is the flood of new software aimed at the early years educational setting. Unlike books, software is expensive, and difficult to evaluate without purchasing it first. Two points probably need to be underlined. Firstly, check the educational ICT press for reviews, and secondly look for advice from your local LEA support staff or colleagues in other settings who may have experience of the software. In educational journals it is always useful to look at articles written by teachers who are reporting how they have used particular software packages within a curriculum framework. Most of the references in this essay have been reports of this type, and they provide an invaluable starting point for considering the potential use of software. Whilst these aren't foolproof, they can sometimes avoid a limited budget being wasted.

When you have the software, it is important to remember that it needs to be evaluated for the purpose you intend using it for. The information produced by BECTa and found at their website may be useful as may similar information found on the internet. A particular problem can be software from other countries, that makes use of heavily accented language or even non-standard English. It must also be said that some of the so called 'educational' software in shops is of very poor quality and of very dubious educational worth. The increase in multi-media machines has also meant that schools are making greater use of more sophisticated encyclopedia type software. Whilst this is often very useful, it can be highly selective and extremely partisan when dealing with information. It is an interesting exercise to look up the information provided about Cuba on a range of information packages; the variation of information and the 'slant' it takes can be quite extreme. Equally, it is frequently difficult to find software in shops that conforms to the recognized standards of gender, culture and individual fairness that we expect to find in school books. Jackson (1990) who noted the importance of finding software and ICT situations, which avoided gender stereotyping and gave girls positive experiences with computers in education, could also have been talking about racial stereotyping. Whereas school literature has tackled this problem, it is still waiting to be tackled in the world of software. On the whole I feel there is very little substitute for buying recommended and reviewed software from a good educational software supplier.

Finally, we need to mention fun! During a visit to one class of 6-year olds I was very interested to see a group of them working at the computer, absolutely engrossed in an interactive story book. Somehow it seemed more than reasonable that when the story was finished and the narrator's voice said, 'goodbye', a little chorus of voices answered, with one hopeful voice adding, 'See you tomorrow'. If the software we are using doesn't maintain interest and engage pupils' imaginations then one has to ask what we are using it for?

Hardware

It is perhaps extremely important to point out that computers are not the only 'hardware' within the field of ICT. Whilst this essay concentrates on computers, it is important to acknowledge that electronic activity centres, keyboards, switch operated toys, video machines and simple floor robots are amongst the wide variety of ICT hardware available.

One of the great misfortunes for schools has been the diversity of computer operating systems they have had to contend with. Schools frequently have three or four different computers each needing its own software and sometimes its own peripherals. The gradual movement towards standardization on the PC is both welcome and necessary if we are to equip pupils for the reality of the world they are going to work in. Where schools are investing in new hardware, there is little sense in replicating this diversity. The answer is simple; schools need to re-equip with standard PCs. They represent a cheaper, more widely supported and more cheaply maintained option than machines aimed at an 'educational market'. The major question that remains for schools is whether they should buy desk top machines or consider the possibilities presented by laptops or pocket book machines. This obviously depends on how computers are going to be used; the obvious benefit for some pupils of having a portable computer is perhaps less obvious in an early years setting, although as Tatlock (1996) demonstrates, it should not be written off lightly.

Yet it is important to note that schools need to look carefully at the hardware they actually have and the use they make of it. Simply because hardware is old doesn't prevent it being used in a useful way. The simple addition of switches or other input devices can transform an old machine into a useful classroom resource. It also offers the teacher the possibility of using an older machine as a dedicated word processor or painting machine.

Whilst schools standardize their primary hardware such as computers, they need to approach the question of input devices a little more creatively. For the youngest pupils, the 'qwerty' keyboard may be both intimidating and difficult to manipulate. Alternative keyboards, such as the well known 'concept keyboard', are widely available. Whilst the standard mouse is relatively easy to manipulate, the bigger tracker balls sometimes provide greater control for young children. Perhaps the most interesting issue in hardware (and paralleled in the question of software) is that many schools are recognizing many of the technical adaptions made to support pupils with special educational needs also have an application for early years pupils. The central question is whether the adaption achieves the required effect of making the child a successful operator of the hardware. It is important to mention the increasing range of other peripherals available to schools. With scanners and cameras becoming cheaper, they offer the school the opportunity to produce a wide range of curriculum materials that use contexts familiar to the children they are aimed at. It is significant that already we have special schools producing their own reading schemes because they were unable to find a scheme that met their needs. The impact of hardware such as scanners and digital cameras makes the development of school specific curriculum material for early years pupils a very real possibility.

A final issue to be noted is the question of output. In the past, printing was slow and of poor quality. The recent development of cheaper and more efficient colour printers offers schools the opportunity to produce good quality hard copies of children's work. Yet there is also a lot to be said for encouraging young pupils to recognize that a print out is not always necessary. Most schemes of work in early years settings recognize that skills such as saving files onto a disc can be achieved by very young children, and this allows pupils to keep a complete record of their work, whilst actively selecting what they want hard copies of. The increasing significance of the internet as a way of displaying children's work may be indicative of a growing realization that how and where we display pupil's work, like much else in the world of ICT, is also undergoing change.

Classroom Organization

There is no simple rule for the classroom organization that is needed to support good practice in the use of ICT, on the contrary, it relates very much to the context of the classroom. What is essential is that teachers develop a style of organization that integrates ICT within their normal classroom practice. This organization should ensure that all pupils have access to ICT as a matter of entitlement. This means that teachers avoid the most obvious blocking practices such as only allowing pupils to use the computer when they have completed other work, or when they have behaved well. In addition, there has to be an awareness of the dangers presented by attitudes that may encourage boys rather than girls to use the resources or that may imply only the more able pupil can use computers properly. There has been an increasing realization that school policies for ICT need to encourage positive practices that ensure computers are used to promote social experiences and the development of cooperative learning skills.

A key factor for teachers to consider in their ICT teaching is differentiation. In the same way that teachers use differentiation to ensure that pupils make progress in other curriculum areas, ICT demands the same approach. Having clear learning objectives for individual pupils is an essential step to helping them make progress. Where teachers sometimes experience confusion is in establishing the difference between the content of the ICT curriculum, and the learning objectives within a piece of software. If our objective is to help the pupil develop their mouse control, then the software we use to do this is almost immaterial. We may use a simple painting programme, acknowledging that any development they make in their understanding and competence in art is an additional or unintended achievement. This means we value what they achieve, but recognize that it wasn't our primary aim. The question we need to ask is not about art or the quality of their picture, but rather how good their mouse control is and whether they need to progress to a more complex objective.

Hand in hand with accurate differentiation is a consistent, reliable and school-wide system for recording or tracking the developing knowledge, skills and under-standing of pupils. There are so many lists of the skills and objectives within the ICT curriculum available that no school needs to 're-invent the wheel', unless they see a particular staff development benefit flowing from such an exercise. What is important is that teacher's see the part that pupils can play in recording and evaluating their own achievements. A local school that I know quite well has a simple rule, the pupils have a list of skills that they have to achieve across each key stage, and they have a responsibility for keeping their own lists. The teachers then use the pupils' lists as the basis for assessment and discussion. Another school gives each pupil a disc at the beginning of each year, and the pupil saves their own work whether it happens to be pictures or text files. Every couple of weeks they choose something from their disc to be printed out and filed in their evidence file. This pro-cess with 6- and 7-year-old pupils is constantly reinforcing the message that they share the responsibility for recording and evaluating their own achievement.

As can be seen from the comments above the organization of the classroom becomes a crucial element in allowing us to differentiate and record. The reality is that issues such as how much support pupils receive, or how we organize their access to ICT are factors that need to be considered when thinking about our classroom organization. The intervention of adults in the use of ICT needs to be measured and thought through in much the same way that it is with reading. There needs to be some care taken that children are encouraged to solve problems without adults taking over the situation. Where access to ICT is provided on a free choice basis, there is a need to ensure that all the professionals and para-professionals in the classroom are able to operate and help with the ICT resources.

It is hard to divide classroom organization, differentiation and recording progression in a subject area; quite rightly teachers see these areas as vastly over-lapping. The key seems to be to ensure that as educators we treat ICT as a curriculum subject or area, not as an 'optional extra'. This will help us focus on what we need to do to ensure that each pupil receives their entitlement to a challenging and differentiated ICT curriculum.

ICT and Pupils with Special Educational Needs

It would be difficult to discuss the importance of ICT for pupils in the early years of their education, without mentioning the role of ICT in making education access-ible for pupils with Special Educational Needs (SEN). Professionals involved in special education led the early development of ICT, particularly in primary educa-tion in England and Wales. Therefore it is not really surprising that much of the most acclaimed primary software that has had a huge effect on children's learning, has origins in software development groups such as SEMERC. In much the same way the pioneering work of companies, such as inclusive technology to make hardware accessible to all pupils, has had implications in the mainstream class-room. (The web sites of the two groups named are included in the References and provide a wealth of information about both ICT and Special Educational Needs.)

Yet despite the comments above, I am firmly of the belief that in ICT more than in any other area of education, pupils with special educational needs compete with their peers on more favourable terms. The technology that produced the concept keyboard for pupils with SEN did not produce an educational ghetto; on the contrary, it allowed all children easier access to the wonders of ICT. We should applaud the fact that speech activated software developed initially for visually impaired adults is now being used to encourage all youngsters to create their own story books, even before they have mastered the art of writing or reading. The ability of ICT to respond so rapidly to pupils ensures that they are learning within an extremely responsive environment. If teachers harness this responsiveness to soft-ware that matches the pupils' needs, employing hardware that gives them easy access, and developing the experience as a social learning occasion, we are surely seeing ICT as a powerful learning tool for all children, not just those with special needs.

If a by-product of ICT is to produce pupils who are able to recognize the benefits of ICT for all, and who see their fellow pupils with special or individual needs in a situation of success and participation, this alone will be a huge step forward for society. The centrality of the teacher in the early years environment is not simply to facilitate access to the ICT curriculum; rather it is to give pupils an expectation that ICT is a tool that they should have access to in every learning context throughout their school careers. If they give their pupils this expectation, they will have changed education for them totally.

Internet and E-mail

The one new development in ICT that has undoubtedly got the potential to change all our lives is the Internet and its associated option of e-mail. Whilst schools are still coming to grips with the government's proposal to connect all schools, libraries and hospitals to the 'information superhighway', other schools have become active participants on it. Increasing numbers of schools have their own web sites, as a cursory glance at any LEA's web site will show you (Kent for instance being a good example). Here we can see pupils' work being displayed to the world, and we can see the school at work.

Increasingly, projects sponsored by the British government and the European Community, such as Netd@ays, are encouraging schools to form transnational links. This development has an impact on pupils who become increasingly aware of different cultures with an immediacy that has never before been possible at such a sustained level. Beith (1998) suggests that children in early years settings have much to gain from early exposure to the Internet, particularly confidence in using technology to support their learning. This confidence was brought home to a group of my university students recently, who were talking to an 8-year-old boy about his school's use of e-mail to communicate with a French primary school. He pointed out that he was in daily communication with his e-mail pen-friend in New York; and whilst the contact with the French children was interesting, he really enjoyed the daily swap of e-mails with New York. It is hard to imagine just how the world will look to young people who have always had e-mail and the Internet as part of their lives.

No consideration of the Internet is ever complete because of the dynamic nature of the medium, but it is important for schools to consider the child protection issues inherent in any work in such an unregulated environment. I could not do justice to such an issue in this limited space, and therefore simply flag it up for consideration. There is a great deal of information on how to protect children from unwanted material available from sources both on the internet and within national organizations such as BECTa, and prudent professionals need to consider this carefully.

Initial Teacher Training, Continuing Professional Development and ICT

Perhaps the realization on the part of the present government that teachers are entitled to meaningful professional development of high quality in ICT, is a belated recognition that the limited national progress in ICT was created and sustained by politicians, not educators. Government policy, as reflected in Circular 4/98, DfEE

(1998), addresses an anxiety with information technology that has predominated in teaching for too long. At long last there is a coordinated plan to educate and enskill both serving teachers and students undertaking initial teacher education. Whilst the transformation won't take place instantly, over time we should see fewer teachers who claim to be 'technophobes', and more teachers who are comfortable incorporating another teaching tool into their classrooms.

The development of a coordinated plan for continuing professional development in ICT for teachers needs to address what I hope has been a recurring theme in this essay. ICT is a constantly developing area. Few professionals in the field are able to predict with any accuracy what the next technical development will be, and fewer still can predict what the application of that development will mean for education. The eventual aim of any programme of CPD for teachers must aim to provide them with a continually developing sense of competence in the field; allowing them to adapt and experiment with ICT applications for the benefit of their pupils.

The development of the Internet offers all the professionals involved in early years education new opportunities. The most obvious of these is access to the thousands of pages of information and opinion about issues of relevance to their professional practice. Whilst it is reasonable to accept that there is much dross on the Internet, there is an increasing body of reference material available through it which is of good quality. The Internet is also increasingly being seen as a means of providing open and distance learning; with increasing limits being placed on courses offered by universities, the opportunities for professionals other than teachers to undertake inservice education is becoming more limited. It is likely that telematics will become increasingly important in the coming years, and this in turn will provide opportunities for all the professionals involved in early years education to undertake courses of advanced professional development.

Conclusion

I am sure that accessing ICT within the early years curriculum presents educators with challenges. Yet ICT can offer pupils a resource of skills and knowledge which will be both an essential part of their future studies, as well as of their work and leisure. Perhaps like reading and mathematics, ICT is justifiably being recognized as part of the core curriculum.

In trying to draw these comments to some conclusion I at first tried to find some deep educational reference to underline the gravity of the impact made by ICT. Yet, if we turn to the comments of the inventors of the computer who worked in Manchester fifty years ago their comments reflect something that the two little girls of the title felt. Excitement. Tom Kilburn, talking about the work that went into developing 'baby', the first programmable computer at Manchester University captures two elements that make ICT so important in learning, '. . . the most exciting time was June 1948 when the first machine worked. Without question. Nothing could ever compare with that' (1992).[2]

When the two girls, heard the lion go roar in the computer programme, they were excited, and whether they knew it or not, nothing would ever be quite the same in their lives again.

Notes

1 Burns, C. (1995) reporting a conversation between two pupils looking at a conventional book after using interactive storybook software on the computer.
2 Further information can be found at the following web site, http://www.cs.man.ac.uk/mark1/kilburn.html

References

BEITH, M. (1998) 'Never too young', *Interactive*, **17**, pp. 8–10.
BETTS, G. (1996) 'Finding their place', *Interactive*, **8**, pp. 18–20.
BILTON, H. (1995) 'The llTtle ones', *Educational Computing and Technology*, **16**, 2, pp. 10–12.
BURNS, C. (1995) 'Talking IT up', *Educational Computing and Technology*, **16**, 2, pp. 16–18.
BURNS, I. (1996) 'The joy factor', *Interactive*, **5**, pp. 6–8.
DfEE (1998) *Circular Number 04/98: Requirements for Courses of Initial Teacher Training*, London: HMSO.
JACKSON, A. (1990) 'Information technology and the early years', *Early Years*, **11**, 1, pp. 23–8.
JOHNSTON, C.B. (1997) 'Interactive storybook software: Effects on verbal development in kindergarten children', *Early Child Development and Care*, **132**, pp. 33–44.
KEELING, G. (1995) 'Shirts, skirts and screens', *Interactive*, **2**, pp. 8–10.
OFSTED (1995) *Information Technology: A Review of Inspection Findings 1993/94*, London: HMSO.
PESCOD, D. (1995) 'Let's write a book!', *Interactive*, **3**, pp. 6–8.
SCAA (1996) *Nursery Education: Desirable Outcomes for Children's Learning on Entering Compulsory Education*, London: HMSO.
TATLOCK, S. (1996) 'Put IT in your Pocket', *Child Education*, **73**, 5, pp. 24–5.
TAYLOR, C. (1996) 'Teaching reading with talking story books', *Computer Education*, **84**, pp. 24–7.
Web Sites:
Inclusive Technology http://www.inclusive.co.uk
SEMERC http://www.granada-learning.com

13　Early Childhood Institutions as a Democratic and Emancipatory Project

Peter Moss

> [Early childhood institutions] as well as our images of what a child is, can be and should be, must be seen as the social construction of a community of human agents, originating through our active interaction with other people and with society.... [Early childhood] institutions and pedagogical practises for children are constituted by dominant discourses in our society and embody thoughts, conceptions and ethics which prevail at a given moment in a given society. (Dahlberg, 1995)

> We asked what prompted the people of Reggio Emilia to design an early childhood education system founded on the perspective of the child. He [Bonacci, Mayor of Reggio-Emilia in the 1960s] replied that the fascist experience had taught them that people who conformed and obeyed were dangerous, and that in building a new society it was imperative to safeguard and communicate that lesson and nurture and maintain a vision of children who can think and act for themselves. (Dahlberg, 1995, p. 8)

The State We Are In

The language of early childhood services today is increasingly the language of technology, management and the market — interventions and outcomes, providers and purchasers, plans and programmes. The metaphor, as the American early childhood expert Lilian Katz (1993) has pointed out, is the processing plant or factory:

> It seems to me that early childhood programmes are increasingly in danger of being modelled on the corporate/industrial or factory model so pervasive in elementary and secondary levels of education ... factories are designed to transform raw material into prespecified products by treating it to a sequence of prespecified standard processes. (pp. 33–4)

The language is neither accidental nor surprising. For the increasing priority given to early childhood services in recent years is driven, at least in the Anglo-American world, by economic concerns and the consequences of economic change and located within a context where market forces and relationships are prioritized. An increasingly rampant, unconstrained and global Anglo-American capitalism, a neoliberal project of worldwide economic deregulation and free markets (Grey,

1998), combining with rapid technological change, has brought in its trail increased inequalities, insecurities, exclusions and dislocations, while at the same time under-mining the post-war welfare state with its principles of solidarity, shared risk and redistribution. Nation states, increasingly powerless to control free-booting capital, instead increasingly seek to lure it to their shores through the offer of productive, educated and compliant labour forces, consisting of women and men in their 'prime working years' (i.e. 25–50) (for a discussion of the compression of employment onto this age group and, more generally, parental employment trends, see Brannen et al., 1997; Deven et al., 1998). Early childhood services are now seen as one way to ensure the availability of such labour forces, both here and now and in the future. In the words of a recent American report, which resonates in the United Kingdom also,

> As the global economy takes hold, politicians and business leaders — **heretofore largely uninterested in young children** — are voicing concern and demonstrating readiness for action. Facing an increasingly competitive global economic market, they are worried about economic productivity. . . . Given this climate, quality early care and education services have been advocated as a cost-effective approach to maintaining a stable, well-prepared workforce today [through providing care for workers' children] — and preparing such a workforce for the future. (emphasis added) (Kagan et al., 1996, pp. 12–13)

But the role of early childhood services is not just understood in directly economic terms. They have a social task to perform too, as part of a larger project which seeks more effective methods of social control to limit the damage caused by deregulated free market capitalism. In sum, as 'money scours the world for the highest return (generating) colossal insecurity, the role of government is to main-tain order in their territories and package their populations into skilled docile workforces with the correct attitudes in the hope that international finance may offer jobs through inward investment' (Atkinson and Elliott, 1998). In this context, not only are services increasingly understood in economic and market terms, but the people working in them are understood as low skilled technicians, whose job it is to act as neutral transmitters (reproducers) of required and predetermined knowledge and values to children and of simplified versions of their technology to parents.

Early Childhood and the Project of Modernity

The current approach to early childhood services is produced not only within a particular economic context. It is also located within a particular philosophical context — the Project of Modernity (Habermas, 1987). Modernity is a historical period beginning in Western Europe in the sixteenth or seventeenth century (there is no agreement on dating) with a series of profound social-structural and intellec-tual transformations, and which achieved maturity as a cultural project during the

Enlightenment, and as a socially accomplished form of life with the growth of industrial society (Bauman, 1991; for a history of modernity, see Toulmin, 1990). Modernity has proposed a way of understanding the world as an objective reality, 'out there' ready to be found and known through the application of rationality and objective scientific method. It has subscribed to a belief in the possibility of linear progress, mastery over nature, absolute truth, rational planning of ideal social orders, universal laws and principles and there being only one possible answer to any question (Bauman, 1991; Harvey, 1989). It has held control, order, predictability and certainty as prime virtues.

It is not my purpose in this chapter to argue that the views of early childhood services outlined above are necessarily wrong or misguided. Nor to dismiss or support Modernity and its ideals. Rather, I want to argue that all of those engaged with early childhood have choices to make, about how we understand what early childhood and its institutions are, can be or should be; that these choices are related to further choices we must make about how we understand who young children are, can be or should be; and that we can also choose whether we want to view the world through the lens of the project of modernity or alternative lenses. This last area of choice is perhaps the most challenging of all since so powerful and deeply embedded are the assumptions of modernity that they permeate not only our society and culture, but us as individuals. So deep indeed are they embedded that we may no longer recognize them as assumptions but take them for granted as the only true way of viewing the world, so avoiding the philosophical chore of deciding what questions to ask in favour of the technical task of finding solutions to taken for granted questions: as the Italian historian Carlo Ginzberg (1999) observes, we live in a world where 'we are constantly being offered solutions before we have asked the critical questions'.

Early childhood institutions (and here I am deliberately choosing the term 'institution' rather than 'service' for reasons that will subsequently become clearer) and the pedagogical and other projects they undertake can never be reduced simply to the merely technical or managerial, for they are always located within the ethical, the philosophical and the political. 'What works?' a question much admired by politicians and policy-makers today, may be *an* important question to ask, but it is not *the* only question with which we need to be struggling. Equally if not more important are such questions as 'what do we think early childhood services are?', 'who do we think young children are?', 'what do we want for our children?' and 'what sort of world do we live in today?'.

Situating Myself

Before proposing an alternative understanding of what early childhood institutions might be, I should sketch in some of the choices I make — where I choose to situate myself — and which lead to this particular understanding. First, I choose to view the world through the lens of the project of postmodernity. Unlike modernity's belief in an objective, knowable, unified world, 'out there', discoverable through the application of reason and scientific method, in the project of postmodernity the world is assumed to be *socially constructed*, with all human beings active particip-ants as co-constructors, engaged in relationship with others in *meaning making* rather than truth finding. Instead of a single true reality, there are many 'perspectival realities', socially and linguistically constructed (Gergen, 1993). Science and scientific method are not rejected but are viewed as one perspective, one type of knowing, the inclusive 'and/also' being preferred to the exclusionary 'either/or'. Postmodernism not only raises questions about representation and legitimation, but sees complex-ity, diversity, context, ambivalence, uncertainty, multiplicity as features of the world to recognize and value rather than to control out of existence:

> What the controversial idea of postmodernity most often refers to (even if only tacitly) is first and foremost the ineradicable plurality of the world; plurality which is not a temporary station on the road to the not-yet attained perfection . . . but the constitutive quality of existence. . . . The world is ambivalent, though its colonizers and rulers do not like it to be such. Certainties are no more than hypotheses, histories no more than constructions, truths no more than temporary stations. . . . Ambivalence is not to be bewailed. It is to be celebrated. It is the limit to the power of the powerful. (Bauman, 1991, pp. 98 and 179)

Politically, my understanding of what early childhood institutions can or should be is shaped by three concerns. First, the state of contemporary democracy. The collapse of Communism has made the problems in contemporary liberal democracy all the more apparent, in particular widespread disengagement and disillusionment with traditional politics and political institutions, and increasing cynicism about the role and performance of the elected representatives who populate these institutions. One response has been to reform these institutions, for example, through decen-tralization of power from the central institutions of the nation state; another, the emergence of new forms of political action, 'new social movements'. But are there other possibilities for the practice of democracy, new forms of democratic institution which can also develop a more inclusive political process addressing issues that affect the lives of everyone, children and adults alike?

Second, the importance of what the American political scientist Robert Putnam calls 'social capital' — trust, reciprocity, respect and other features of social organ-ization which, he demonstrates in his study of Italian regions, are an important condition for the economic and political success of a society. Putnam (1993) argues that a major condition for producing social capital is extensive networks of civic associations, which constitute 'an essential form of social capital', instilling in their members habits of cooperation, solidarity and public-spiritedness; 'the denser such networks in a community, the more likely that its citizens will be able to cooperate for mutual benefit' (p. 173). The types of civic associations that Putnam identifies are very much adult-focused: football clubs, choral societies, cooperative organiza-tions and so on. Can this concept be extended to institutions involving children?

Third, the major challenges facing us today are not only economic perform-ance and competitive ability. A comprehensive agenda of such challenges might also include problems of coexistence, reflected in a century of genocides and wars of unparalleled magnitude and barbarity, environmental degradation of life-threatening proportions, growing inequalities and social exclusion with huge numbers of people living in abject and unnecessary squalor and poverty, and the need for a form of capitalism that can offer a better balance between economic productivity (narrowly defined) and the well-being of people, society and the physical environment. These challenges, with their complexities, inter-relationships and difficult judgments, call for people — children and adults — with analytical, reflective and ethical abilities, capable of problematizing, deconstructing and reconstructing, challenging dominant discourses and doing this always in democratic and dialogic relationship with others. Simply to produce successive generations of highly productive workers (productivity being narrowly defined in terms of return on capital and shareholder value), increasingly committed to and enmeshed in long working hours and the workplace, may win capital investment — but in the process degrade our ability to care for ourselves, others and our environment. So can we produce not only productive workers but critical thinkers, with the ability and courage to think and act for themselves?

Who Do We Think Young Children Are?

Before considering how these perspectives contribute to the production of a particular understanding of what early childhood institutions might be, one final piece of the argument needs putting in place. How, as human agents, we choose to understand or construct early childhood institutions is related to how we choose to understand young children and early childhood. The idea that childhood (like institutions for children) is a social construct — that 'children's lives are lived through childhoods constructed for them by adult understandings of childhood and what children are and should be' (Mayall, 1996, p. 1) — is hardly original, indeed has now reached the status of an 'industry standard' and has been the subject of much writing and research in the vibrant sociology of childhood (cf. Prout and James, 1997). Not only does it draw our attention to our subjectivity, as adults, in studying children, but it questions all ideas of the essential or universal child, passing through an immutable and standardized sequence of 'child development'.

We can say that the construction of the early childhood service increasingly dominant in the current economic context and driven by the project of modernity is closely related to an inter-related set of understandings about who the young child is and what early childhood is (for a fuller discussion, see Moss and Petrie, 1997; Dahlberg et al., 1999). First, children are considered to be primarily the private responsibility of parents or, to be precise, of mothers; in our society, we still view the care of children as mainly women's work even now when most mothers are employed. The child–parent relationship becomes more prominent as the welfare state gradually retreats and welfare becomes increasingly privatized and marketized, a process that has been prominent in the early childhood field over the last 15 years.

This process has particularly problematic consequences for children, since they are unable to take full responsibility for their own welfare. It exposes them to the full forces of the market with its inherent inequalities and insecurities. And while the dominant discourse produces parents as *consumers* of marketized services for children, the questions raised by this construction have gone largely unaddressed: if parents are the consumers, what is the position of the children who use and experience services? Should *children's* access to services depend on the ability of *parents* to use the market? Are the interests of children and parents necessarily always commensurate? Should parental choice be the pre-eminent value in considering services for children? To what extent is choice a realistic concept, given that many services are already rationed by cost, location, availability and knowledge? Overall, is the market an appropriate model for children's services, with its basic function of rationing resources, its inevitable consequence of winners and losers and its assumption that consumers and users are synonymous?

So, as a society we seem very confident talking about the relationship between the child and their parents within the nuclear family. But when it comes to the relationship between children and society, or more broadly children, parents and society, we are much less certain: in fact, I would argue that there is no clear understanding of this relationship, nor of children as a social group in society. The questions here are about whether children themselves, individually *and* as a social group, have a direct relationship with society and its institutions, raising issues of rights, citizenship and participation.

To sum up, therefore, the first dominant idea constructs children as dependent and privatized, as being in relationship to the family, and in strongly individualistic terms — but neither as a member of a social group nor in relation to society.

The *second* widespread and influential idea about children can be illustrated if we consider how children usually make the news. Look at the newspapers any week and see how children are represented: as the subjects of abuse or the perpetrators of crimes, as failing pupils or unruly nuisances. Look too at the pervasive and unproblematized use of terms like 'children in need', not only in legislation and service delivery, but in media events and fund raising. (Most Scandinavians do not use the term 'children in need', because they see it constructing the child in a way that they choose to avoid.)

In addition to the privatized and dependent child, therefore, we construct the child as poor, weak and innocent, or as primitive, uncontrollable and threatening. Although apparently opposites, both of these constructions are closely linked: both draw on ideas about the child as nature or as a *tabula rasa*, starting with and from nothing, *becoming* a realized, socialized and adult human being. The metaphor for *childhood* is a ladder of development, from incompleteness to maturity, climbing out of childhood into adulthood; while the metaphor for the *child* is an initially empty vessel, to be filled over time with knowledge, identity and correct values poured in by adults — the young child as re-producer.

In this construction, education is usually understood to mean the transmission or depositing of an established and agreed body of existing knowledge, what Freire (1985) calls the banking concept of education in which 'knowledge is a gift bestowed by those who consider themselves knowledgeable on those they consider know nothing' (p. 46). It is also understood very much in foundational terms, of equipping young children for what will follow, to be judged in terms of long-term outcomes. In this outcome-driven approach, the concern is less with the childhood that young children are living, and mainly with the school children and adults they will become:

> events and experiences hold significance only if our narratives of education and child development name them as stepping stones on the paths towards positive or negative developmental outcomes. ... [We] value activities that we believe will have a long-term payoff at the expense of activities that seem frivolous or pointless because they are not correlated with success later in life. (Tobin, 1997, pp. 13–4)

Viewed in this way, we value childhood increasingly in terms of its contribution to adulthood, not as a life stage of importance in its own right. We treat children as 'becoming' adults, meriting our care and protection, but not as equal human beings. The early childhood service is the means for processing young children into adults, as well as for producing other adult-related outcomes, such as 'childcare'.

There are of course many other understandings or constructions of children and childhood — what they are, can be and should be — produced within different temporal, historical and philosophical contexts. I want to look at one set of constructions which might be summarized as follows:

- Children as citizens, with a recognized place in society as well as the family;
- Children as social actors, active participants, with a voice to be listened to;
- Children as learners from birth, as co-constructors of knowledge and identity;
- Children as critical thinkers, with ideas and theories that need taking seriously and the capability to think and act for themselves;
- Children as powerful pedagogues, within a pedagogy of relationships in which children are understood to be actively engaged in co-constructing their own and others' knowledge and identities.

This understanding of children is summed up for me by Loris Malaguzzi (1993) the first head of the early childhood services in Reggio-Emilia:

> Our image of children no longer considers them as isolated and egocentric, does not see them only engaged in action with objects, does not emphasize only the cognitive aspects, does not belittle feelings or what is not logical and does not consider with ambiguity the role of the affective domain. Instead, our image of the child is rich in potential, strong, powerful, competent and, most of all, connected to adults and other children. (p. 10)

The view of children as co-constructors (rather than re-producers) of knowledge is fundamentally important. It is quite at odds with the 'banking model' of learning and the child as re-producer of predetermined knowledge. It understands that 'what children learn, all their knowledge, emerges in the process of self and social construction since children do not passively endure their experience but become active agents in their socialization, co-constructed with their peers' (Rinaldi, 1993, p. 105). It is a view of children as meaning makers, but always in relationship with others, seeking *an* answer, rather than *the* answer.

The Early Childhood Institution as a Forum in Civil Society

So, how might we understand early childhood institutions as fit places for active, co-constructing young children, who are citizens with relationships and a recognized place both inside and outside the family? In a recent book (Dahlberg et al., 1999) colleagues and I have proposed and explored the construction of early childhood institutions as having the potential to be forums or public spaces located in civil society where children and adults can engage together in projects of social, cultural, political and economic significance.

'Civil society' has several contradictory meanings in political science. Our understanding of 'civil society' is similar to the definition of Cohen and Arato (1992) — 'a sphere of social interaction between economy and state, composed above all of the intimate sphere (especially the family), the sphere of associations (especially voluntary associations), social movements and forms of public communication' (p. ix). We would, however, view the 'intimate sphere' as a distinct and fourth area, apart from but in relationship with the state, the economy and civil society. 'Civil society' can therefore be seen as a place between or alongside these other three areas, and their institutions (government at different levels; the market, work organizations and trades unions; households and families). It is where individuals can engage together or associate outside the formal structures of state, market and family, in activities of common interest which may be of many kinds — cultural, social, economic, and political: 'the words "civil society" name the space of uncoerced human association and also the set of relational networks — formed for the sake of family, faith, interest and ideology — that fill up that space' (Walzer, 1992, p. 89).

'Forums' or 'public spaces' we see as an important constituent of civil society, overlapping with Putnam's idea of 'civic associations', contributing to the generation of 'social capital'. They are actual physical spaces where people can come together to engage in activities of common interest and collective action. But they should also be understood as providing through their openness, their activities and their procedures possibilities and opportunities for participation, encounter, dialogue and critical enquiry. In short they provide a location for the practice of democracy, serving 'to recapture the idea of critical democracy and community' (Giroux, 1989, p. 201). Forums or public spaces provide opportunities for active citizenship, through engaging in dialogue about issues of social, cultural, political and economic significance. By doing so, people can 'share their stories and struggle together within social relations' (ibid.) so as to deepen their understanding of these issues; they can have their say in the 'formulation, stipulation and adoption' of decisions about matters of public importance (Benhabib, 1992). An active democracy requires this type of engagement by active citizens in forums or public spaces, which can therefore be understood as important democratic institutions.

Our understanding is that early childhood institutions can be understood and produced as forums or public spaces in civil society: but they are *not* inherently so. Once again, it is important to stress that we have to make choices about how we understand and produce these institutions. *What they are, their role and purposes, is not self evident.*

What Are the Projects of the Early Childhood Institution?

There are many possible answers to this question. We should never take for granted what these projects are. The choice must ultimately be the subject of continuous, participatory and critical processes of democratic debate and decision making. In conclusion, I want to focus on possible *political* projects. By doing so I am not implying that social, cultural or economic projects are any the less important; but I want to compensate for the neglect of this political dimension in most early childhood discourse. And within the many possible political projects, I want to foreground two areas — the practice of democracy and emancipation.

Early childhood institutions have the possibility of being new political institutions for the practice of democracy, where people (parents, politicians, practitioners, researchers — and children) 'come together to speak, to engage in dialogue, to share their stories and to struggle together within social relations that strengthen rather than weaken possibilities for active citizenship' (Giroux, 1989, p. 201). About what sort of issues? A long list could be drawn up, but three areas seem immediately important: questions about childhood (e.g. What do we want for our children? What is a good childhood? Who do we understand young children to be?); about pedagogical work (e.g. Do we really see the child? What do we understand by pedagogical work, and by good pedagogical work?) and about parenthood (e.g. What constitutes a good balance between employment and caring? Are current conditions of employment conducive to satisfying parenthood? What are the responsibilities of women and men with respect to children and their care?). Through producing a space to address such questions, the early childhood institution can promote a vivid, visible and critical pedagogical practice and a politics of childhood and parenthood whose starting point is an insistence on the public importance of these matters.

Closely related to this democratic project is what might be called an emancipatory project, understood as supporting the ability of children and adults to be critical thinkers, with the confidence, capability and motivation to think and act for themselves. A pedagogy based on co-construction, in which children's ideas and theories are always treated seriously but not unquestioningly is an important part. Emancipatory practice also finds expression in other ways: by making pedagogical practice the subject of constant public dialogue, analysis and reflection, where the purpose is to deepen understanding rather than evaluate against some universal norm or standard; and by creating a forum for the development of a politics of childhood and parenthood.

Many early childhood institutions have engaged in democratic or emancipatory projects, without necessarily labelling their activities in this way. But some of the most important and sustained examples can be found in the early childhood institutions in the Northern Italian city of Reggio-Emilia, which over recent years have acquired international renown. As the quotation at the beginning of this chapter makes clear, they grew as part of an explicitly political and emancipatory project, to challenge fascism and 'to nurture and maintain a vision of children who can think and act for themselves'. Reggio has also produced over the years some important 'pedagogical tools' that sustain a vibrant, open and rigorous democratic and emancipatory practice: the procedure of pedagogical documentation, the role of specialist staff such as *atelierista* and *pedagogista*, the time built into the pedagogues' working week to analyse, debate and reflect on pedagogical practice (cf. Edwards et al., 1998; Dahlberg et al., 1999).

But these technical features are the surface manifestations of something much deeper, a pedagogical practice located in a profound understanding of young children in relation to the world and a philosophical perspective which in many respects can be understood as postmodern.

Some of the elements of that practice, understanding and perspective include: choosing to adopt a social constructionist approach; challenging and deconstructing dominant discourses, realizing the power of these discourses in shaping our thoughts and actions, including the field of early childhood pedagogy; rejecting the prescription of rules, goals, methods and standards, and in so doing risking uncertainty and complexity; having the courage to think for themselves in constructing new discourses and, in so doing, daring to make the choice of understanding the child as a rich child, a child of infinite capabilities, a child born with a hundred languages; building a new pedagogical project, foregrounding relationships and encounters, dialogue and confrontation, reflexion and critical thinking; border-crossing disciplines and perspectives, replacing either/or positions with an and/also openness; and understanding the contextualized and dynamic nature of pedagogical practice, which problematizes the idea of a transferable 'programme' or a universal project (Dahlberg et al., 1999).

What Reggio and other examples show is that we can choose to go beyond early childhood *services* reproducing predetermined outputs and premised on relationships between giver and taker, provider and purchaser, technician and passive recipient. Instead, we can choose to have early childhood institutions — places *for* children, for the celebration of plurality rather than the application of standardization, providing opportunities for democratic and emancipatory practice for citizens, opportunities that citizens (children and adults) may determine as social actors in relationship with others, opportunities that may produce outcomes that are unexpected and subversive, challenging and transformatory, ambivalent and wondrous.

References

ATKINSON, D. and ELLIOTT, L. (1998) 'Anxious? Insecure? You'll get used to it' in The *Guardian*, 6 June.

BAUMAN, Z. (1991) *Modernity and Ambivalence*, Cambridge: Polity Press.

BENHANBIB, S. (1992) *Situating the Self*, Cambridge: Polity Press.

BRANNEN, J., MOSS, P., OWEN, C. and WALE, C. (1997) *Mothers, Fathers and Employment*, London: Department for Education and Employment.

COHEN, J. and ARATO, A. (1992) *Civil Society and Political Theory*, Cambridge, MA: The MIT Press.

DAHLBERG, G. (1995) Everything is a beginning and everything is dangerous: Some reflections on the Reggio Emilia experience', Paper given at an international seminar *Nostalgio del Futuro* in honour of Loris Malaguzzi, Milan, October.

DAHLBERG, G., MOSS, P. and PENCE, A. (1999) *Beyond Quality in Early Childhood Education and Care; Postmodern Perspectives*, London: Falmer Press.

DEVEN, F., INGLIS, S., MOSS, P. and PETRIE, P. (1998) *State of the Art Review on the Reconciliation of Employment and Family Life and Quality in Care Services*, London: Department for Education and Employment.

EDWARDS, C., GANDINI, L. and FORMAN, G. (eds) (1998) *The Hundred Languages of Children*, 2nd edn., Norwood, NJ: Ablex.

FREIRE, P. (1985) (English edn.) *Pedagogy of the Oppressed*, Harmondsworth: Penguin Books.

GERGEN, K. (1993) 'Towards a postmodern psychology', in KVALE, S. (ed.) *Psychology and Postmodernism*, London: Sage.

GINZBURG, C. (1999) *History, Rhetoric and Proof*, Waltham, MA: Brandeis University.

GIROUX, H. (1989) *Schooling for Democracy: Critical Pedagogy in the Modern Age*, London: Routledge.

GREY, J. (1998) 'Bad times coming', in The *Guardian*, 27 May.

HABERMAS, J. (1987) *The Philosophical Discourse of Modernity*, Cambridge: Polity Press.

HARVEY, D. (1989) *The Condition of Postmodernity*, Oxford: Blackwell.

JAMES, A. and PROUT, A. (eds) (1997) *Constructing and Deconstructing Childhood: Contemporary Issues in the Sociological Study of Childhood*, 2nd edn. London: Falmer Press.

KAGAN, S., COHEN, N. and NEUMAN, M. (1996) 'Introduction: The changing context of American early care and education', in KAGAN, S. and COHEN, N. (eds) *Reinventing Early Care and Education: A Vision for a Quality System*, San Francisco: Jossey-Bass.

KATZ, L. (1993) 'What can we learn from Reggio-Emilia?', in EDWARDS, C., GANDINI, L. and FORMAN, G. (eds) *The Hundred Languages of Children*, Norwood, NJ: Ablex.

MAYALL, B. (1996) *Children, Health and the Social Order*, Buckingham: Open University Press.

MALAGUZZI, L. (1993) 'For an education based on relationships', *Young Children*, 11/93, pp. 9–13.

MOSS, P. and PETRIE, P. (1997) *Children's Servies: Time for a New Approach*, London: Institute of Education University of London.

PUTNAM, R. (1993) *Making Democracy Work: Civic Traditions in Modern Italy*, Princeton NJ: Princeton University Press.

RINALDI, C. (1993) 'The emergent curriculum and social constructivism', in EDWARDS, C., GANDINI, L. and FORMAN, G. (eds) *The Hundred Languages of Children*, Norwood, NJ: Ablex.

TOBIN, J. (1997) 'The missing discourse of pleasure and desire', in TOBIN, J. (ed.) *Making a Place for Pleasure in Early Childhood Education*, New Haven CT: Yale University Press.

TOULMIN, S. (1990) *Cosmopolis: The Hidden Agenda of Modernity*, Chicago: University of Chicago Press.

WALZER, M. (1992) 'The civil society argument', in MOUFFE, C. (ed.) *Dimensions of Radical Democracy: Pluralism, Citizenship, Community*, London: Verso.

14 Early Childhood Education in the Postmodern World

Philip Gammage

Background and Context

Childhood

'Childhood' is largely a social construct. In ways connected with our own experience and values, we recognize it, label it, hold expectations of it. It is not a fixed entity for all time, but socially shaped and identified by us within a collective milieu of beliefs. Historically, different societies have invested different meanings in it at different times and the period called 'childhood' has varied through the generations, depending partly on religious belief, upon the rites of passage at puberty and the acknowledged livelihood activities and apparent lifespan of the group concerned. In the past, some religious groups, such as Christian Puritans, saw all children as born into the 'seedbed of sin' and took it as their firm duty to ensure early (and avowedly rigid) discipline as part of the path to grace. However, some groups have viewed children as inherently 'innocent' and have taken steps to protect that presumed innocence. Paradoxically, at some times and in some societies, both views have been held simultaneously, as, for instance, in Victorian England when a combination of sentimentality, genuine concern and strict discipline all jostled for a place in parts of the public psyche, if not within individual value systems themselves.

Whatever the case, childhood was a dangerous time and death, disease and malnutrition frequent visitors, so that, even with large families, the reality was that many a child had to face the likelihood of an early grave. Consequently much religious teaching focused on obedience and the need for early redemption. Living with the likelihood of death is not an historical phenomenon, either. Even to this day it is estimated by UNICEF that some eight million children a year die 'unnecessarily' throughout the world, because of the exigencies of poor diet, inadequate housing and medicine, inappropriate labour and conditions of cruelty; a serious indictment of the world of adults in the new millennium!

Nevertheless, many parents in the world would appear to view their children somewhat more kindly than did the early Puritans and perhaps less naively than certain classes of Victorian England. However, even in countries of relative affluence certain forces of modernity may operate in ways which are seen as breaking the trust implied by the 'innocence' of childhood. For instance, despite the undoubted benefits of information technology, the all-powerful pervasiveness of the media and their centrality in the postmodern world cause serious worries. There are those for whom the media are at times held in some distaste, since exposure to the worst aspects are thought to have devastating effects upon children's attitudes and values. In short, there are people who claim that childish 'innocence' may actually need to be actively protected to some degree, though usually any protection is left to the discretion of the family and active censorship eschewed in most western societies. Nevertheless control of the media, whether it lies in the hands of big business 'overlords', or in the hands of unscrupulous politicians, is an issue which will increasingly affect us all and our children. The child's knowledge will be crucially dependent upon and filtered through systems over which the ordinary family has little control.

The period of childhood innocence is also physically shorter than in the past; for, since the late nineteenth century, medical records in the western world document the 'secular trend in decline of age at menarche'. This means that girls reach puberty earlier than they did. In Britain the estimated 'decline' is from about 17 plus years in the late 1880s to about 12 plus years now. Boys also show a similar, but somewhat later aged, trend, reaching physical maturity earlier than their predecessors. The implications of this earlier maturity are considerable. For instance, normal variations in age of menarche would ensure that a significant proportion of girls in primary school (perhaps 20 per cent) have reached some form of sexual maturity; a feature not countenanced by those involved in early schooling a century ago. It is certainly a feature not lost on advertisers and manufacturers; many of whom are increasingly 'geared' to exploiting the earlier sexual maturity of the modern child.

The Family

Concepts of (and the actual structures of) families are also changing throughout the world. Within the European Union as a whole about 80 per cent of parents with children still at home are married, though many of these are remarriages and there are huge variations between countries (Ruxton, 1996). In the UK, it is said that just over half of all children reared in families after the year 2000 will be brought up in step-families of one sort or another. Moreover, throughout the richer parts of the world sizes of families are falling (currently about 1.8 children per family in the UK) and the rates of divorce are increasing rapidly, with the current expectations of about a 40 per cent demise in contracted marriages within UK, USA, Australia and Canada and with one in two children born in Sweden and Finland being already born 'out of wedlock'. (In the UK and France, it is approximately one in three.) Indeed, a strong 'Scandinavian pattern' now is for cohabitation, children and then (possibly) a marriage contract, in that order.

It may now be, as Penelope Leach (1996) says, that FUNCTIONS are markedly more important than STRUCTURES when one considers the role of the modern family; those functions being primarily the ones of good quality attachment, concern

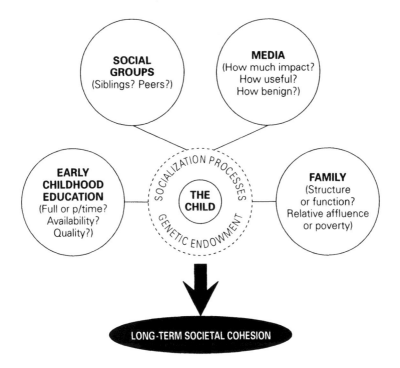

Figure 14.1:   Influences on and from the child

and support for the child in a way characteristic of 'going that extra mile', or being on the child's side. There is an enormous weight of evidence from the social and medical sciences showing how crucial these functions are for later adult self-esteem and survival.

Add to the foregoing the rapid change in our knowledge of genetics and of medicine, our potential to eliminate certain diseases like cystic fibrosis, perhaps even certain forms of cancer; our ability to save and nurture the extremely handi-capped; our ability to prolong our reproductive capacity; and so on. Thus one sees a context in which a great deal of the change in the values, in the family itself, in the welfare of children and in the roles of women force societies to plan differently for their children than they might have done previously. In short, early childhood in the postmodern world occurs within the context of fast changing values and some-what fluid social structures; and needs addressing as one of the major issues of our time (see Figure 14.1). This is particularly appropriate when one realizes that many care systems grew up haphazardly and that they (and systems of formal education) were 'designed' at a time when salient definitions were largely male originated and male dominated, when most mothers were invariably at home 'servicing' the family, when divorce was rare, when fulltime male employment was the norm and when television and the Internet did not exist!

Jobs, Technology and Early Childhood

Most of the countries comprising the 29 members of OECD (and many others) now recognize that approximately the first eight years of life constitute a meaningful period which can legitimately be called 'early childhood'. Some (e.g. Spain since 1993) have actually legislated for certain types of care and provision from birth, and the Scandinavian countries, in particular, have enviable systems of means-tested provision, of supplementary family support, of maternal and paternal leave from birth and work/creche availability, where needed. This is partly because, in many technologically advanced countries, whether we approve or not, women are accessing the work force in ways essential for the economy and at times faster and in more adaptable styles than are men. Indeed, the notion of a job for life, or even any job at all, may well become an impossible dream for many of us during the coming century, perhaps especially so for certain groups of less educated men. Information technology is already altering national boundaries, facilitating the movement of money and resources in ways which may limit the ability of certain cadres to 'work' at all! Heavy industries are shrinking, becoming more fully mechanized, or simply outmoded, and with them are lost the chances of jobs for many who are not intellectually, technically or situationally 'flexible'. Yet work, in some form or other, appears to matter for humans as a psychological necessity. There is much in it which relates to identity, self-worth and happiness, as well as to the actual stability of society. (Collective personal self-worth and societal stability would seem to be critically interrelated.)

We know also that, throughout the world, these advances in technology, increased mobility, economic pressures, changes in values, the availability of more efficient contraception, the longer life expectation (to cite but a few) may well be concomitant aspects to that earlier cited rise in divorce and to the changing expectations of relationships between males and females. This pattern of change is remarkably similar and consistent throughout the western world; and many governments are only just beginning to grasp that new styles of work, of family, of education, of mobility, of corporate finance interact with value systems in ways which will profoundly affect societal cohesion and notions of society itself in the longer term.

Family Values and Socialization

In the postmodern world, many definitions and values are seen as less fixed and are sometimes exposed as not 'God-given', but simply designed to support certain groups at the expense of others. Profound questions lie at the heart of standard or traditional assumptions about what constitutes a 'family', and what constitutes a stable relationship. Terms like 'family values' can be shown to be very situationally and contextually specific and not as enduring as some might think. (Are the much-lauded Victorian family values desirable, when they demeaned, elevated and infantilized women all at the same time?) At the same time, there is a wealth of evidence to show that children who experience family disruption, loss of consistent love and, especially those who suffer from the poverty associated with some forms of family breakdown, are generally more likely to suffer social, educational and health problems than a comparable sample whose families remain intact. This is not to apportion blame: simply to ask who helps support, socialize and educate this growing group of children; and what systems of support and education must be altered and unified to ensure a caring, cohesive and just society? At the 'sharp end' of the economy and of social order it might appear that time is not on our side and that massive reappraisals of work patterns and our responsibilities to our children are in order (Ball, 1994 and RSA, 1998).

Other features of postmodernism, too, may be causing massive changes.[1] Typical of these is that our perspectives on intelligence appear to be undergoing radical modification: likewise our views of male and female 'innate' abilities. Despite that, it is still clear that some politicians and policy advisers have not always 'caught up with research' and persist in outdated views. They perceive care and education as separate, see care as something which is largely the province of a mother at home and education itself as some simple 'transmissive', or didactic, 'telling them' process not connected with rates of development, choice, opportunity or self-esteem. They adopt crude measures of 'standards', or vie with other countries in inappropriate comparisons of achievement, without sufficient examination of the cultural context in which they occur. Such crude comparisons often flout the first laws of comparative study and of ecological awareness. They ignore the interaction of a host of contextual cultural variables; they persist in an over-simplistic input–output view of education and care in which the subtleties of process and individual empowerment are lost. Such perspectives have little real connection to the need for flexibility, social adaptation or creativity in modern societies. They tend to be short-term, 'output myopic', focusing on the immediate product, rather than the importance of the long-term, of the fundamental need to establish enduring dispositions in children which will help them enquire and take responsibility for themselves. They certainly do not take sufficient account of, for instance, the developmental and social indices of early reading failure in boys, or the later burgeoning, sporadic, even endemic, male school drop-out and unemployment in the twenty-first century. They may misjudge or fail to recognize the social justice in or the power of the 'women's movement', usually do not see that individual self-worth is the essential weapon in any fight against crime, drug addiction and dictatorship. They rarely acknowledge the changing family as a feature of such staggering importance that providing new ways of helping secure and support all our children should be our first preoccupation, outweighing the politics of defence, power and economy.

Despite the British rhetoric of equality and 'entitlement' (one of the oft-quoted vestments girding the 1988 Education Reform Act) many have not even begun to reach the stage, which certain Victorian philanthropists did understand, whereby we secure the availability of good care and education as one of the critical means to a just and humane society. If they do perceive some of this 'through a glass darkly', then at best they see children as little bits of economic investment, as competitors who will take the country forward in some ill-defined (and often inappropriate) race to the top! Yet, one might argue that just and loving treatment of all our children are issues which will totally alter the power and the economy of the society AND its potential for genuine human development in the future.

The Mass Media

Within all this the influence of the mass media (as touched on earlier) is pervasive and sustained, often catering for the lowest common denominator in public taste, usually recognizing, despite occasional worthy government or public attempts to constrain it, that profit is the abiding central concern of those involved. British children of three years or so watch about 23 hours of television and video per week, dropping to about 16 hours during primary age. In the USA, however, it may be as high as 40 hours prior to school age. Television may have much to commend it, but media violence is an issue of general public concern in many countries, though the 'jury is still out' in respect of its impact (Boyer, 1991; Gulbenkian, 1995). Peer groups, once thought to be the province mainly of teenage life, have been clearly found to have a marked impact upon the clothes, toy, cereal (and even possibly of the drug) choices of the young, ably assisted, of course, by images from marketing and the media.

Overall, it may be that to survive as a society with dignity and integrity (as well as economic success) through the next millennium we will require consistent, caring, benign educational influences on our children, those that emanate from well-trained staff in schools or institutions of family and child care working in concert with the family and the community. We will need to recognize how crucial are the first five or six years of life and invest in it at the same rate as we have, hitherto invested in the later stages. As Reiner reportedly said to US governors in a convention in the USA, 'Why does the money only kick in after it's mostly no use?' (Lewis, 1997).

Constraints and Policies

Paying the Piper

One cannot assume a direct connection between a country's (or state's) wealth and its overall willingness to invest in public education. For instance, 'Most US states have a higher capability of providing educational services than many countries that have provided far more for their children' (Svestka, 1995). Nor does the simplistic examination of GDP proportions spent on education tell us much, since it appears that most countries in the OECD and the European Union spend between about 4 and 8 per cent of the GDP annually on education overall (CERI/OECD, 1996). These figures are also difficult to disaggregate entirely, because different countries allocate their early childhood care budgets in different ways and, in some cases, derive additional monies from different sources placed under other headings than either 'social' or 'education'. Different countries clearly apportion the relative amounts differently within the budget, too, and such apportionments have a massive effect upon the extent and quality of early childhood provision; vide, Denmark, Finland and Norway. These latter have relatively high general income tax bases plus locally (Kommune) raised taxes; and such differences may explain why their early childhood care and educational provision appear so generous in comparison with those of the UK, Australia or USA.

We should also note that different countries have differential levels of spending between one stage of education and another. Traditionally, in most countries, secondary education and further education have taken a major share of the finance. It would appear that there are modest, if urgent, changes now taking place partly to redress this imbalance, particularly as policy makers reappraise the long-term costs of delinquency, crime and associated social breakdown. Such policies include markedly different attitudes to the role of the state in personal welfare. In some countries it is seen as an 'intrusion', or 'nanny state', as its populist description is in the UK. In others it is seen as essential and humane support and almost unquestioned. Such attitudes eventually translate into the ballot box and into the nature of the tax system.

Large heterogeneous countries with different minority, ethnic and migrant groups may have considerably more difficulty in achieving even a modest consensus (e.g. USA or Canada) than might countries that are relatively homogeneous, like Denmark or Finland. For instance, both countries use a relatively high tax base to support extensive 'free' (means-tested) early childhood education, school, university education and health for all their peoples. Philosophical traditions of identity, egalitarianism and unity appear to lie behind such practices. Also different beliefs about the value of children clearly give rise to different emphases and preoccupations for their policy makers.

Common Concerns

From small-scale preliminary analyses for OECD (Gammage and Little, 1995; Gammage, 1997) it appeared that common broadly identifiable concerns could be detected in certain western countries approaching revision (or currently revising) their early years policy. Different cultural traditions must not be minimized, and they together with different economic systems, different ministerial responsibilities and changing attitudes to childhood clearly give rise to different emphases and preoccupations at quite different points (see Figure 14.2).

For instance, Scandinavian traditions of the centrality of a play-based, aesthetically oriented curriculum up to about 7 years or so would not find much favour currently in England, despite the fact that, at later stages, the Scandinavians tend to do better than we do in international comparisons of certain aspects of school achievement (such as reading and foreign languages). It is notable that Finland, with its tradition of 'child-centred' approaches up to age 7 or so, and one

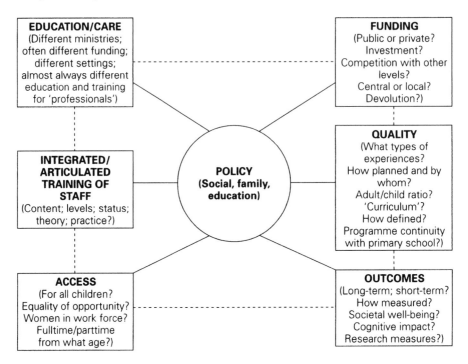

Figure 14.2: Problems of definition and value in ECE

well underpinned with strong oral and musical expectations too, seems to produce more consistent and able forms of literacy than does an England obsessed with reading schemes and base-line tests at age 4. Similarly, France, with its secure 120 year tradition of écoles maternelles for all those two-and-a-half years and above, would find it difficult to understand why Britain persistently lags behind many countries in the education and care of its very young. Perhaps it is because in Britain there is still detectable a tendency to see education 'merely' as a commodity which can be bought and sold.

Countries more clearly defined as social welfare societies (like Denmark) would appear to be able to call upon quite different philosophical beliefs to advocate the care of their youngest and most vulnerable members of society, whereas solutions to potential need in England are often couched in the form 'make-do-and mend', in the language of redress, of supplementary grants, special needs, or of targetting specific geographical areas (zoning). Large-scale philosophical debate about educational principles or ideas seems almost a thing of the past in England; less so in the rest of Europe, North America or Scandinavia. In addition, the British professionals involved (teachers and carers) seem to have been more vilified than understood, have been systematically excluded from policy-making and alienated by policies of crude comparison, over-zealous/inappropriate inspection and fundamental mistrust.

Professional Education

In England teacher education itself has been caught up in this 'blame the teacher' approach and has become allied to the 'input–output' model of business and commerce; and much of the child development and sociology underpinning good professional practice has been deliberately ridiculed by ministers and inspectors alike and effectively all but removed from the initial training curriculum. The language of the education and care debate is more miserable than measured, with certain 'progressive' ideas being publicly labelled as 'toxic' by senior civil servants, such as the Chief Inspector of Schools, in 1998. It may be, too, that Britain is still unable to escape the bones of a class system which once perceived education as a privilege, rather than as one of wholesale commitment to full-cost provision as the essential for a just society, a society capable of real flexibility and the ability to face long-term social change.

A glance at Belgian or Finnish training for teachers and carers of early years shows by comparison how desperately mechanistic the British system has become. It is still possible in the university education departments of, say, Leuven or Oulu to discuss topics such as loving children appropriately, personal motives for entering a caring profession, the role of self-esteem in child development, of the importance of psycho-dynamic theory. The British, however, now seem obsessed with literacy and numeracy 'hours', with refusing to recognize the crucial role of play in the development of the child and are, it is said, even thinking of removing the traditional 'playtime break' for many young children. Indeed, in a recent sample the afternoon playtime break seems to have already disappeared in about 30 per cent of British infant schools (Blatchford, 1998). What would they make of Finnish children's periodic playbreak every fifty minutes, or the relatively short school day?

Policy Emphases

Figure 14.2 is an *aide mémoire*, a map, setting out the key issues and concerns in the form of 'constraints', whilst acknowledging that they are different both in kind and in emphasis. In many cases, too, they have a 'knock-on' effect and are not fully discrete or isolated one from another. For instance, emphasis on cognitive outcomes, rather than social ones, may affect views of quality of education and of access (equality of opportunity) and may, in its extreme form, deny the connection between cognition and emotion in our reasoning. Questions of devolved or central control and accountability will also affect perspectives on equality of opportunity, taxation, local 'community ownership' and funding. However, the fundamental question would seem to be that concerning the division (or integration) of education and care. How might high quality care map onto parents' needs and flow into high quality education? Is it possible to have one without the other? Such questions have a long history throughout the world. They have certainly preoccupied policy makers from the early 1960s (e.g. Head Start, commenced in the USA in 1964), to those of the StartRight committee of the Royal Society of Arts in the UK (Ball, 1994). It would seem possible to provide care that is not especially educative. It is doubtful, however, that high quality early childhood education is possible without involving a measure of high quality care. The arguments are complex and 'culturally embedded', heavily influenced by perceptions of values, individual responsibility, views of attachment, psychological development, and so on. More and more, however, countries are training their early years carers and educators together, recognizing the seamless nature of early learning and of the associated professional tasks. There are many 'turf disputes' and demarcation perceptions yet to be overcome, but the articulation of the two careers is, for many countries, now fact, not fancy.

Research and Childhood

One thing is certain; a wealth of psychological research shows that early learning is crucial (Trevarthen, 1993 and 1994), that the child is massively competent from birth, that appropriate stimulation matters and appears to affect the neuron–synapse connections. The child is uniquely programmed for language development early in life and for massively accelerating learning. But the child also depends upon good modelling. Much evidence, since the days of Bowlby and before, points to the critical role of attachment in emotional health. We may no longer believe that it is solely the MOTHER'S responsibility, but we know that damage to self-esteem and sometimes later adult dysfunctionality does seem to follow disturbed attachment (Holmes, 1993). We also know that failure to provide the right environment can cause long-term personal and sometimes serious social damage, that delinquency may be predicted very early by certain 'markers' which correlate with a lack in the meeting of appropriate child needs (Silver, 1997).

Children themselves are more mature and more sophisticated than in the past, especially in relation to technology, but there are fewer opportunities for unsupervised play activities out of doors. Whilst they may be heavier and more mature than previously, they may also be more vulnerable. Certainly they will often have surprisingly sedentary lives in much of North America, Europe and Australia; and obesity among children has increased and is of some concern to paediatricians and health professionals.

Summary

This brief chapter attempts to remind us that childhood is a social construct critically affected by the ideas, fashions and technology with which we live. It shows that the family is likewise a 'moveable feast', that divorce, 'serial monogamy', cohabitation, step-families and extended families of various types are now commonplace; and that (in Leach's (1996) words) 'structure is less important than function'. It avers that social and economic change is now so fast that there is urgent need to address the question of how we provide love and care for our children from birth. Institutions fit for our children must become commonplace. It shows that certain key 'constraints' or emphases appear to be fashionable and affect policy in many nations. Above all it is concerned to emphasize that care and education are interwoven to such an extent that it no longer makes sense to make separate provision. In short, we now need to deploy the same energy and zeal in establishing good, flexible early childhood provision as our forebears brought to the establishment of elementary education one and two centuries ago.

Note

1 Indeed, the core of 'postmodernism' is essentially this: a time when rules, customs, beliefs, values and ideas are subjected to reanalysis, when a greater awareness of their context-dependent, subjective nature is revealed.

References

BALL, C. (1994) *Start Right: The Importance of Early Learning*, London: Royal Society for the Encouragement of the Arts, Manufacturers and Commerce (RSA).

BLATCHFORD, P. (1998) 'The state of play in schools', *Child Psychology and Psychiatry Review*, **3**, 2, pp. 58–67.

BOYER, E. (1991) *Ready to Learn*, Lawrenceville, NJ: Princeton University Press.

CENTRE FOR EDUCATIONAL RESEARCH AND INNOVATION (CERI) (1996) *Education at a Glance*, OECD Indicators: 4th edn., Paris: OECD.

GAMMAGE, P. (1997) *Early Childhood Care and Education: A Position Paper*, Paris: OECD.

GAMMAGE, P. and LITTLE, J. (1995) *The Importance of Early Childhood Education and Care for Children's Later Development*, Paris: OECD.

GULBENKIAN TRUST (1995) *Children and Violence*, Commissioned report, London: Gulbenkian Foundation.

HOLMES, J. (1993) *John Bowlby and Attachment Theory*, London: Routledge.

LEACH, P. (1996) Talk given at British Association of Early Childhood Education conference (BAECE) sponsored by Boots, in Nottingham, 23 May.

LEWIS, A. (1997) Editorial in *Kappan*, April, **78**, 8.

ROYAL SOCIETY of ARTS (1998) *Redefining Work*, London: RSA.

RUXTON, S. (1996) *Children in Europe*, London: NCH Action for Children.

SILVER, P. (ed.) (1997) *From Child to Adult: The Dunedin Multi-disciplinary Health and Development Study*, Oxford: Oxford University Press.

SVESTKA, S. (1995) *Financing Pre-school for All Children*, ERIC Digest, EDO-PS-95-16, Urbana Champaign, IL: University of Illinois.

TREVARTHEN, C. (1993) *Playing into Reality: Conversations with the Infant Communicator*, Winnicott Studies, **7**, Spring, pp. 67–84, London: Karnak Books

TREVARTHEN, C. (1994) 'How children learn before school', Talk given to BAECE at Newcastle University, 2 November.

15 The Role of Research in Explaining the Past and Shaping the Future[1]

Kathy Sylva

In this chapter I shall draw on four research paradigms for exploring early childhood education and care. Each has been chosen to represent a wide array of research methods; all have contributed, and will contribute, to policy and practice. I shall concentrate on children's learning through the formal and informal curriculum because it is clear that children experience a curriculum (in its broadest sense) in many kinds of preschool settings, including the home.

Longitudinal Studies on the Impact of Early Learning

These studies are known as 'impact' research because they show the effects of early childhood programmes on children's subsequent social and emotional development as well as on their academic achievement. The findings are so well rehearsed that I will devote little space to them. The best example is Schweinhart and Weikart's (1993) powerful research showing the long-term and measurable benefits of attendance at a structured preschool programme (High/Scope) in the two years before school entry. This study is especially rigorous because children were randomly assigned to 'educational' or 'home control' groups when they were 3 years old. The random assignment ensured that differences in outcome at follow-up were not brought about by differences at the start of the programme.

Although an evaluation of just one curriculum taught in just one centre, the High/Scope research is a powerful demonstration of the (potential) benefits of a structured educational programme which includes substantial parent involvement (Figure 15.1). Subsequent cost benefit analysis of the High/Scope programme showed $7,160 (US) was saved for each $1,000 invested in early childhood education. (See Figure 15.2 for detailed costs and benefits.) The message for policy makers all over the world was that investment in high quality early childhood education could save government money later on. Politicians and policy makers, including the World Bank, responded with government funds to support statutory and voluntary initiatives.

Studies of single programmes such as High/Scope would not be scientifically creditable were they not replicated by many others (Daniels, 1995; Howes, Phillips and Whitebrook, 1992; Phillips, McCartney and Scarr, 1987). We now have a

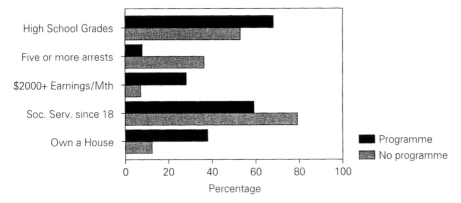

Figure 15.1: High/Scope Perry Preschool Study: Outcomes at age 27
Source: From Schweinhart and Weikart (1993)

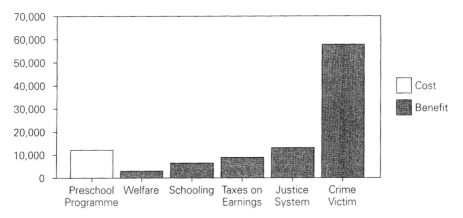

Figure 15.2: High/Scope Perry Preschool Study: Cost and savings (1992 $ value)
Source: From Schweinhart and Weikart (1993)

powerful tool in meta-analysis which draws together numeric results 'from many studies into one statistical frame (Slavin, 1995). Lazar and Darlington's (1982) landmark study used meta-analysis techniques on 11 high quality research studies and found that early preschool provision led to lasting benefits for children. White (1985) used similar techniques on more than 300 studies and came to a similar conclusion. These meta-analyses have shown that the important benefits of pre-school education include social and emotional outcomes, not only academic ones. I have argued (Sylva, 1994) that the most lasting contribution of early education to children's development is the way it shapes motivations, self-concept and social commitment — not formal 'school' skills.

Longitudinal Studies on the Processes which Lead to
Differential Impact on Children's Lives

Although many studies in the first paradigm have shown the benefits of preschool education, researchers who study the comparative effect of different curricula search for educational processes which might bring about the substantial impact found in longitudinal follow-up. Recent research has sought links between the outcomes of preschool experience (e.g. reading, writing or children's self-esteem) and the curricular processes in the preschool learning environments which may give rise to them. Researchers using this second paradigm study children at preschool, then follow them on to primary school and even adulthood. If some children 'do better' (i.e. have better outcomes), their early preschool experiences are investigated to look for educational processes which might be the link between preschool attendance and later success in life.

I'll illustrate this research paradigm with a study carried out by Maria Emilia Nabuco in Portugal (Nabuco and Sylva, 1995). The researchers compared children's outcomes according to which kind of preschool programme they had attended. In this study the effects of three different curricula were studied: the High/Scope, the Modern Movement and the Formal Skills programmes were each implemented in 5 preschools. A large sample of their 'graduates' were followed into their primary schools. Over 220 children participated in the study, first at 15 preschool centres and later when they moved on to 19 primary schools. Results showed that the High/Scope children had higher academic outcomes in primary school (reading and writing). Moreover, the children who had attended Formal Skills preschool programme showed more anxiety and perceived themselves to be less socially

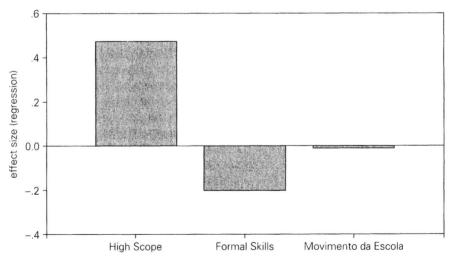

Figure 15.3:   Effect of curriculum on reading
Source: From Nabuco and Sylva (1995)

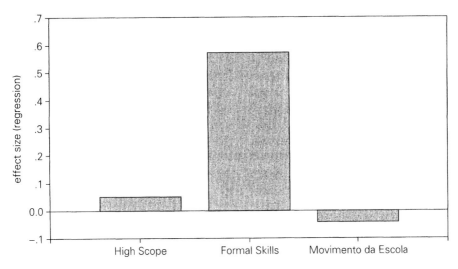

Figure 15.4: Effect of curriculum on anxiety
Source: From Nabuco and Sylva (1995)

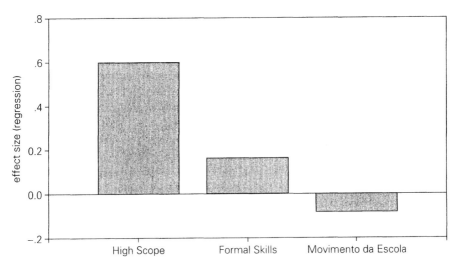

Figure 15.5: Effect of curriculum on writing
Source: From Nabuco and Sylva (1995)

acceptable when they were primary pupils. Perceived acceptance and competence were measured on Harter and Pike's (1983) scale of self-esteem and anxiety was measured on Tremblay's scale of pro-social behaviour (Figures 15.3, 15.4, 15.5, 15.6).

A subtle means of describing the educational processes of 'successful' pre-school programmes is to carry out detailed observations on children and staff. Using systematic observation, Nabuco found differences between the High/Scope

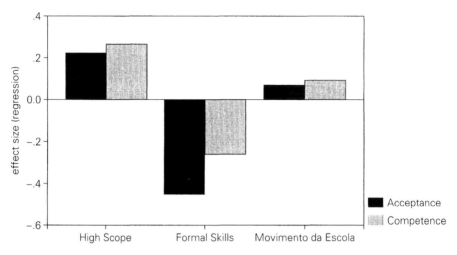

Figure 15.6: Effect of curriculum on acceptance and competence
Source: From Nabuco and Sylva (1995)

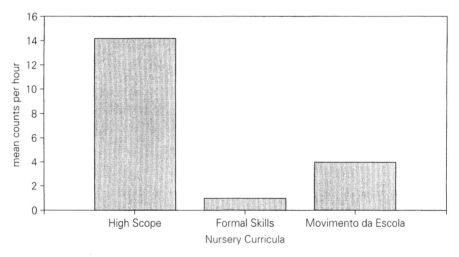

Figure 15.7: Pretend play by curricula
Source: From Nabuco and Sylva (1995)

nurseries and the other two curricula: she observed more songs, rhymes and child-to-child 'chat' in the High/Scope nurseries, activities rich in language and culture, than she found in the other two programmes. Furthermore children in the High/Scope nurseries engaged more in problem solving and enjoyed a balance of choice, both 'free' and 'guided' by adults. Children in the Formal Skills group had little free choice during the preschool day while children in the Modern Movement group had the most choice of all. It appears that the High/Scope nurseries were based on a curriculum process model which encouraged the activities summarized in Figures 15.7–15.13.

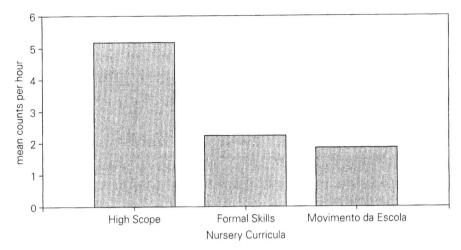

Figure 15.8   Adult leads story/rhyme/song by curricula
Source: From Nabuco and Sylva (1995)

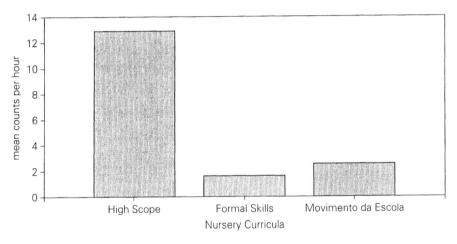

Figure 15.9:   Examination and problem solving by curricula
Source: From Nabuco and Sylva (1995)

Researchers working in the first two paradigms use careful baseline measurement so that the gains found in children's longitudinal development are those which are 'value added' by the preschool stage of education. However, the impact design exemplifed in this second paradigm is an improvement on earlier research such as Schweinhart, Barnes and Weikart's, (1993) in that: (i) it investigates the experience of children from several preschool centres, not just one; (ii) it studies educational processes by observing the day-to-day experiences of preschool children and staff to document curricular processes; (iii) it compares the effects of different programmes. Thus, preschool education, like other forms of education, can be studied using 'indicators' and 'impact' (Riley and Nuttall, 1994).

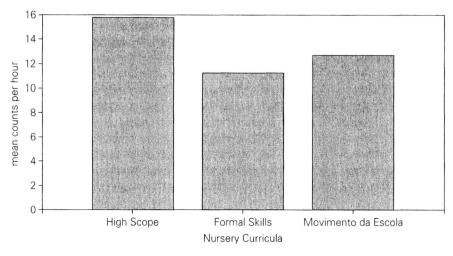

Figure 15.10:   Informal conversation by curricula
Source: From Nabuco and Sylva (1995)

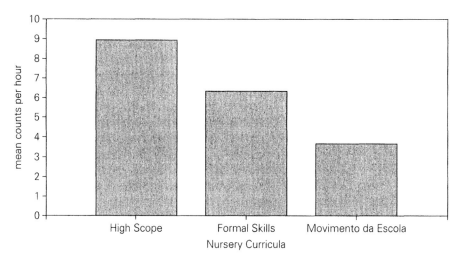

Figure 15.11:   Small scale construction by curricula
Source: From Nabuco and Sylva (1995)

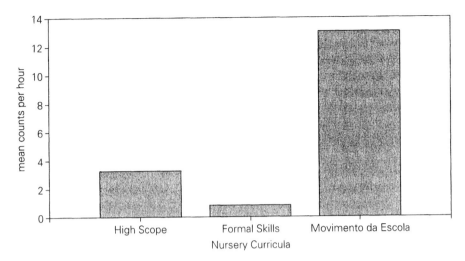

Figure 15.12: Manipulation by curricula
Source: From Nabuco and Sylva (1995)

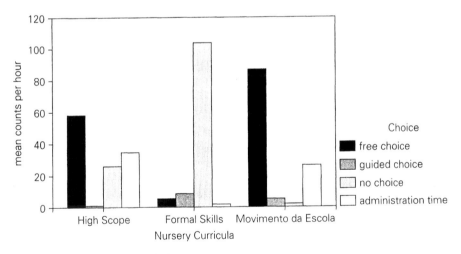

Figure 15.13: Choice by curricula
Source: From Nabuco and Sylva (1995)

Discourse Analysis

Whereas twenty years ago research into learning focused on children solving cognitive tasks on their own, at the start of a new century we focus on children's collaborative learning with adults and peers. This shift reflects the theoretical move away from conceiving of the learner as a solitary being (Piaget) to the learner as a co-constructor in the social context (Vygotsky, 1978). We now investigate children's cognitive development in joint activities which are carried out in everyday settings, particularly those in which cultural 'objects' and cognitive 'tools' are practised and transmitted. This new, more cultural, approach assumes that children develop differently in different cultures and that adults offer different goals and 'tutorials' to them.

> Individuals transform culture as they appropriate its practices, carrying them forward to the next generation in altered form to fit the needs of their particular generation and circumstances. (Rogoff, 1990, p. 98)

The third paradigm is exemplified by the methods of discursive psychology and conversational analysis. These have been used to good effect for analysing knowledge transmission in school (Edwards and Mercer, 1989) and family settings (Edwards and Middleton, 1986). In this paradigm the acquisition of knowledge in its broadest sense is viewed as the product of ordinary, repeated and regulated activities within social domains. School, family and community are places where selected types of discourse are acquired and practised. Researchers studying the 'conversations of learning' use utterances in the spoken text as the unit of analysis, although some very innovative researchers use the conversational activity as the unit of analysis instead of the isolated utterance.

I take as the prototype in this third paradigm, research carried out in Italy by Pontecorvo (1993; 1995). She has recorded, transcribed, then analysed conversations to show how children learn the rules and mores of social life. For example, Pontecorvo has shown how children acquire argumentative structures, a useful cultural tool, which enables them to achieve their aims and find a place in the family hierarchy. She and her colleagues studied children acquiring and using the argumentative roles of 'proposer', 'supporter' and 'defender'.

The following excerpt shows one child acquiring skill at defending herself in a family dispute. The 5-year-old girl, Gaia, resorts to the 'counterfactual' to divert attention from her actual misdeed. In this excerpt you will see that Gaia has drunk all the cola. Her older brother points out this misdeed at at the dinner table and Gaia responds to this by exaggerating her misdeed in order to deflect censure and turn it into a family joke.

Excerpt 8: Coca cola — at the dinner table

[Father, mother, boy (11 years), girl (5 years)]

Father: ma la coca è finita?
But is there no more coke?

Girl: seh::

Boy: Gaia l'ha finita *tu*tta. Oggi pomeriggio l'ha aperta e se l'e *fin*ita
tu:tta qua:nta! (scandendo le parole)
**Gaia has finished it up. Today afternoon she has opened it and
she has finished it all.**

Father: Gaia? Guarda che e tanta quella=quella cosa di
Gaia look, all that coke it is too much

Mother: e U fa male
and it's bad for your health

Girl: no guarda
No look

Boy: e io non mi so' bevuto piu niente
and I couldn't drink anything afterwards

Girl: papa::papa: guarda che ho iniziato stamatti:na
**Daddy, daddy, look I began *this morning* (Gaia lies to exagger-
ate her crime and deflect censure).**

Mother: capi:to
You see

Father: peggio mi sento
That's even worse

Boy: eh infatti
Yeah exactly

Girl: (ride)
(laughs)

Father: no perche nessuno controlla evidentemente
Clearly nobody looks after her

Mother: eh:: no anche perche se anche volessero non riescono . . . a con-
trollare Gaia nel senso che [Gaia e un po':
**Well no because even if they wanted to they can't look after
Gaia 'cause Gaia is a bit. . . .**

Girl: (ridendo) e vero
(laughing) that's true

Boy: eh eh (ridono tutti e due imitando sol) ci ride pure capito
she laughs too, y'see (they both laugh imitating the girl)

From Pontecorvo et al., 1993

In this excerpt, a 5-year-old girl uses an exaggeration to deflect criticism from her parents. Laughingly, her father joins in the joke by saying 'Nobody looks after her', as if it's not really the girl's fault that she consumed all the cola because she is not 'properly' cared for.

'Learning' in Pontecorvo's research refers to the acquisition of social roles, rules and ways to get around them as Gaia did. It's a far cry from the learning of academic skills which is the focus of much research using the paradigms presented earlier. Pontecorvo and her colleagues have shown how social contexts differ in the argumentative topics and techniques adopted by children. At home the children argue about discipline; their parents remind them of household rules (e.g. 'all that coke is too much'). In contrast, children show more mature argument structures in the preschool setting. At school children were observed to use counter-factual structures to describe an imaginary and, as yet, unexperienced future. Why might children use more sophisticated counter-factuals in the nursery? The skill and motive to 'take a stand' must originate in the family, as Pontecorvo has shown, but the 'distancing' required by social life at the nursery might require the use of more mature linguistic and cognitive forms. Again, the informal curriculum of the home and the more formal curriculum of the preschool complement each other but are not the same.

This third research paradigm focuses on children and adults in 'natural' conversations; it goes beneath the surface of behaviour to discover meanings and motives which cannot be discovered by using the first two paradigms. Whilst Nabuco and Sylva studied educational processes in the preschool classroom by using systematic, quantified observation, Pontecorvo's work delves even deeper. By using a combination of quantitative and qualitative analysis, she and her colleagues reveal subtle moves such as Gaia's in complex social interactions. On the basis of this kind of research, we can speculate on means by which children learn about themselves and how to succeed in the social world. Still it is difficult to generalize these findings; larger more systematic studies are needed, perhaps using interventions to devise causal pathways for development.

Narrative Research

There is an exciting new vein of early years research exemplified by Vivian Paley's work (1992) on classroom narratives. In one of her ethnographic books Paley describes the way one teacher (the author) encouraged cooperation amongst her preschool pupils in Chicago through a combination of storytelling and group discussion. It all began when Paley introduced a new classroom rule, a rule which changed social life dramatically . The rule was: 'you can't say *"you can't play"* '. The teacher introduced the rule through stories. Once children explored and accepted this rule, brought alive by the storyteller 'Magpie' and his friends Annabella and Prince Kareem, a transformation in tolerance and cooperation took place amongst children in the classroom. Paley's ethnographic and narrative study shows that the classroom is a micro-culture based on shared, although disputed, meaning constructed partly from class 'stories' told by teacher and elaborated by children.

Paley's informal educational 'intervention' lasted one year and its success is well documented through the case study of her own class. Paley's words speak more clearly than mine:

> . . . . , I am more aware of the voices of exclusion in the classroom. 'You can't play' suddenly seems too overbearing and harsh, resounding like a slap from wall to wall. How casually one child determines the fate of another.
>
> also 'Are you my friend?' the little ones ask in nursery school, not knowing. The responses are questions. If yes, then what? And if I push you away, how does that feel?
>
> By kindergarten, a structure begins to be revealed and will soon be carved in stone. Certain children will have the right to limit the social experiences of their classmates. Henceforth a ruling class will notify others of their acceptability, and the outsiders learn to anticipate the sting of rejection.
>
> Must it be so? This year I am compelled to find out. Posting a sign that reads YOU CAN'T SAY YOU CAN'T PLAY, I announce the new social order and, from the start, it is greeted with disbelief.
>
> Only 4 out of 25 in my kindergarten class find the idea appealing, and they are the children most often rejected. The loudest in opposition are those who do the most rejecting. But everyone looks doubtful in the face of this unaccountable innovation.
>
> Fervently the children search for detours and loopholes as we debate the issues and, eventually, I bring the matter before the older students in the school. They too cannot imagine such a plan working. 'You can't say you can't play?' It is very fair, they admit, but it just isn't human nature.
>
> Fortunately, the human species does not live by debate alone. There is an alternate route, proceeding less directly, but often better able to reach the soul of a controversy. It is story, the children's preferred frame of reference. This time, however, I will be the storyteller, inventing Magpie, a bird who rescues those who are lonely or frightened and tells them stories to raise their spirits.
>
> (From Paley, 1992, pp. 3–4)

So I tell the children a story. 'Some of you know Mrs. Wilson, who teaches with me. Her building shares a backyard with two other buildings. All the children in all the buildings play in that one yard and they follow a simple rule: Everyone can play. When a child comes out the older ones ask, "Do you want to play?" And if someone is mean or fights a lot they tell him or her not to do it and they keep saying it until the child remembers to play nicely.'

The children are fascinated by my story. 'What do you think of Mrs. Wilson's backyard?' I ask.

'It's very nice.' 'Those are really nice kids.' 'I wish I live there.' 'So do I,' I say. 'Could this happen in a classroom?' 'Maybe,' says the boy who worried about my rule causing more fighting. 'It's very fair. But people aren't that fair as the rule is.' 'Anyway, I think it is fair if girls want to play alone,' a girl says softly. 'Or boys can play alone,' adds the boy next to her. 'But what if a girl is curious?' I ask the boy. 'Let's say she has no brothers and she wants to know more about boys. Or what if a boy is curious about the way girls play.'

His answer satisfies everyone: 'Ask the girl if she has a brother and if she says no she can play. And if it's a boy with no sisters then the girls should let him play. That would be fair.' (From Paley, 1992, p. 36)

In Paley's research, the researcher filters what is important in her class from what is not. There are no formal rules about what is entered as 'data' in the computer (as is the case in the first two paradigms) or what is fleeting and ignored. Paley interweaves the imaginary tales of 'Magpie' and 'Mrs Wilson' with real class discussions of how all the children think and feel. What strikes the reader is the vibrant account of the class as a community, a community which argues passionately about and strives towards morality. Paley's work attests to what is possible when an imaginative teacher sets her mind on changing classroom social mores and interactions. Paley's book exemplifies classroom research adhering to a paradigm which does not follow the path of scientific objectivity. The researcher fuses stories, autobiography and classroom fieldnotes to present a holistic, personal account. Perhaps validity is less important than authenticity here?

What Do the Different Research Paradigms Tell Us about Quality in Curriculum?

I turn now to the concept of fitness for purpose. A parent exasperated (or delighted) with their child might look to Pontecorvo for explanation as to how they got that way. A nursery teacher wishing her children to be more accepting of their peers would turn to Vivian Paley's research for practical help and inspiration. An administrator responsible for 20 day care centres might find the work by Nabuco and Sylva useful in deciding which curriculum she might offer in training for staff. And finally, a government debating educational policy would do well to consult the literature on the long-term impact of early education, especially the meta-analytic studies of White and the cost benefit studies of Schweinhart and Weikart, before it came to a decision about national investment in preschool education.

I'll now propose that some research is not fit for certain purposes. Studies which investigate the natural learning experiences of children, such as that of Pontecorvo or Paley, can illuminate good practice, even promulgate it, but cannot demonstrate its impact on children's later development. Furthermore studies in just one classroom, even one as splendid as Paley's, cannot be generalized easily to other classes in other contexts. We need to know when a given programme or strategy can be replicated, by whom, and with what effect. We need more meta-analyses to test for generalizability. Even the striking High/Scope study of Schweinhart and Weikart had to be treated with caution until replication by studies such as Nabuco and Sylva reported here. Few single studies are robust enough, if they stand alone, for drawing sound conclusions on which to base policy. Research must be cumulative, each researcher stands on the shoulders of those who laboured earlier using the same or neighbouring traditions. We make changes in our methods, of course, but these must be placed in scientific jeopardy until they've proved their worth. After replicating, we move to other studies to buttress the concepts and to extend them. We must think always of the social context of the children and adults we study and the community they live in. We need firm descriptions of samples, contexts and procedures so other researchers can replicate, adapt or criticize and so practitioners can know when to generalize safely.

What about using research from other nations or cultures? Importing methods and findings across national or cultural borders can sometimes be done but always with caution (Sylva, 1997); there are tests for cultural acceptability and technical means for validating tools developed in other contexts (see Hadeed and Sylva, 1995). These procedures take time and ingenuity.

Checks on internal and external validity are always necessary — all of the paradigms I have described here must satisfy these requirements. Mindless counting makes poor research but so can ethnographic description where the procedures to guard against bias or self-fulfilling prophecy are not sufficiently strong.

Which methods or researchers tell us the most about curriculum? All of them. My own training was in large samples and 'objective' measures but I hope readers have noted my enthusiasm for qualitative approaches using linguistic and ethnographic methods.

Many studies have been reviewed and some exciting new findings presented. How has research contributed to our history and how might it contribute to future practice?

(i) Quantitative, longitudinal studies have demonstrated that the early learning experiences of children in preschool education *can add enormously* to what they learn at home and in the community. Policy makers, in Britain and elsewhere, have taken heed.

(ii) Some curricula, such as High/Scope have demonstrated that their beneficial effects last into primary school and beyond. However, not all curricula lead to positive gains. Practitioners and local policy makers are beginning to respond to this.

(iii) Important learning in preschool includes learning the conventions of discourse such as arguing. We must include these important areas of development in curriculum objectives along with objectives related to academic skills. Those who develop future curricula will learn much from this line of research.

(iv) The 'moral curriculum' is just as vital as the cognitive one. So far, it is being researched via qualitative methods but quantitative paradigms might be brought to bear on so vital a topic. This will be an exciting challenge for researchers such as myself working in the tradition of enlightened positivism or constructivist psychology.

(v)   An understanding of effective early childhood education will require research carried out in a variety of paradigms because no one can provide answers to all our questions about policy and practice. I would argue however that it is dishonest to call for funding on the basis of the outcome studies described in the first two paradigms, then reject these very paradigms as overly 'positivist' or 'simplistic'. Different paradigms are fit for different purposes.

Note

1 An earlier version of this paper was presented at the 'Start Right' Conference hosted in 1995 by the Royal Society for the Encouragement of the Arts, Manufacturers and Commerce (RSA). I am indebted to conversations about research paradigms with Jerome Bruner, Iram Siraj-Blatchford and Tricia David.

References

DANIELS, S. (1995) 'Can preschool education affect children's achievement in primary school?', *Oxford Review of Education*, **21**, 2, pp. 163–78.

EDWARDS, D. and MERCER, N. (1989) 'Reconstructing context: The conventionalization of classroom knowledge', *Discourse Processes*, **12**, pp. 91–104.

EDWARDS, D. and MIDDLETON, D.J. (1986) 'Conversation and remembering: Constructing an account of shared experience through conversational discourse', *Discourse Processes*, **9**, pp. 423–59.

HADEED, J. and SYLVA, K. (1995) 'Behavioural observations as predictors of children's social and cognitive progress in day care', Paper presented at 5th European Conference on the Quality of Early Childhood Education, Paris.

HARTER, S. and PIKE, R. (1982) 'The pictorial scale of perceived competence and social acceptance for young children', *Child Development*, **53**, pp. 87–97.

HOWES, C., PHILLIPS, D.A. and WHITEBOOK, M. (1992) 'Thresholds of quality: Implications for the social development of children in center-based child care', *Child Development*, **63**, pp. 449–60.

LAZAR, L. and DARLINGTON, R. (1982) 'The lasting effects of early education: A report from the Consortium for Longitudinal Studies', *Monographs of the Society for Research in Child Development*, **47**, 2–3 serial No. 195.

NABUCO, M. and SYLVA, K. (1995) Comparisons between ECERS ratings of individual preschool centres and the results of Target Child Observations: Do they match or do they differ? Paper presented at 5th European Conference on the Quality of Early Childhood Education, Paris.

PALEY, V.G. (1992) YOU CAN'T SAY YOU CAN'T PLAY, Cambridge, MA: Harvard University Press.

PHILLIPS, D., McCARTNEY, K. and SCARR, S. (1987) 'Child-care quality and children's social development', *Developmental Psychology*, **4**, pp. 537–43.

PONTECORVO, C. (1995) 'Argumentation et competence linguistique des jeunes enfants', Presented at the 5th European Conference on the Quality of Early Childhood Education, Paris.

PONTECORVO, C., FASULO, A. and AMENDOLA, S. (1993) 'Learning to argue in family shared discourse about the past', Paper presented at Conference 'Discourse, tools and reasoning', Lucca, Il Ciocco, 2–7 November.

RILEY, K.A. and NUTTALL, D.L. (eds) (1994) *Measuring Quality: Education Indicators. United Kingdom and International Perspectives*, London: Falmer Press.

ROGOFF, B. (1990) *Apprenticeship in Thinking: Cognitive Development in Social Context*, New York: Oxford University Press.

SCHWEINHART, L.J., BARNES, H.V. and WEIKART, D.P. (1993) *Significant Benefits of The High Scope Perry Preschool Study Through Age 2–7*, Ypsilanti, MI: High/Scope Press.

SLAVIN, R.E. (1995) 'Best evidence synthesis: An intelligent alternative to meta analysis', *Journal of Clinical Epidemiology*, **48**, pp. 9–18.

SYLVA, K. (1994) 'School influences on children's development', *Journal of Child Psychology and Psychiatry*, **35**, pp. 135–70.

SYLVA, K. (1997) 'The quest for quality in curriculum', in SCHWEINHART, L. and WEIKART, D. *Lasting Differences: The High/Scope Preschool Curriculum Comparison Study Through Age 23*, Ypsilanti: The High/Scope Press.

TREMBLAY, R.E., VITARO, F. and GAGNON, C. (1992) 'A prosocial scale for the preschool behaviour questionnaire: Concurrent and predictive correlates', *International Journal of Behavioural Development*, **15**, 2, pp. 227–45.

VYGOTSKY, L.S. (1978) *Mind In Society: The Development of Higher Psychological Processes*, Cambridge, MA: Harvard University Press.

WHITE, K.R. (1985) 'Efficacy of early intervention', *Journal of Special Education*, **19**, pp. 401–15.

16   Young Children and Their Families: Creating a Community Response

Gillian Pugh

A Vision for the Millennium

A few years ago I was asked to speak at a conference about primary education in the millennium, a talk which was written up (in Pugh and McQuail, 1995) and became known as my 'vision'. I took the year 2010 and described an early childhood centre for children aged from birth to 6 attached to a primary school. The centre was part of a flexible network of services for families with young children, next door to a health centre and providing a drop-in facility for local childminders. There was a range of services for parents, including discussion groups about bringing up children and access to adult education classes and training opportunities, and parents were fully involved in all aspects of their children's learning and in the centre's management.

The centre provided continuity for children from the time they arrived until they started schooling at 6, and the curriculum was entirely suited to their needs. Exciting work was being developed with babies and toddlers, and the staff of the centre had also drawn inspiration from the work of Reggio Emilia in northern Italy, and particularly their emphasis on creativity and communication.

The groups were small with a good ratio of adults to children, and the staff were all well trained, many having taken advantage of the integrated early childhood studies degrees which had provided a sound basis for their teacher training qualifications. Time for continuing professional development was an entitlement of every member of staff.

Investment in high quality early childhood services was assured and, I concluded, Britain had finally become a child-friendly society.

Today, four years and a general election later, how near are we to realizing this vision? I will explore the answer to this question through a case study of the development of one early childhood centre, drawing on the context of national policy.

Over the last year I have been privileged to work on the development of a service for young children and their families in central London that reflects much of what I have learned in a lifetime of research and development work. This chapter attempts to capture some of the excitement of that development. I write as the bulldozers and cement mixers are still on site, and the children and parents are squeezed into temporary portacabins awaiting the birth of the new service in the autumn of 1998. Visitors to the Coram Community Campus in the millennium will be able to make their own judgments as to whether our dreams have come true.

Messages from Research

In over 20 years of working at the National Children's Bureau I had the opportunity to work with policy makers, managers and practitioners in all corners of the United Kingdom and sometimes further afield. Many important messages remain with me from that work, all of them surprisingly obvious at the end of the twentieth century, but most of them still ignored in the way in which society prioritizes its resources.

Research which points to the importance of children's experiences during the first years of their life is now widely accepted (see for example, Ball, 1994), with the first year — as the brain develops — being a critical time in children's emotional and intellectual development. A high percentage of children's learning takes place in these first five years, and it is well established that this is the time when attitudes are formed, when first relationships are made, when concepts are developed, and the foundations for later learning are laid. What constitutes high quality early education is however rather less well understood. Research on the long term impact of early education drawn together by Sylva (1994) points to long-term measurable gains in educational and social development, provided the education is of the highest quality. Sylva points to the importance of aspiration, motivation and socialization and self-esteem in young children's learning, arguing that good early learning encourages and develops 'mastery' without which successful schooling and adult learning is unlikely. Rather than seeing children as weak and vulnerable empty vessels awaiting the nourishment of the National Curriculum, we should see them as 'rich, strong and powerful' (Malaguzzi in Edwards, 1993). Our task in the early years is to provide a quality education that engages them in the process of education.

It is clear too that the role of parents in their children's learning and development is critical, and that whilst most parents want to support this learning, they do not always know how to do so. Both the longitudinal data from the National Child Development Study used in the Plowden report, and the HighScope research (Woodhead, 1985) provide evidence for the powerful effect of parents' aspirations for their children, and of their involvement in and support for their learning.

We also have a growing understanding of the impact on children's development of different styles of parenting. Positive, nurturing relationships between children and parents are an important foundation for children's development, although the circumstances of many family's lives do not make such early beginnings easy. Relationships within families are more important to children than family structures — for example, conflict between parents has been found to be more damaging to children than divorce. Parenting education and support can offer families a range of knowledge, skills and opportunities for sharing experiences, developing self-confidence and discussing approaches towards parenting (Pugh et al., 1994). Although there is little rigorous research in this country on the effectiveness of such courses, a study of 38 parenting programmes showed some encouraging results in respect of parents' attitudes and/or children's behaviour (Smith and Pugh, 1995).

There is also a growing body of research which points to the long-term benefits of preventive work with parents and young children, in both human and financial terms. Simple, relatively inexpensive measures, put into effect early, can save the need for more complex and costly interventions later. The research suggests that wherever possible this support is best provided within open-access, mainstream services — health centres, nurseries, etc — in the local community, rather than specialist referral services (e.g. Statham, 1995; Smith and Pugh, 1996). A review of preventive work with children and young people experiencing a wide range of difficulties — school failure, truancy, criminal behaviour, family breakdown, child abuse, poor mental health — found that three key factors were central to the healthy development of children and young people: the quality of the relationship between children and their parents or main carer; the social and economic support available to families; and access to high quality early education for their children (Sinclair, Hearn and Pugh, 1997).

This view is supported by an authoritative study published by the Carnegie Foundation in the United States (Carnegie, 1994) which points to four main preventive strategies:

- promote responsible parenthood;
- generate quality childcare choices;
- ensure good health and protection;
- mobilize communities to support children and their families.

Mindful of this research and of studies which show that many of the children and families most at risk are not receiving supportive services (Audit Commission, 1994; Department of Health, 1995) the Department of Health is currently attempting to encourage local authorities to shift resources away from a focus only on remedial child protection work towards the kind of family support noted here. This initiative has to date met with only limited success, not least because of the continuing inability of the many professionals working with children — in education, social services, leisure, health and housing departments — to work in a coordinated way and provide an integrated service for children and families. In those areas where greatest progress has been made, services for children 'in need' and support for families are brought together within mainstream services (Pugh and McQuail, 1995; Rea, Price and Pugh, 1995).

Whilst most of the needs of the most vulnerable families can be met through mainstream services, many children and families are still falling through the welfare net and failing to use services. In looking at why this might be, Sinclair et al. (1997) identified the attributes of effective services as the seven 'A's:

- available — parent education and support, good quality affordable day care, open access family centres and health visitors need to be universally available, which at present they are not;
- acceptable — services must be non-stigmatizing, working with families 'where they are at', building on strengths, listening to the views of children and parents, empowering and enabling, encouraging reciprocity and mutual support;
- affordable — which will require subsidies for low income families;
- accessible — not just in terms of physical distance, but in tackling other barriers which tend to put off families with low self-confidence: inaccessible professional jargon, too much written material, different views of 'the problem', inconvenient times for appointments;
- accountable — to users as well as funders;
- appropriate — taking account of children's and families' needs (for example, parents may want an informal drop-in and support before they are ready to embark on more structured education or training);
- across agency — children and parents seldom see their needs as separated into watertight compartments called education, or health or day care. Studies of effective early childhood services show that multi-agency responses to families can meet needs in a holistic way, can promote a joint approach to planning, funding and delivering services, and can make the best use of resources.

The Thomas Coram Foundation

When I joined the Thomas Coram Foundation for Children early in 1997 as chief executive, I found myself in a position to try to put into practice some of this research evidence. Set up by Royal Charter in 1739 as the Foundling Hospital 'for the maintenance and education of exposed and deserted young children', Coram is the oldest children's charity in Britain. Although it retains only a small part of the site in Bloomsbury that was once the Foundling Hospital, it still provides for some of the most disadvantaged children and young people in London, many of them in the care of local authorities. Services include adoption for children with special needs or who have experienced early trauma or abuse, supervised contact services for children separated from their parents, fostering for young people who would otherwise be in custodial care, and supported accommodation for young people leaving care. We are not a big organization — in fact we are tiny by comparison to the better known charities such as Barnardo's — but we do have a tradition of establishing innovatory services which can be used as models for replication elsewhere.

Since 1939 there has also been a service for families in the neighbourhood of our headquarters — a nursery and training centre which evolved into the Coram Children's Centre in the 1970s, and Camden's only nursery school set up in 1936. Shortage of funds and subsidence in the main buildings forced the closure of the Children's Centre in the early 1990s, but by 1997 plans were evolving to redevelop the three acre site — to become the Coram Community Campus.

Coram Community Campus

The Thomas Coram Foundation is situated just south of Kings Cross station, one of the most deprived areas of central London. There is high unemployment, very high levels of homelessness and occupancy of bed and breakfast accommodation, low take up of nursery education, long waiting lists for day care places, and one third of local families are from ethnic minority groups, many from Bangladesh.

The Coram Community Campus, adjacent to our headquarters in Brunswick Square, has over the years housed the 1930s nursery and training centre (now just a parent-run nursery), a Victorian swimming pool (currently used as a furniture store), a nursery school (run by Camden LEA), a second parent run community nursery, two centres for homeless families (run by separate voluntary organizations) and Coram's contact service. By the end of 1996 a successful SRB bid also brought the promise of some funding to set up a project to provide training and support for parents as part of the regeneration of the Kings Cross area. The opportunity to redevelop the campus, through major building works and through bringing all the separate service providers together to provide an integrated service for local children and families, seemed too good to miss. The building works have required the raising of substantial capital sums, and are not the focus of this chapter; the development of services has been no less complex and evolves on a daily basis. This account provides a snapshot written during the spring of 1998.

The vision for the campus has evolved over a number of years and in response to the needs of local families (Crisp and McNeal, 1995). Despite the pioneering work of the Coram Children's Centre in the 1970s, attempts over the last twenty years to develop flexible, multi-agency services responding to need in a holistic way have been remarkably limited (Pugh, 1996; Moss and Penn, 1996; Moss and Petrie, 1997; Makins, 1997). Although the concept of 'early excellence centres' is now government policy, the complexity of bringing together so many agencies and the cost of providing a comprehensive service still makes such centres the exception rather than the norm.

Multi-agency Support

The first challenge for Coram has been to develop a partnership with Camden, the borough in which we are based — to seek political support from the council and a professional partnership with the main agencies. Political support was immediately forthcoming. The leader and deputy leader of the council were enthusiastic, and particularly the deputy leader who was a child psychiatrist and, fortuitously, also chaired the council's under eights committee which gave formal endorsement to the development. Cross-agency developments have been a little slower, in that like many councils Camden is still struggling to find a cross-agency planning mechanism which really works. However, there has been a high level of support from education, whose officers have chaired the nursery centre development group and granted additional funds to the centre; and from leisure; and from the community health trust who plan to base some services on the site. Social services are currently working through their family support strategy, which we hope will include a role for Coram.

Thomas Coram Early Childhood Centre

The other main challenge has been to bring together the parent run community nursery which provided full day care for children from a few months to 5-years-old, for 48 weeks of the year, with the nursery school which provided sessional nursery education for 3- and 4-year-olds during term times only. Anyone who has tried to do this will know just how difficult it can be. Should the head be a teacher? Should the centre be a school with a delegated budget or a community nursery? What complement of teachers, nursery staff and others should there be, and on what levels of pay and with what conditions of service? How many places should there be for babies? If the local authority funding depends on high numbers of 4-year-olds, how can we ensure they come to the nursery and not the local primary schools? What admission arrangements should we adopt? And what levels of charging, for children under 3 and for the 'wrap-around' day care before and after the free nursery education? How many places should be designated for children with special needs? And whatever shall we call it?

It is greatly to the credit of the staff and parents of both nurseries, and the enthusiastic commitment of Camden LEA, that these issues are being thrashed out remarkably smoothly during the nine months during which the building works are going on. The nurseries moved out of the building as two entirely separate entities and will move back in nine months later as one. There is nothing like a deadline for focusing the mind! The Thomas Coram Early Childhood Centre will be designated a Camden school, but with a governing body which reflects the parent management of the community nursery, and the role of the Thomas Coram Foundation. Camden has committed increased funding for the nursery education places as part of an increase across the borough, and social services is funding one of the deputy posts and, through a service level agreement, will buy a number of places for children 'in need'. The advertisement for centre head did not require a teacher, but the successful candidate is a very experienced teacher, coming to Coram from running the Dorothy Gardner Centre, one of the first 'early excellence centres'. The admission criteria and charging policy are being thrashed out on the tightrope between balancing the books and remaining accessible to families on very low incomes. And perhaps most importantly of all the staff of both nurseries are sharing some inservice training on curriculum development, led by one of the project team who developed the curriculum framework *Quality in Diversity in Children's Learning* (National Children's Bureau, 1998) on behalf of the Early Childhood Education Forum.

We are also exploring how to listen to children's views and perspectives, involving them as active participants in contributing to the nursery. Whilst the voices of older children and young people are increasingly heard, there is still little experience of seeking the views of young children, particularly those under 8 years (see, for example, Edwards et al., 1993; Langsted, 1994; Pugh and Selleck, 1996).

Much of the initial focus has been in planning the inside of the integrated nursery, but in this part of central London where so many children live in bed and breakfast accommodation or in flats with no gardens, the outside area is equally important. The nursery children, parents and staff are all involved in plans for developing the outside play area, where there will be room for growing plants, for climbing and riding trikes, for building dens, for quiet play and for sensory areas.

Children with Special Educational Needs

Children with special educational needs will be integrated into the centre, which includes a soft play area and a low sensory room. But specialist services will also be available on the campus. The national charity KIDS, which supports home-based learning, family support, respite care and specialist groups for children with special needs, has been involved in all the discussions on the development of the campus and is moving its north London base onto the site once the building work is finished. Having written a 'good practice' case study of KIDS as part of a national study of partnership between parents and professionals in preschool services in the 1980s (Pugh et al., 1987), I am delighted to be working with them again. As part of the development of the arts centre, described below, art and music therapy will provide new experiences and opportunities for children with physical disabilities and learning difficulties.

Of particular value to children with special needs is the presence of part of Camden and Islington's Child Development Team on the campus. The fact that psychologists, psychiatrists, speech therapists and physiotherapists will have a base in the centre will mean not only that parents and children can work with these health professionals in an easily accessible centre, but that it will be possible to observe and assess children within the mainstream nursery. The installation of a one-way mirror and video facilities will make it possible for a pioneering multi-agency assessment service to be established.

Working with Parents

Although the importance of working with and supporting parents has been evident to those in the early years field ever since the first nurseries were established, it is only in the last few years that there has been much public debate about the importance of parenting and, even then, it has tended to focus on the need to punish parents for the sins of their children. The work of the Coram Parents Centre, because it is currently funded through regeneration money, has of necessity to include the creation of jobs and the training necessary to equip women to access jobs. But the parents centre is developing much more broadly than that, and is offering a range of opportunities from an informal drop-in through to NVQs.

However, even a drop-in is not enough for those whose confidence is at a low ebb, and an important part of the centre's work will be to work out in the community. An influential study by Shinman (1981) found that 25 per cent of families would not use a drop-in centre, playgroup or nursery even when it was within easy walking distance, for fear of their 'welfare', levels of depression, low self-esteem, and the difficulties of getting several small children ready to go out. This study led to the wider recognition of the need for community-based outreach workers to help vulnerable families with low self-esteem to 'plug into' the system (see Aplin and Pugh, 1983; Pugh and Poulton, 1987). Providing informal support to parents who lack confidence is central to the way in which centres such as Coram's make themselves accessible to parents, many of whom then go on to training and employment. Studies of such centres show that the needs of those who refer themselves are often as great if not greater than those who are referred by health visitors and social workers (Smith, 1993; Whalley, 1994).

The work in the parents centre and the nursery centre thus offers parents the possibility of 'plugging in' at whatever level they feel most comfortable. There are informal coffee mornings, discussions about bringing up children, and creative workshops for parents and children together. There are adult education classes — in English as a second language, literacy, keep fit, child development and computer skills. Some of these will go on to award bearing courses and NVQs. There are courses run by psychologists and child psychologists on child development and challenging behaviour; and individual programmes worked out with the social services family support team. There are specialist services for families who are homeless; and the Coram Contact Services provide supervised support to keep children in touch with parents from whom they are separated by divorce or care proceedings.

In collaboration with the community health trust, we are also developing links with health visitors who are beginning to plan child health clinics, well women clinics and parent discussion groups in the parents centre.

A Central Role for the Arts

When the Foundling Hospital was set up in the eighteenth century, some of its earliest benefactors were the greatest painters and sculptors of the day. William Hogarth, Joshua Reynolds, Thomas Gainsborough are amongst a host of distinguished artists who gave their paintings to the hospital in order to raise money for the work with children — a gesture that was not entirely altruistic as, in the days before public art galleries had been established, the great and the good of London visited the hospital to view the pictures, listen to the music in the chapel, and see the children eating their Sunday lunch. There was also a strong musical tradition from the earliest days. George Frederick Handel first performed the Messiah to raise funds for the hospital in 1750, a concert that became an annual event and raised enough money to build the chapel. For those who grew up in the hospital and subsequently in Coram's more recent services, art and music have been an important part of everyday life, a means of communicating when words have seemed inadequate, and a passport on to adult life.

Coram has been keen to ensure that the arts continue to play a central role in the development of the campus and has plans — which must await the completion of the current building work — to develop the disused swimming pool into an arts centre. This will provide us with a base for arts workshops; for artists in residence; for specialist activities, such as a children's theatre and drama, music and dance group; and for using the arts in therapeutic ways, with opportunities for enhancing self-esteem, self confidence and communication. Meanwhile, the arts are integral to all the services on the campus. Following the very successful exhibition from the Reggio Emilia area of Italy — The Hundred Languages of Children — which was particularly powerful in the way in which it conveyed children's communication through the visual arts, we are working with a group of colleagues from across the UK to create a more permanent base for taking this work forward.

Training and Professional Development

The key to high quality work with young children is a staff team committed to reflecting on and improving their own practice. The availability of an on-going programme of training and professional development will therefore be a central plank of the centre. As the role of the centre develops it will also play an important part in Camden's early years training strategy, providing cross-borough and multi-agency training. Coram is already an accredited centre for social work training and will become an accredited NVQ centre. We are also working with the City Literary Institute on the parenting education work, and with other close neighbours — Kingsway College, the University of North London and the London University Institute of Education — on other training initiatives. The combination of these various factors, and the observation facilities noted above, suggest the real possibility of creating a 'climbing frame' of training opportunities ranging from NVQ level 2 through to masters and doctorate level qualifications.

Research and Evaluation

If services are to respond to the needs of children and parents, and if we are to understand the process of development so that we can learn from both our successes and our mistakes, it is important that research and evaluation are in place from the beginning. The Joseph Rowntree Foundation are funding a two year evaluation of the processes involved in the setting up of this model of service provision, and of the early outcomes for children and parents. We hope to use this research as the basis for similar developments in other inner London boroughs.

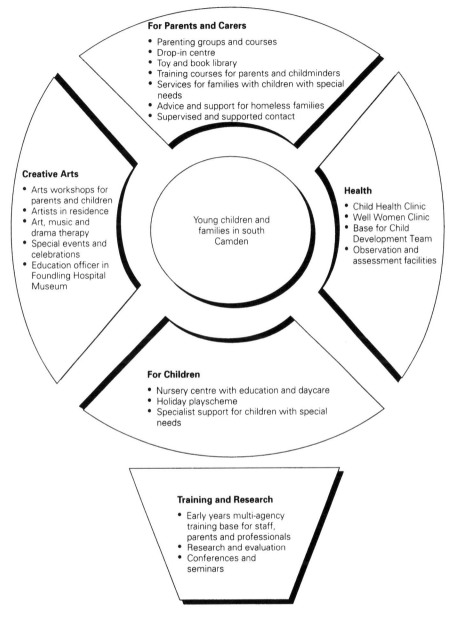

Figure 16.1:   Coram Community Campus

So What's Special Then?

In a sense, the answer to this question is everything and nothing. Everything because we are developing a service that uniquely suits the children and families living in south Camden and uses the facilities that we have at our disposal (see Figure 16.1). Nothing because all over the country early years practitioners are doing some elements of what we are doing. But for me, what makes the Coram services special is the chance that we have to weave so many different coloured threads together, by:

- working in partnership with so many statutory service providers — education, social services, health and leisure services;
- working in partnership with other voluntary agencies, with our own voluntary agency — the Thomas Coram Foundation — owning the site and facilitating the overall development;
- responding to local need, and involving parents and children in the development of services;
- providing high quality mainstream open access services in an area of high need;
- providing specialist support for children and parents within this open access service;
- providing adult education and training opportunities;
- enabling parents to work alongside their children in the nurseries;
- providing both integrated and specialist services for children with special needs;
- exploring the role of the creative and performing arts in the lives of young children and families;
- and by underpinning all our work with training, and with research and evaluation.

In Conclusion

So, to return to my 'vision', how much has been achieved and what remains to be done?

Looking back to four years ago I realize how much of the practice that I dreamed of is already, or will soon be, happening on the Coram Community Campus and in many other centres around the UK. The needs of children are being addressed as a whole through agencies working together and, in particular, there is no artificial divide between care and education. There is continuity of care and education from a few months old up until 5 — provided the local primary schools do not entice parents to take their children out of the centre early. The hours are flexible to meet the needs of parents who are working or studying, and there are a whole range of opportunities for parents to access support or training or to become involved in their children's learning. For staff and parents alike there is a 'climbing frame' of training opportunities being developed. And the requirement on the local authority to provide an Early Years Development and Childcare Plan means that complex centres such as ours should eventually become the norm rather than the exception.

Many of the recommendations that I made for changes in government policy have also begun to happen. There is better coordination between departments with the Department for Education and Employment taking the lead, and there is now a national childcare strategy. But it is at central government level that most remains to be done. Well before the year 2010 I would hope to see the age at which formal schooling starts raised to 6, and the introduction of an appropriate child-centred curriculum which recognizes the particular needs and learning patterns of young children. Linked in to this would be the development and funding of a proper early years training strategy, ensuring that all who work with young children are properly trained and have access to continuing professional development (see Abbott and Pugh, 1998). I would also expect a range of initiatives which would make it easier for parents to combine work with bringing up young children — a properly funded childcare strategy, family friendly employment policies and parental leave arrangements.

As we go into the millennium we have much to rejoice about, but we cannot afford to be complacent yet.

References

ABBOTT, L. and PUGH, G. (eds) (1998) *Training to Work in the Early Years — Developing the Climbing Frame*, Buckingham: Open University Press.

APLIN, G. and PUGH, G. (1983) *Perspectives on Home Visiting National*, London: Children's Bureau.

AUDIT COMMISSION (1994) *Seen but Not Heard: Coordinating Community Child Health and Social Services for Children in Need*, London: Audit Commission.

BALL, C. (1994) *Start Right: The Importance of Early Learning*, London: Royal Society for the Encouragement of the Arts, Manufacturers and Commerce (RSA).

CARNEGIE FOUNDATION (1994) *Starting Points: Report of Carnegie Task Force on Meeting the Needs of Our Youngest Children*, Carnegie, New York: Carnegie Foundation.

CRISP, S. and MCNEAL, J. (1995) *The First Steps: Consulting Local Parents*, London: Thomas Coram Foundation.

DEPARTMENT OF HEALTH (1995) *Child Protection: Messages from Research*, London: HMSO.

EARLY CHILDHOOD EDUCATION FORUM (1998) *Quality in Diversity in Early Learning*, London: National Children's Bureau.

EDWARDS, C., GANDINI, L. and FORMAN, G. (eds) (1993) *The Hundred Languages of Children*, New York: Ablex.

LANGSTED, O. (1994) 'Looking at quality from the child's perspective', in Moss, P. and PENCE, A. (eds) *Valuing Quality in Early Childhood Services*, London: Paul Chapman.

MAKINS, V. (1997) *Not Just a Nursery: Multi-agency Early Years Centres in Action*, London: National Children's Bureau.

MOSS, P. and PENN, H. (1996) *Transforming Nursery Education*, London: Paul Chapman.

Moss, P. and Petrie, P. (1997) *Children's Services: Time for a New Approach*, London: Thomas Coram Research Unit.

Pugh, G. (ed.) (1996) *Contemporary Issues in the Early Years*, 2nd edn., London: Paul Chapman.

Pugh, G. and McQuail, S. (1995) *Effective Organisation of Early Childhood Services*, London: National Children's Bureau.

Pugh, G. and Poulton, L. (1987) *A Job for Life*, London: National Children's Bureau.

Pugh, G. and Selleck, D. (1996) 'Listening to and communicating with young children', in Davie, R. and Upton, D. (eds) *The Voice of the Child*, London: Falmer Press.

Pugh, G., Aplin, G., De'Ath, E. and Moxon, M. (1987) *Partnership in Action*, volume 2, London: National Children's Bureau.

Pugh, G., De'Ath, E. and Smith, C. (1994) *Confident Parents, Confident Children: Policy and Practice in Parenting Education and Support*, London: National Children's Bureau.

Rea Price, J. and Pugh, G. (1995) *Championing Children*, Manchester: Manchester City Council.

Shinman, S (1981) *A Chance for Every Child*, London: Tavistock Publications.

Sinclair, R., Hearn, B. and Pugh, G. (1997) *Preventive Work with Families: The Role of Mainstream Services*, London: National Children's Bureau.

Smith, T. (1993) *Family Centres and Bringing Up Your Children*, London: Children's Society.

Smith, C. and Pugh, G. (1996) *Learning to Be a Parent*, London: Family Policy Studies Centre.

Statham, J. (1994) *Childcare in the Community*, London: Save the Children Fund.

Sylva, K. (1994) 'The impact of early learning on children's later development,' in Ball, C. *Start Right: The Importance of Early Learning*, London: Royal Society of Arts.

Whalley, M. (1994) *Learning to Be Strong*, London: Hodder and Stoughton.

Woodhead, M. (1985) 'Pre-school education has long term effects: But can they be generalised?', *Oxford Review of Education*, 11, 2, pp. 133–55.

Conclusion: Drawing the Threads Together

Lesley Abbott and Helen Moylett

The end of the first millennium; the beginning of the next. We finish one century; we start the next. Physically these statements seem true enough. Intellectually and emotionally beginnings and endings and their boundaries may be more confused. We hope that while journeying through this book you have felt the postmodern sands shifting beneath your feet; that you have read chapters that challenge and sometimes seem to contradict one another; that you have wondered about your own theories and practice; but that at the same time you have realized that underneath those sands is some firm rock — the firm rock of conviction about the importance of children learning to be learners. That conviction seems to be what the past, the present and the future might share. Clearly there is no brave new world of early education that will suddenly be created in the Year 2000 — that brave new world already exists. Perhaps we just need to understand it better to make it more widespread.

Understanding, though, is often difficult and challenging and involves far more than merely intellectual, or even practical, effort. Rosemary Peacocke concludes Chapter 1 with a poem that implies the futility of adults trying to find or recapture 'the centre' of the world as children understand it — perhaps because we have long since forgotten or repressed it. However, what we can and should do is engage with children somewhere nearer the centre of their world; engage with them playfully and yet seriously (see Parker-Rees Chapter 6, Abbott Chapter 7); engage with them in ways which expose our dreams as well as theirs; engage *with* them in the learning process. The meaning of the word 'with' is important here. It implies equality, unconditional positive regard and getting stuck in, not a remote watchfulness. Tina Bruce in Chapter 3 talks about classrooms having 'heart and soul as well as mind'. We hope readers have found this book engaging their hearts and souls as well as their minds. Without those we will continue to see children solely as human capital (see for instance the quote from *Excellence in Schools* page 1 Introduction). Politicians need to be reminded that:

> A nation is not a firm. A school is not part of that firm efficiently churning out the 'human capital' required to run it. We do damage to our very sense of the common good to even think of the human drama of education in these terms. It is demeaning to teachers and creates a schooling process that remains unconnected to the lives of so many children. (Apple, 1990)

Philip Gammage in Chapter 14 warns us of the danger in seeing children as 'little bits of economic investments, as competitors who will take the country forward in some ill-defined (and often inappropriate) race to the top!'

Of course the present Labour Government has recognized the interconnectedness of various different aspects of children's lives. The Social Exclusion Unit, the Out of School Care initiative and Early Years Development Partnerships are examples of this awareness. However, despite welcoming the government's commitment to families, particularly those living in disadvantaged areas, we wonder how far they can avoid the constraints of the British class system. Polly Toynbee (1998) a New Labour supporter, questions the meaning attributed to 'family' in the current political climate:

> Family for the Tories was anti-sex and moral control. For Labour it's a code for poor families failing to survive, a language for helping families without stigmatizing them. 'Family' and 'parenting' sounds like everyone — but Labour really means 'them' not 'us'. (*Guardian*, 24 July 1998)

One might claim that there is nothing wrong with wanting to help those less fortunate than oneself — many great human advances have happened as a result; but so has much disastrous missionary work. We hope that Education Action Zones, for instance, prove to be more successful than the old Educational Priority Areas set up in the aftermath of the Plowden Report. EPAs suffered from being based on a deficit model which implied that the disadvantaged had to change because they needed to know better, while the middle class establishment had no need for self examination and would remain the same. It is envisaged that the EAZs will operate as action forums 'which will include parents and other representatives from the local business and social community, as well as representation from the constituent schools' (DfEE, 1997). However they still seem to emphasize a narrow model of educational achievement. The clear message from the writers of this book is that narrow models exclude rather than include whilst ignoring the mountain of research available about children's learning.

Some fundamentally inappropriate and outdated ideas about children's learning remain unchallenged by current political initiatives. The notion that children are people in waiting still permeates political and educational thinking. The idea that childhood is socially constructed for instance and that children might be active co-constructors means that we can choose to see our youngest children as powerful people in their own right. However take, for example, the way the Sure Start project was announced in July 1998. In *The Guardian* the byline was 'Outreach workers to visit newborn as a first step to get them ready for school' (15 July 1998).

Early childhood is *not* a waiting room for school! Many of the contributors to the book refer to countries where children experience a structured programme of early education and care which is seen as valid in its own right and which is certainly not a watered down version of the school curriculum. We suffer in Britain from an approach to curriculum which has always, despite many best efforts to the contrary, ended up 'adapting' a secondary subject-based model for younger and younger children. We seem to be steadfast in our refusal to see early childhood as a stage in its own right. Nutbrown (1998) points to the way in which the top down model has even changed the language of early education.

Of course the early years must, in some senses, be a preparation for school but we need to be careful that 'preschool' does not become the dominant idea that 'preparation' does not become the watchword that play does not become denigrated and work elevated in an attempt to make young children more like older ones and, therefore, more like adults. As Moss (Chapter 13) points out, we have some ambivalent attitudes to children seeing them as privatized and dependent as well as 'poor, weak and innocent, or as primitive, uncontrollable or threatening'. He claims, like David (Chapter 8), that these ways of seeing children stem from our refusal to see them as powerful people in their own right. Clearly as we get older the vast majority of us learn to conform, to apparently control our holistic messy ways of learning that do not separate emotion, bodily function and intellect. However, as many of this book's contributors point out, psychologists like Gardner have been showing us that learning remains messy; that the school system fails in its inability to address concepts such as multiple intelligence.

So those of us who work in early education have some important choices to make as we move into the next millennium. We can tinker with the status quo — reforming what we have or we can be more radical and decide to be transformers rather than reformers. We need to seize the chance that a new government committed to reform can give us to extend and understand the good practice that already exists. Because, of course, there are wonderful things happening for some of our youngest children already — there are examples in this book and we have written about them elsewhere (Abbott and Moylett, 1997; Abbott and Rodger, 1994). All young children have a right to the very best educare.

Who is going to provide this universally excellent educare? Woven into all the contributions to this book is the need for specialist training for early years workers. As the Start Right report concluded in 1994 'The calibre and training of professionals who work with children are key determinants of high quality provision'. Many government initiatives like Sure Start call not only for integration of services but also for workers who can be part of multi-disciplinary teams and who have the flexibility to meet changing needs. As teacher trainers we are heartened by recent changes in our own field.

At the time of writing in our own university, the BA (Hons) in Early Childhood Studies, one of the first of the multi-disciplinary degrees, enters its sixth year in its part-time form, and its third year as a fulltime course. Its graduates are now in positions of responsibility in local authority inspection and registration, in management of family and day-care centres, childminder training, health care, social work, parent support and teaching. Their presence will increasingly be felt, as new and expanded integrated services are developed.

First year students on the new BEd (Hons) Early Years route will undertake an 'advanced study of the early years' and will become the new 'early years specialist teachers' of the future — trained to be 'involved' in all settings providing education for 4-year-olds and very soon 3-year-olds too! We wonder exactly what 'involvement' will entail, but we are confident that the multi-disciplinary training and practical experience in a wide range of settings, will prepare them for whatever role they are required to undertake.

For the first time primary postgraduate students are training to take on an early years specialist role. Amongst the degrees with which they commence the course, will be those in Early Childhood studies, now recognized by the Teacher Training Agency alongside primary curriculum subjects as an appropriate foundation for teacher training!

These new approaches to teacher training are welcome and we hope helping to modulate what Mary-Jane Drummond in Chapter 5 refers to as that particular teacher tone of voice, so caustically satirized by Joyce Grenfell, so ubiquitously heard in mainstream classrooms! However, some teachers talking in different voices is one thing, sorting out the more general training muddle is another. Pugh (1998) points to 'the confusion over training, the piecemeal way in which courses have developed, the low status that many carry, the lack of funding for students enrolling on them and the generally low level of qualification that besets the field . . .' This will not surprise those who are aware that the majority of educare services for children under 4 are staffed not by teachers but by a:

> largely unqualified army of more than 200,000 child care and education workers. In England and Wales alone there are roughly 100,000 self-employed childminders and at least 50,000 playgroup leaders and assistants in some 20,000 playgroups. Workers with young children and their families are also found in day nurseries, nursery and primary schools, crèches, parent and toddler groups, family centres, parent support and home visiting schemes, toy libraries, playbuses and many other types of provision. (Hevey and Curtis, 1996, p. 212)

The only education or training opportunities available to these staff are parttime, low cost and not formally assessed. Throughout this book writers have been asking us to rethink our ideas about children and their learning. At the same time, we also need to rethink our ideas about their educarers. If we give high status to early childhood as a phase in its own right then we should give high status to *all* our youngest children's educarers. With high status comes recognition of skills and knowledge and organized professional development and training.

The concept of a 'climbing frame' of professional development with easily accessible entry and exit points has been developed in Abbott and Pugh (1998). In this model courses would share some important underlying principles which would lend coherence and continuity to any professional development path across, round or up the climbing frame. Clearly, there is much work still to be done in order to erect a climbing frame that is sturdy and attractive to educarers, in place of the old bits of adventure playground, some of which looks quite exciting but which anyone can see is neglected, has bits missing and is dangerous for too many people to use at once.

The 'climbing frame' continues to be developed in a number of ways. The establishment of Early Years Development and Childcare Partnerships with a requirement 'to develop a training strategy which assesses training needs, and sets out how these needs can be met' (DfEE, 1997) is a first step. The Early Years Training group which has met regularly for many years at the National Children's

Bureau and has overseen the development of the integrated, multi-disciplinary degrees in early childhood studies, recognizes the need to integrate all training to work with children before they start school, across the statutory, voluntary and private sectors. A National Training Organisation (NTO) to oversee the training needs of early years workers is encouraging but, sadly, it does not include teacher education within its remit.

The training debate will doubtless continue well into the new millennium influenced, we hope by some of the ideas in this book. We hope it will inspire readers with the courage to be transforming rather than reforming and that reading it may help them to make some space for reflection. We agree with David's view that:

> Probably the most important implications for training, apart from high levels of knowledge in a range of relevant disciplines, involve the need for early childhood educators to be able to centre (to view the world from another's viewpoint); to 'problematize' their favoured theories and to engage in reflexivity (examining how their own thinking, views and actions influence their ecological niche). Thus, training should not be about acquiring facts and knowledge, but about exploring bodies of knowledge and submitting them to critical analysis in the light of real-life experience. There should be opportunities for experiencing and reflecting on teamwork with other adults, leading to open, depersonalized self-evaluation of strengths and weaknesses. In particular . . . there should be discussion of ways in which societies construct different versions of early childhood and the services deemed appropriate as a result. (David, 1998, p. 25)

Whether you read this book for personal interest, or use it in training others, we hope that you will be inspired by the doors the writers open. We hope that it will inspire you to open some doors of your own; to look through at what could be and to take those first steps into a different place; to make the end also the beginning. Our children are born courageous, they need us to be courageous too.

References

ABBOTT, L. and MOYLETT, H. (eds) (1997) *Working with the Under 3s: Responding to Childrens Needs*, Buckingham: Open University Press.

ABBOTT, L. and PUGH, G. (eds) (1998) *Training to Work in the Early Years*, Buckingham: Open University Press.

ABBOTT, L. and RODGER, R. (eds) (1994) *Quality Education in the Early Years*, Buckingham: Open University Press.

APPLE, M. (1990) *Ideology and Curriculum* (2nd edition), London: Routledge.

DAVID, T. (1998) 'Changing minds: Young children and society', in ABBOTT, L. and PUGH, G. (eds) *Training to Work in the Early Years*, Buckingham: Open University Press.

DfEE (1997) *Excellence in Schools*, London: HMSO.

HEVEY, D. and CURTIS, A. (1996) 'Training to work in the early years', in PUGH, G. (ed.) *Contemporary Issues in the Early Years* (2nd edn), London: Paul Chapman.

NUTBROWN, C. (1998) *The Lore and Language of Early Education*, Sheffield: University of Sheffield.

PUGH, G. (1998) 'Early Years Training in Context', in ABBOTT, L. and PUGH, G. (eds) *Training to Work in the Early Years*, Buckingham: Open University Press.

TOYNBEE, P. (1998) The *Guardian*, July 24.

Notes on Contributors

John Abbott was formerly the Director of the Education 2000 Trust, and for the past two and half years has been the President of the 21st Century Learning Initiative, based in Washington, DC. The Initiative is a transnational program to synthesize the best of research and development into the nature of human learning, and to examine its implications for education, work and the development of communities world-wide. He started his teaching career at Manchester Grammar School, and was later headteacher of a comprehensive school.

Lesley Abbott is Professor of Early Childhood Education at the Manchester Metropolitan University where she heads the Early Years Multi-Professional Centre. She was a member of the Committee of Inquiry into the Quality of the Educational Experience offered to 3- and 4-year-olds (The Rumbold Committee) and the Royal Society of Arts Early Learning Inquiry. She has given evidence to the Education Select Committee and advised the present government on the future of early years training. She is firmly committed to multiprofessional training and the development of a 'climbing frame' of training opportunity for all those involved in the educare of young children. This commitment led to the development of one of the first multiprofessional degrees in the country — the BA(Hons) in Early Childhood Studies. Her major research interest is play, about which she has written and published in this country and abroad. Her publications include *Play in the Primary Years* and *Quality Education in the Early Years*. She directed the research project 'Educare for the Under Threes' and co-edited the Early Interactions series *Working with the Under Threes — Training and Professional Development and Responding to Children's Needs*, Open University Press (1997) with Helen Moylett. She has co-edited with Gillian Pugh *Training to Work in the Early Years — Developing the Climbing Frame*, Open University Press (1998). She has been responsible for the evaluation of the European Funded 'Pathways to Professionalism' project and is currently monitoring the new 'specialist early years teacher' routes in her own university. She directed the project which led to the production of the Firm Foundations — Professional support materials. She is currently working on the production of video, training and resource materials for parents and professionals working with children under 3.

Paul Baker is a Lecturer at Manchester Metropolitan University, where he teaches in both Special Educational Needs and Information and Communications Technology. Prior to teaching at the University he taught in a number of different Special Schools with pupils who were experiencing a range of learning and behavioural difficulties. He was the headteacher of a school for pupils with physical disabilities when he moved to the University. He has a particular interest in teacher education at all levels. Currently he is leading a new B.Ed main subject in Special Needs in Literacy and Numeracy within the initial teacher education programme of the university. It is hoped that this will be the first initial teacher education course which will award both a degree and a nationally recognized qualification in the education of pupils with specific learning difficulties. Whilst at the university Paul has been involved in a number of trans-European programmes, and spent a year as a visiting lecturer at Siauliai University in Lithuania.

Sir Christopher Ball is Chancellor of the University of Derby and a Patron of the National Campaign for Learning. Director of Learning at the RSA (1990–97), he was formerly Warden of Keble College Oxford (1980–88). Chairman of the Board of the National Advisory Body for Public Sector Higher Education (1982–88) and President of the Association of Colleges for Further and Higher Education (1990–92). He is the author of a number of books and reports on learning, including *Fitness for Purpose* (SRHE, 1985), *Aim Higher* (RSA, 1989), *More Means Different* (RSA, 1990), *Learning Pays* (RSA, 1991), *Sharks and Splashes: The Future of Education and Employment* (New Zealand Institute of Policy Studies, 1991), *Profitable Learning* (RSA, 1992), and a report on Early Learning entitled *Start Right* (RSA, 1994). In April 1996 the Campaign for Learning Personal Learning Action PLAN, *Make it Happen*, was published, developed from his original draft.

Caroline Barratt-Pugh is a Senior Lecturer in the Department of Language Arts Education at the Edith Cowan University, Perth, Western Australia. She is particularly interested in bilingualism and early literacy in home and school settings. She has been involved in teaching and research in these areas for a number of years. Caroline started her early years career as a nursery nurse and then became a teacher in Bradford, Yorkshire. She joined the Early Years team at the Manchester Metropolitan University in 1987 and has been in Australia since 1992.

Tony Bertram is Senior Research Fellow and Co-Director of the Centre for Research in Early Childhood at University College Worcester. He is also Director of a national research project entitled 'Effective Early Learning' (the EEL Project) which aims to evaluate and improve the quality of early education in a wide range of education and care settings and President of the European Early Childhood Education Research Association, which he co-founded. He taught in first schools and primary schools for 13 years, and was a headteacher for 7 years prior to working in higher education. His research interests remain very much with young children and those who work with them. He has carried out a number of projects including the training of early years teachers in Europe, the admission of children to school and male educators of young children. His current personal research project is focusing on the evaluation and development of effective early childhood educators. Working with Professor Christine Pascal, they are currently launching a major new research and development initiative called 'Accounting Early for Life Long Learning', which focuses on the enhancement of young children's attitudes and dispositions to learning and emotional well being in early childhood settings. He has written and lectured widely on the above topics in the UK, the USA, South America and across much of Europe.

Tina Bruce trained as a Froebel nursery infant teacher and as a teacher of children with hearing impairment at the University of Manchester. She taught in mainstream and special school settings and was the teacher 'Mrs B' in the Froebel Nursery Research School, with the Research Fellow Chris Athey at the Froebel Institute. She became Director of the Centre for Early Childhood Studies there, directed the Froebel Blockplay Project, and with The British Council helped to set up the first kindergarten Training College in Cairo. She was given the International Award 'Outstanding Woman in Education' by the University of Virginia, and has been a keynote speaker and guest lecturer at the 6th Early Childhood Convention in New Zealand. Her books include bestsellers *Early Childhood Education, Time to Play* and *Childcare and Education*. She is currently Visiting Professor at the University of North London which validates the MA in Early Childhood Education with Care taught at Pen Green. She is married to Professor Ian Bruce, Director General of the Royal National Institute for the Blind, and has two children at university.

Tricia David is a Professor of Education at Canterbury Christ Church College, where she directs the Centre for International Studies in Early Childhood and she is at present coordinator of the college's Centre for Educational Research. Tricia has worked in the early years field for over 30 years, in a variety of roles including: researcher, community educator, teacher educator, nursery and primary teacher and headteacher, UK national president of OMEP (World Organisation for Early Childhood Education), and as one of the co-founders of the national umbrella group the Early Childhood Education Forum. She currently edits the *International Journal of Early Childhood* and has written and edited a number of articles and books, of which *Researching Early Childhood* (with Carol Aubrey and Linda Thompson, Falmer Press, 1999) is the most recent. Tricia is at present leading a team funded by the Esmée Fairbairn Foundation, exploring approaches to early literacy in France and England.

Mary-Jane Drummond is a Lecturer in Primary Education at the School of Education, University of Cambridge, where she teaches on a variety of courses for teachers and other educators from all over East Anglia. Her special interests are early childhood care and education and the formative assessment of children's learning. She is also a member of the advisory group of the Early Childhood Unit at the National Children's Bureau and has been closely involved in their interdisciplinary training and development work. She is an editor of the *Cambridge Journal of Education*, and a member of the editorial board of *Forum*. She has acted as external evaluator to a number of early years projects (in Norfolk, Bedfordshire, Hampshire and Hertfordshire). She is a member of the team of researchers at the

School of Education now writing up their work on the research project Positive Alternatives to Exclusion. She was the editor of the Early Childhood Education Forum publication *Quality in Diversity in Early Learning: A Framework for Early Childhood Practitioners* (1998, National Children's Bureau).

Philip Gammage was trained as a teacher at Goldsmiths College many years ago. After teaching infants and juniors for about 10 years, he studied psychology and comparative education, eventually ending up with a PhD and a senior lectureship at Bristol University. He has held several posts, including that of Dean and Professor of Education at Nottingham University and currently holds the foundation de Lissa Chair in early childhood research at the University of South Australia and the State Department of Education. He has experience of working in 14 countries and of acting as a consultant for OECD. He is an unreformed advocate of 'child-centred' approaches to learning and believes fervently that care and education have to be combined in humane ways if our societies are to develop happily and harmoniously in the future. Philip is past president of the British Association of Early Childhood Education, has written several books on children and schooling and is an inadequate but keen violinist.

Glenys Kinnock was educated at Holyhead Comprehensive School, and graduated from University College Cardiff. She has been a teacher in secondary, primary and infant and nursery schools. Glenys was elected to the European Parliament in June 1994 and represents the consistency of South Wales East. As well as being a Member of the Development Committee, she is Vice-President of the Africa Caribbean and Pacific/European Union Joint Assembly, and is a Rapporteur for the Working Group on the Future of EU/ACP relations. Glenys is a member of the Employment Committee, and of the Human Rights sub-committee and she has been appointed as the European Member of Parliament responsible for liaison with the UK Government's Department of International Development. Glenys was appointed the EU's Special Representative in the 1998 Cambodian Elections.

Glenys's specific interests are in gender issues, children's rights, and strategies to ensure sustainable development. She has visited many developing countries and has specific interests in Southern Africa. Her interest in human rights has taken her to Burma where she met Aung San Suu Kyi. She is President of One World Action, the Development NGO. She is also President of College Harlech, Vice-President of Steel Action in the European Parliament, and Vice-President of the United Nations Association, Cardiff and District.

Glenys Kinnock has written books about Eritrea and Namibia and, in 1993, her collection of interviews with British women, *By Faith and Daring* was published. In 1996, she produced *Could Do Better — Where Is Britain in the European Education League Tables*?' She is a Fellow of the Royal Society of Arts.

Peter Moss is Professor of Early Childhood Provision at the Thomas Coram Research Unit, Institute of Education University of London. His research interests include early childhood and the relationship between employment and family life, with a particular interest in cross-national work. Between 1986 and 1996, he was coordinator of the European Commission network on Childcare and Other Measures to reconcile Employment and Family Responsibilities, where he was responsible for a wide range of work on services for children under 11, parental leave and men as carers for children. He has also written about the 'problem with quality', arising from the concept being value-based and relative. A long-term, and continuing, advocate of the need for an integrated and coherent early childhood service (for children 0–6), his current interests are in the relationship between institutions for younger and older children and the relationship between organization, practice and philosophy.

Helen Moylett is Senior Lecturer in Education Studies at the Manchester Metropolitan University where she teaches on a range of initial and inservice courses including the BEd and the BA Early Childhood Studies degrees. She has worked in a number of inner city Manchester primary schools, in both early and later years settings, both as a classteacher and as an advisory teacher. She was one of the first home-school liaison teachers in Manchester and continues to pursue her interest in this field through her research and work with students. She is particularly interested in the ways in which practitioners can reflect upon and research their practice with a view to improving it. Together with Lesley Abbott she has co-edited two books in the series Early Interactions: *Working with the Under Threes — Training and Professional Development and Responding to Children's Needs*, Open University Press (1997). She is currently working on the project 'Educare for the Under Threes' which involves the production of video, training and support materials for parents and early years professionals. She is the chair of the Stockport Early Years Development and Childcare Partnership and is committed to the development of training opportunities for all those involved in the care and education of young children.

Rod Parker-Rees worked as a nursery and reception teacher and at the National Primary Centre in Bristol before joining the University of Plymouth's Rolle School of Education in 1993 as subject leader for primary design and technology. He has helped to develop an Early Childhood Studies main subject pathway in the Rolle School of Education's BEd degree and now teaches mainly in early childhood studies. His main research interests include playfulness, design and technology in the early years, how representation and modelling can support children's thinking and the role of talk in young children's learning. Recent publications include: 'The tale of a task: Learning beyond the map', in POLLARD, A., THIESSEN, D. and FILER, A. (eds) *Children and Their Curriculum: The Perspectives of Primary and Elementary School Children* (Falmer Press), and 'Making sense and made sense: Design and technology and the playful construction of meaning in the early years', *Early Years*, **18**, 1.

Christine Pascal is Professor of Early Childhood Education and Co-Director of the Centre for Research in Early Childhood at University College Worcester. She is currently directing two national research projects entitled 'Effective Early Learning' (the EEL project) and 'Accounting Early for Lifelong Learning' (the ACE project) which aim to evaluate and improve the quality of early education in a wide range of settings. She taught in infant schools for 10 years prior to working in higher education and maintains regular involvement with children and teachers through her research and in-service courses. She was a member of the Committee of Inquiry into the Quality of the Educational Experiences offered to 3- and 4-year-olds (The Rumbold Committee) and the Royal Society of Arts Early Learning Inquiry. She is currently a member of the DfEE and QCA Early Years Advisory panels. She is a former President of the British Association of Early Childhood Education and now Vice-President. She has acted as a consultant in Europe, Scandinavia and South America and in 1990 co-founded the European Early Childhood Education Research Association.

Rosemary Peacock After some teaching experience and two children later, Rosemary became headteacher of an infant school in Oxford. Seven years on she became a member of HM Inspectorate and in due course was made Staff Inspector for the early years. More recently she has been involved with a variety of activities, all connected with young children — advising the media, working with researchers — EEL and PEEP projects — advising the Select Committee in the House of Commons, and lecturing and teaching in USA. She is also busy locally within the Oxford CE Diocese advising church schools, and is the Chair of the Oxford Early Years Development and Childcare Partnership. Two of her special interests in the early years are language and literacy and spiritual development. Can it be significant that one of her children grew up to be philosopher and the other became ordained and works with teachers?

Gillian Pugh has been Chief Executive of the Thomas Coram Foundation for Children since early 1997, having previously been Director of the Early Childhood Unit at the National Children's Bureau. She has published books and training materials on policy development, on coordination of services, on curriculum, on parental involvement and on parent education. Recent publications include *The Contribution of Mainstream Services to Preventive Work with Families* with Ruth Sinclair and Barbara Hearn (1997), *Contemporary Issues in the Early Years* (2nd edition, 1996) and *Training to Work in the Early Years — Developing the Climbing Frame* with Lesley Abbott (1998). Gillian was a member of the Rumbold Committee on the education of children of three to five, of the RSA Start Right enquiry and of the Audit Commission study of early education. She set up and chaired the Early Childhood Education Forum, and was a founder member of the Parenting Education and Support Forum.

Margaret Stevens has taught all ages in the primary school. She was an early years teacher for over 20 years working in a range of schools. In recent years she has been involved in teacher education and local authority inservice work and was responsible for the establishment and development of the Primary Base/Resource centre at the Manchester Metropolitan University. For the past two years she has been working as an OFSTED Nursery Inspector and has undertaken more than 50 inspections in a wide variety of nursery settings in the midlands and the north of England. Having recently undergone the inspection process herself, needless to say with a glowing report, she is able to empathize with centre staff for whom the experience is often a stressful and daunting one!

Kathy Sylva is Reader in Educational Studies at the University of Oxford Department of Educational Studies. After earning a PhD at Harvard University she moved to Oxford where she taught psychology while serving on the Oxford Preschool Research Group. Her book *Childwatching at Playgroup and Nursery School* broke new ground by questioning an unbridled 'free play' ideology. With Teresa Smith and Elizabeth Moore she evaluated the High/Scope preschool programme with its emphasis on 'plan, do, review' in each session. She moved to London to begin research on assessment and curriculum in primary schools. In *Early Intervention in Children with Reading Difficulties* she and Jane Hurry showed that Reading Recovery is a successful intervention and cost-effective as well. She has returned to Oxford and is one of the leaders of the DfEE research on effective provision of preschool education. A dominant theme throughout her work is the impact of education not only on 'subject knowledge' but on children's problem solving, social skills and commitment to their own learning.

Mark Vandevelde is a student at Sharnbrook Upper School in Bedfordshire. With the support of his school Mark has exploited electronic sources of knowledge including the Internet to become a pioneer of independent learning. Mark has developed a number of media-related interests. He has produced and presented programmes for his school's television station, drawing upon a network of collaborators spanning three continents. His role in spearheading the creation of online education centres for the learning community won him his school's enterprise award. He has developed a reputation as a formidable interviewer, and has featured on local and national radio. He was one of a team of three students who won an Institute of Management award for public speaking. His writing has won national competitions, and has been published widely, including in *The Times Educational Supplement*. His other interests include music and photography.

Mark Vandevelde's digital portfolio is available on the web at http:// ds.dial.pipex.com/town/estate/wd17/markvandevelde/.

Index